# PRACTICAL TIPS FOR AMERICANS TRAVELING ABROAD:
# IGNORE THEM AT YOUR OWN RISK

## GLADSON I. NWANNA (Ph.D)

**World Travel Institute**
**Baltimore, Maryland**

Copyright © 1999 by Gladson I. Nwanna

Library of Congress Cataloging-in-Publication Data

Nwanna, Gladson I.
       Practical tips for Americans traveling abroad : ignore them at
       your own risk / Gladson I. Nwanna.
             p.   cm.
       Includes index.
       ISBN 1-890605-09-3
       1.      Travel.  I. Title.
       G151.N94 1998
910--dc21                                    97-19149
                                            CIP

Cover Design by Steven R. Morris

Printed in Canada

# Acknowledgement

A lot of people have helped me with this book, giving me everything from encouragement and typesetting to editorial advice and help. I would especially, like to thank, Mrs. Phyllis Desbordes for her editorial support and other valuable suggestions and Ms. Nicole Cook for her efforts in the design of the cover.

My gratitude and indebtedness also go to the organizations and firms that gave me permission to reproduce some of their proprietary works. These include:

**Agora, Inc.:** The material was excerpted from *The World Catalog*, and from *International Living*, one year subscription price is $34; both publications by Agora Inc., 824 E. Baltimore St., Baltimore, MD 21202; (410) 234-0515. Reprinted by permission. [Reference Code used in the text **IL**]

**Runzheimer International:** Reprinted by permission. All rights reserved by Runzheimer International. [Reference Code used in the text **RI**]

# Preface

With careful and the right form of preparations Americans abroad can look forward to a safe, enriching and exciting trip and stay in their host, foreign country . On the other hand, their trip abroad could become wasteful, expensive, boring, embarrassing and a nightmare if the traveler is not adequately informed. Unfortunately, for many more who will travel abroad without the opportunity to read this book their trip might become costly, filled with surprises, regrets and nightmares. Most of this will result from them not making the right form of preparations.

The key to a successful trip overseas will depend, to a large extent, on how well you invest in preparing for such trips; particularly, in familiarizing yourself with a variety of conditions, laws, rules, regulations and requirements as they apply to home and abroad. One of the qualities of this book is that it addresses these issues in a realistic and practical fashion for the international traveler, especially Americans Traveling Abroad.

The uniqueness of this book include the fact that most of the information and suggestions stem from first hand experiences of several international travelers with whom I was fortunate and privileged to meet with and share ideas and experiences. Incidentally, it is hard to find a traveler to a foreign county who has returned to his or her host country without a memorable experience that he or she wished had not happened or could have been avoided. There are those planning to travel abroad in the future who invariably appear interested in learning everything possible to ensure a hitch-free trip, but like their predecessors might take a few things for granted could spoil their trip abroad and potentially cost them, both financially and emotionally. Similarly, there are those potential travelers who are unaware of the "little things" that could save them money, time and possibly their lives. It is these "little things", based on first hand experiences that this book is all about.It is hoped that it will make it possible for you to enjoy your trip abroad without incidents.

Certainly you cannot be too prepared for travel to a foreign country especially if it is directed towards learning as much safety, time and money-saving information as possible or preparation that portrays prevailing and/or unique social, economic, cultural and political conditions and norms abroad.

This book has other unique features that separate it from the "typical" travel book or guide available today in the market. Most of the information in this book:

- is relevant to all categories of International travelers.

- is relevant to Americans and non-Americans alike traveling abroad, as well as those residing abroad. Several of the topics discussed and tips provided have no boundaries and are applicable to anyone traveling to a foreign country.

- is relevant to first time  travelers, as well as seasoned travelers, business, disabled, older, and student travelers, and minors traveling unaccompanied;

- includes safety, money, shopping, security, and health tips;

- includes tips on getting financial and other forms of assistance overseas;

- includes tips for traveling and transporting pets;

- includes information on foreign adoptions, international child abduction and hostage situations;

In addition, the Appendix section have numerous addresses, telephone numbers  and other valuable information often sought after, but very often not readily accessible to International travelers, including country by country information.

It is my expectation that the information contained in this book will make a big difference in ensuring a safe, enjoyable, rewarding and hitch-free trip for millions of American and overseas-bound travelers. I hope that you can benefit from my experiences and mistakes and those of other international travelers whose ideas and experiences I have also benefitted from. Above all, I would hope that the information in this book will translate and ensure for you and your loved ones a safe, uneventful, less embarrassing, fun-filled and exciting trip abroad. If it does, I would certainly like to hear from you. Suggestions and letters should be mailed to Public Relations Department, WTI, P.O. Box 32674, Baltimore, Maryland 21282-2674.

# Editor's Note:

I believe you will agree that we live in changing times, including changing political, social, cultural and economic climates, both at home and abroad that may impact on international travels. Whereas most of the information contained in this book will remain valid perhaps through the ages, some is bound to change. I have anticipated that to be the case; hence, I have provided you with relevant references, including addresses and phone numbers of government and non-government agencies and organizations that will keep you up-to-date.

## DISCLAIMER:

Neither the publisher nor the author can accept responsibility for errors or omissions that may occur, nor will they be held responsible for the experiences of readers while they are traveling. The information contained in this book is meant to serve only as a guide and to assist you in your travel plans. This information is neither all inclusive, exhaustive nor cast in bronze. You are advised to verify and reconfirm all information mentioned in this book with your travel agent, travel advisor, travel bureaus and with embassies and consulates of the country (ies) you plan to visit before embarking on your trip.

# TABLE OF CONTENTS

# APPENDICES

# ENTRY/EXIT REQUIREMENTS

**Visas:** Different countries have different visa requirements and may not allow you into the country without one. However, while some countries do not require visas from Americans, many others do. Most countries charge a fee for their visas. Remember, visas are usually stamped in the passport, so you must have a valid passport before applying. You may, also, be denied a visa if your passport has a validity of less than six months and/or if other entry requirements have not been met.

Some countries impose time restrictions on their visas; that is, you may be required to use the visa by starting off your journey and/or entry to the country within a given time period (typically 90 days). In some cases, the visa period may also include the length of time you are allowed to stay in that country. Once the visa period has expired, you may have to re-apply.

**U.S. Customs:** Familiarize yourself with the U.S. Customs Services' regulations and requirements. It could save you a lot of effort, time and money. This is especially important for those travelers contemplating returning to the U.S. with food items, animal products and other merchandise purchased abroad. The U.S. Customs publications referenced in Appendix 1C are a must read for those travelers.

**Visa and Other Entry Requirements:** Although a U.S. passport and/or visa may not be required for Americans traveling to some countries, it is required for travel to most countries in the world. For those countries not requiring visas, there  may be other requirements that must be met. Each country has its own set of entry and exit requirements.

The U.S. Department of State publication, <u>Foreign Entry Requirements,</u> found in most public libraries, gives basic information on entry requirements and tells where and how to apply for visas. The best authority on a country's visa and other requirements, however, is its embassy or consulates. It is  recommended that you check with them before applying. Allow plenty of time to obtain the visas. An average of two weeks for each visa is recommended, but some countries may require at least a month. Do not forget that you may be able to get a second passport to travel on in the event your other passport is tied up with the visa application. When you make visa inquires, ask about the following:

*       Entry/Exit Visas
*       Visa price, length of validity, and number of entries.
*       Financial data required, proof of sufficient funds, proof of onward return ticket.
*       Immunizations required.
*       Currency regulations.
*       Import/export restrictions and limitations.
*       Departure tax. Be sure to keep enough local currency to depart as planned.
*       AIDS clearance certification. An increasing number of countries require certification that visitors are free from the AIDS virus.

As an international traveler, it is advisable to apply for a visa in person and at foreign consulates or embassies near you, especially considering that your presence may be needed for an interview. Furthermore, this will allow you to straighten things out as well as ensure that the visa has been issued properly. It is also advisable that you obtain your visa(s) before you leave home. If you decide to visit additional countries en route, it may be difficult or impossible to obtain visas. In several countries you may not be admitted into the country without a visa, and may be required to depart on the next plane if you arrive without one. This can be particularly frustrating if the next plane does not arrive for several days, the airport hotel is full and the airport has no sleeping accommodations.

Should you decide to apply for your visa by mail remember to enclose the application form, the visa fee, your passport, photograph(s) and any other documents required. Should you chose to have your passport mailed to you, do enclose adequate postage money and request that it be returned to you by registered mail. Do not forget to find out what forms of payment are acceptable since some embassies do not honor personal checks.

Remember, some countries require both entry and exit visas and, depending on the country, you may be better off securing a multiple or double-entry visa before departure. Travelers with only a single entry visa may find it particularly difficult to leave the country in the event of an emergency. While planning your itinerary, beware that some Arab countries will refuse to admit you if your passport shows any evidence of previous or expected travel to Israel. If you have such notations in your passport or plan to visit some of these countries in conjunction with a trip to other countries, contact a U.S. passport agency for guidance.

**Tourists**: Some countries, including Kuwait, Oman, Qatar and Saudi Arabia do not permit tourism. All visitors must be sponsored either by a company in the country to be visited or by a relative or friend native to the country. Countries requiring visitors to be sponsored usually will require them to obtain exit permits from their sponsors as well. It is advisable not to accept sponsorship to visit a country, unless you are sure you will also be able to obtain an exit permit.

**Departure Tax**: Some countries require all departing passengers to pay a departure tax or some type of tax or levy. You should, as part of your inquiry on entry, verify if this applies and if so, keep enough local and/or "hard" currency to ensure departure as planned.

**Overstaying**: Overstaying the validity of your visa or tourist card is considered a violation in several countries. If you think, you might overstay, it is advisable to contact the local immigration office to find out whether you would be allowed to do so and what the requirements may be. In some countries, you may be granted an extension after submitting a formal application. Usually, the sooner you make such determination and/or put in your application, the better.

**Customs Declaration:** If in doubt, make it a habit to always declare to the customs and/or immigration anything you cannot afford to have confiscated, including all items of personal jewelry.

**Validation on Passports**: As an international traveler one observation you will quickly make is the number of times your travel documents, particularly your passport, will be requested by one authority or the other. The other observation is the number of times some form of sticker or stamp is placed or imprinted in your U.S. passport. This is not unusual. The important thing is that you should not hesitate to have any of these validations. In fact, in most cases you should ask whoever is requesting your passport if a validation by them is not required. The validations that you should always look out for and ask about include: (a) visas (entry and exit) unless they are not required, in which case you will be told and (b) all currency transactions.

Do remember, however, that in some countries, some of these validations may not necessarily be made directly into your passport. They may come in the form of a sheet of paper enclosed or attached to your passport or tourist card.

## SAFETY MATTERS

**Trouble:**  While abroad, should you find yourself in trouble (especially with local law enforcement officials) or with any other type of problem (stranded, sick, lost documents, emergency), immediately contact the nearest U.S. Embassy or Consulate. When in trouble with the local law enforcement authorities, visit call, or request the presence of the U.S. Ambassador, Consul or an official from the Embassy or Consulate. While they might not help you resolve all of your problems, they are the best help available.  It is recommended that you register with the nearest U.S. Embassy or Consulate upon arrival.  Check Appendix A for a list of U.S. Embassies and Consulates all over the world.

**Insurance:**  Obtaining adequate insurance coverage must always be paramount in the minds of every international traveler. Coverage to be considered should include automobile, life, medical, trip interruptions and cancellations, bankruptcy, luggage and personal effects insurance. The need for insurance will vary from one traveler to another.  Of course, if you don't plan to drive, you obviously do not need an automobile insurance. If you plan to take your own car as opposed to renting one, you may find that your existing insurance policy(ies) will not cover you in case of a loss. Whatever the case, should you plan to drive abroad, first ensure that you are comprehensively insured by a reputable company and that your insurance policy is valid and will be honored in the country you are visiting.

While shopping for or evaluating your health insurance needs, remember that a good medical insurance should provide you with total coverage, including full coverage for hospital stay, medications and any medically related treatment you might incur, short or long-term. Health policies must also include the cost of transportation to the United States in the event of emergencies and serious conditions, including that of a traveling companion.

Because damaged and lost luggage has become a common experience for many travelers, you may consider insuring these and other accompanying possessions and valuables, especially given the limited coverage, if any, provided to travelers by their carriers. Although you may not recover your losses in full, a good insurance coverage will inevitably minimize your loss. Time-conscious travelers who are concerned about the financial loss due to unscheduled trip cancellations or interruptions, may consider purchasing a trip cancellation or a trip-interruption policy.

There is, of course, life insurance, which is even more important while you are in transit or are abroad. Although you may already carry a life insurance policy, this may be another time to examine the adequacy of your existing policy.

All in all, your pre-travel plans should include researching and getting the necessary insurance coverage. A good insurance broker should be able to help you in avoiding duplication of policies and coverage. Your travel planner, advisor, travel agent and tour operators will be of assistance to you in this area. Also, check your existing automobile, medical and life insurance policies. You may already be partially or fully covered and may or may not need additional coverage. You may, also, find that you are adequately covered by your credit card company (for those who may be charging their tickets). If you are not sure of what is covered or the extent

5

of the coverage, contact your credit card company. Also check with your travel agent; some of them now provide free flight insurance for their ticket clients.

Very often travelers overlook the fact that they may already be adequately covered with double and triple indemnity clauses for accidental death and/or dismemberment by the airline, the travel or auto clubs. Most major credit card companies such as American Express, Mastercard, Visa Carte Blanche, Dinners Club and Discover automatically provide between $100,000 and $350,000 of flight insurance (accident and life) to cardholders who charge their trips to their cards. Cardholders desiring higher coverage can also buy them from these companies at a fairly reasonable rate. These card companies also provide insurance coverage for delayed or lost luggage up to $500 for checked luggages and up to $1,250 for carry-on baggages. It is important to remember that in the event of an accident or death while riding as a passenger, international airlines are liable for up to $75,000 if the ticket is bought in the U.S. The amount is different for tickets bought abroad.

When all is done do not forget to carry your insurance card and a photocopy of your policy with you, including the telephone numbers of your insurance company and agent in case a need arises. Be financially prepared as well, Some insurance companies may require that you settle your expenses overseas and then apply for reimbursement. Some of the policies mentioned here can be easily purchased through your local insurance brokers. Remember, the more comprehensive the coverage (combination policies) the better. A list of some companies that provide travel-related insurance, including short-term policies, is provided in Appendices V and W.

**Security Precautions:**  As a security protection,  it is advisable for the international traveler to always maintain a low profile while in a foreign country. This is particularly important for Americans and those visiting countries in the Middle East, Africa, Asia and South America. You can have a perfectly enjoyable vacation without revealing or showing off your citizenship or parading yourself as an American.

If contemporary or past events are indications to draw from, it is clear that not all countries nor all the citizens of a given country are friendly with Americans, or with America as a country for a variety of reasons. Unfortunately, it is difficult to tell when and where this may be the case.

However, you can stay out of an area of controversy and uncertainty and have yourself a safe and peaceful trip by minding what you say, when and where you say it, and what you do, how, when and where you do it and what you carry, as well as how and where you carry it. To improve your personal security (a) minimize stopover time you spend at airports, avoiding those airports that are known to have security problems; (b) try to book direct flights, scheduling flights preferably on wide-body jets (two aisles) since they are more difficult for hijackers to take over and control; (c) request window seats since passengers in aisle seats are more likely to be abused by hijackers, (d) try not to discuss your travel plans in public places, rather restrict information about your travel plans to those who need to know.

**Dangerous Goods/Articles:** The following materials are often regarded by airlines and by law as articles or goods subject to special conditions. They are generally not allowed to be carried on board airplanes and, if allowed, must be transported as cargo.

- Infectious substances (materials that may cause human disease)
- Explosives, munitions, fireworks and flares
- Compressed gases of any kind
- Magnetized materials
- Corrosive materials
- Radioactive substances
- Oxidizing materials and peroxides (e.g. lead powder)
- Toxic materials and irritants (e.g. tear gas)
- Readily flammable solids and liquids such as gasoline or matches
- Other dangerous goods and substance

**Safety from Thieves:**[IL] Tourists are often easy and lucrative marks for thieves. Special precautions will lessen the opportunities for thieves. Here's a list of things you can do:

- Carry most of your money in traveler's checks insured for theft.

- Never leave your belongings unattended in airports, hotels or restaurants.

- Taxi drivers, can also be thieves. If a taxi driver does not turn his meter on, ask him to turn it on or get yourself another cab. Otherwise, he may take you to your destination and charge you a higher fee. If he tries to" rip you off," get his cab number and report him to law enforcement.

- If you agree to let someone carry your luggage and load it into a taxi watch him closely. He could run off with your bag or pretend to load your bags into the taxi while holding some back. You may not realize you've been robbed until you reach the hotel or destination.

- When registering in hotels, do not put your brief case on the floor. That makes it a perfect target for a quick grab.

- Keep your valuables in the hotel safe.

- Always lock your doors and windows when you leave your hotel room, especially those leading to the balcony.

- When eating in the hotel restaurant or lounge never leave your hotel key on the table. A thief can note the room number, go to your room and rob you when he knows you are out.

- If you are in town for a convention and are required to wear a name tag, remove your name tag when you are not in a meeting. Otherwise, thieves will notice your name, find out your room number from the desk clerk, and rob your room while you are out.

8

■   Never let a stranger into the hotel room even if he claims to be on the hotel staff. Call the desk to make sure the person is legitimate before you open the door.

■   In crowds, walk against the flow of traffic even if you get dirty looks. That makes a pickpocket's job much harder.

■   If someone jostles you in the crowd, turn around immediately while checking for your wallet. Pickpockets move fast.

■   Don't keep your passport and cash in the same place.

■   If you carry a purse, carry your money in a pocket. Cash should be kept in front pants pockets or skirt pockets. Pickpockets go for the purse and back pocket first. Money belts are even better. If they are well-attached, they are difficult to pick.

■   Try to get a **shadowed baggage tag**, so that thieves cannot easily memorize your name and address.

■   When shopping, do not put your package down on the ground to get your money out. Put them in front of you where you can see them or keep then in an over-the-shoulder bag. Keep your bag toward the front of your body while walking. If it's too far behind you, someone can reach in and take something out without your knowing it.

■   Sleazy clubs, topless bars, and strip joints are notorious for scams. Foreigners are easy prey. For example, if you buy a bottle of champagne for a "lady," the bartender, after she's had a few drinks, may exchange the bottle for a half-empty one. By the end of the night, you are charged an exorbitant price for six bottles, while you probably only drank one full bottle of champagne.

■   If you lose your checkbook and it is returned, make sure that no checks are missing.

9

**Carrying Parcels and Letters for Others:** As hard as it may sometimes appear, avoid carrying parcels or letters on behalf of third persons whether or not such a person is traveling along with you on the same plane (or other means of transportation). It is highly dangerous to carry something, if you do not know its contents. Personally, if I must carry a parcel or letter for a very dear friend or relative, I insist on knowing the contents and on doing the actual packing. You can have your entire vacation or trip completely ruined by becoming a victim of a parcel or package with suspicious or illegal contents. Claiming ignorance or emphasizing your "Good Samaritan" spirit will not help you.

**Security and Hotel Rooms:** Do not assume that your hotel room is always safe, whether, as relates to safe guarding your valuables or for personal safety. Important valuables should be carried with you at all times or locked up in the hotel safe. To get a safe deposit box, ask the desk clerk at the hotel. For travelers lodging in facilities without safe deposit boxes, the choice should be obvious. Carry your valuables with you. You will be amazed at how fast an item of yours can disappear. Poverty is real in several parts of the world, and hotel employees are not exceptions. An item considered so unimportant by you might be very valuable to a poor hotel employee.

**Pickpockets and Baggage Thieves:** These are two of the several types of menacing hosts and hostesses you will likely encounter during your trips abroad. They come in all forms and shades. They carry no name tags or special identifying features except that they are almost everywhere, but more in some places than in others, particularly at airports, train and bus stations and in crowded public gatherings. Many are well trained in the art, and operate as part of a gang, while some others may be just independent operating amateurs. Surely, you would like to be able to identify them so as to stay away. Unfortunately, it may be difficult. It could be that four year old girl or boy hovering around you, that 16 year old offering to help carry one of your bags, that miserable-looking woman carrying a baby in one hand, with the other hand extended to you, or that well dressed and well spoken gentleman or woman, seemingly knowledgeable about everything around town, including your immediate need. However they are described, it should be clear that they are your worst enemies. They are capable of making you re-live all the problems faced by many travelers. Of course, pickpockets, baggage thieves and their derivatives can be found in every country, including the U.S., and their motives are the same: to take what is yours and get away with it by any means necessary. How you will deal with them in the U.S. is, therefore, no different from the approach you will use abroad? Well, not necessarily. As you journey from one country or community to another, you will find that their **modus operandi** is different. Whereas, in some places, the law is there to protect you; in some countries you will find very little real help or consolation, even from law enforcement. You may even find blame for not being careful enough. Well, maybe the latter might make sense, at least to the extent that it motivates you to learn about the tricks and take necessary precautions.

Although pickpockets and baggage thieves occasionally operate overtly and with some degree of violence or force, most go about it in a subtle way. For the most part, their key strategy is DISTRACTION. Remember DISTRACTION. In other words, they will distract you by whatever means will work and then rob you. There are numerous ways and techniques pickpockets and baggage thieves use in an effort to distract. There are stories of people using mustard or ketchup by "unintentionally" smearing it on your clothes. Some will create sudden situations and emotions such as pointing and looking to the sky for an unseen and unknown phenomenon, indirectly encouraging you to do the same. Some even stage events and games that will attract the unsuspecting. Some will engage you in conversations long enough for you to loose your sense of where you are. There are the familiar forms of distractions used by pickpockets, including crowding you bumping into you, stepping on your toes, or cornering you so tight that you can hardly feel differently or notice any serious picking taking place. Throughout your trip you have to bear in mind that many of these individuals are very smart and they believe you can be distracted. You help them by giving them the opportunity, the time and the place. What can you do to minimize your becoming a victim?

(a) Avoid crowded areas and events (2) Stay away from dark alleys, poorly lit and isolated places, including train compartments with only very few

11

people. Remember they tend to pick more on those who appear helpless and weak. (c) Avoid conversations with groups of unknown individuals, particularly during shopping (d) Refuse unsolicited assistance and when you must do so, be careful. If you need help with your luggage, do the approaching and surrender the heavier and least valuable luggage, not your wallet or hand bag, (e) Stay focused and keep walking to your destination. If you have any stains or whatever, you can certainly check it out somewhere else (for example, in your hotel) not on the street. (f) Carry your valuables in a secure and hidden place where somebody must totally demobilize you to get to without you noticing. A number of travelers pouches, particularly money belts, are becoming very popular and many do provide better protection. (g) Do not make a habit of telling people time when they ask. If it is so important, they can always ask some other person or invest in a cheap watch. (h) Do not make change for people. Certainly they can go to the bank. (i) Watch where you sit or stand even in trains and buses. It is better to have your back to the wall if you can. (j) Try to blend and to look like everyone around you. Conspicuous looks and actions only expose you. You don't have to carry name tags and look like a tourist to be a tourist or to display your valuables and money to appreciate why you must have them. (k) Do not ask strangers to watch your luggage or bags, no matter where and no matter how short a time. (l) Be aware of your immediate environment and the people there. A careful look at faces and actions around you should be able to trigger an appropriate action on your part. A place with too many loiterers and strollers is not particularly an attractive place to be. It is often a fishing zone for pickpockets. (m) Avoid carrying your wallet or purse in a rear pocket. Carrying these items in front of you in clear view and crossed over with your arms is definitely better protection. Inside pockets are even better, particularly if they have zippers. Money belts (waist, leg and shoulder belts) have became popular with tourists. Every pickpocket-conscious traveler should consider getting one of these belts or making one for themselves.

And for those happy-go-lucky travelers who, despite all warnings and advice to the contrary, will drink and get drunk, you are perhaps the most vulnerable.

**Safety Precautions for Women Alone**[IL] Unfortunately, women need to take special precautions when traveling abroad, especially when traveling alone. Attitudes toward women vary from country to country, but here are a few general precautions that women should take when traveling:

- If you're traveling solo, use public transportation whenever possible. The incidence of rape and robbery of lone women in cabs are alarmingly high. As an American, you are an even greater temptation.

- Do most of your traveling during the day. If you must go out at night, travel with an acquaintance, especially in southern Europe where the men tend to be sexually aggressive toward women.

- The less you carry around with you, the easier it will be to run if necessary. Do not overburden yourself with packages or luggage.

- Don't wear expensive jewelry or clothes, especially when you're alone.

- Men in Italy and Spain like to pinch. Stand with your back against the wall in elevators, and if you're traveling with a friend, ask him to walk behind you in crowds. If you figure out who's pinching you, turn around and say "Enough." That usually will put an end to it.

- Have your key ready before you reach your room so you won't be fumbling for it in the hallways.

- Don't flirt with men on the hotel staff unless you're serious about it. They have a key to your room and may not be able to resist the invitation. If you hear anyone trying your door, call the front desk immediately. If you don't have a phone, be loud and aggressive. Yell. Threaten to notify the police.

- Ask for a hotel room near an elevator so that you won't be walking

13

down long dim corridors alone at night.

- Try staying at a bed-and-breakfast instead of a hotel

**Hitchhiking**: Avoid the temptation, unless it is your normal way of life and your preferred means of transportation, in which case you are fully aware of the thrills as well as the risks that go with it. There are many personal safety considerations and risks to worry about in a foreign land and you do not want to complicate them or add to the risks. Should you find yourself destitute or stranded, call or request assistance from the nearest police office and the U.S. consulate. Much better, plan well and avoid those things that may necessitate hitchhiking in the first place, such as carrying adequate funds and emergency contact telephone numbers. Remember, hitchhiking may be frowned upon and may be illegal in some countries or prohibited in certain areas. Despite the problems and risks inherent in hitchhiking, this practice appears relatively safer and more common in Europe than in other regions of the world.

**Beggars and Homeless Persons**: As you journey round the globe, you will find beggars and homeless persons just as you will find them here in the U.S. This is common in large urban centers. It is uncertain, what to expect from these groups as their mode of operation varies from country to country. Without a doubt, they can be a nuisance and a pest to travelers and in some cases, a source of embarrassment. It's really up to you how you deal with them. In many countries, they will touch you, pull you, insult you, harass you and even rob you. Very often, a small token gift will satisfy them. Ironically, although they may complain of lack of food, most will not accept food, but would rather prefer money. However, you deal with this group of people, be careful not to lose sight of your valuables as many are, in fact, <u>bona</u>-<u>fide</u> professional pickpockets, luggage thieves and muggers. Many of them, including women and young children, are not what they claim to be, but rather are part of a robbery or extortion ring or gang in disguise. Stories of parents actually training their children in the act of begging, as a way of life are common. Also common is the reality of poverty in several parts of the world, contributing in part to these illegal practices.

14

<u>Tricksters</u>: Perhaps next to pickpockets, tricksters are another group determined at fowling up your trip. They will come in all shades and colors, some well dressed, knowledgeable and well spoken, and others just the opposite. They will prey upon your confidence and desperation with promises to do wonders for you or to render services you never requested. Essentially, Beware! What they want is your money. You will probably find more tricksters in South Asian Countries than in other parts of the world. These individuals are nothing but con men, women and children who, in a flash, will render you penniless as they disappear with your money and valuables. Just be on the lookout for unsolicited assistance of any form or type. Besides, always be suspicious of unsolicited samaritans. Their motives are often unpredictable and "unsamaritan." Your best approach is to avoid them and, if approached, to simply say, "No thanks" and walk away. Do not let them distract you or get you to participate in their discussion.

<u>Visiting Remote Areas:</u> As an international traveler, you may have reason(s) to travel outside the urban centers to remote rural areas and villages, sometimes solo, or as part of a group. If this is part of your overseas plan, you need to take certain safety measures. Incidents of armed robbery, vandalism and in some cases rape abound in some of these areas, particularly in some of the countries in Africa and South America. Some of the reported incidents take place even during the day. While many of the incidents are random acts, some target foreigners. Here are some actions you may take to minimize becoming a victim: (a) Do your home work! Research as much as possible about travel conditions in that part of the country you plan visiting, particularly, any incidents or history of crimes against foreigners. The nearest U.S. embassy or consulate in the area will be a good source. (b) Notify the nearest U.S. embassy or consulate of your presence in the country and about your planned trip. They might provide you with additional, valuable information about the area, including alternative precautionary arrangements. (c) Avoid any mode of transportation and attire that conspicuously identifies you or your group as foreigners. (d) Traveling as a group, is certainly more advantageous than traveling solo. (e) Avoid late evening or night travels. (f) Seek the help of the local law enforcement. They can provide you with additional information about the area, including routes. (g) Importantly, consider investing in

15

armed escorts. You could readily find them or get good recommendations from the U.S. embassies or consulates, from the local law enforcement or your hotel guest desk. In some countries, the local police office, for a fee, will provide you with such assistance. Local firms providing security services, off-duty police officers and retired law enforcement officers are also available in some countries. The escort arrangement may include, the escorting officer(s) riding with you in the same car, van or bus or riding ahead of you, in their own vehicle. It is often hard to say which is a better arrangement since there are cost implications. Nevertheless, their share presence and better understanding of local travel conditions is an advantage worth considering and pursuing by a foreigner.

**Vagabonds:** In your trip around the world you will, from time to time, run into vagabonds. These individuals parade and roam around inside and outside the airports, ticketing offices, government buildings and offices, and many other places where travelers and non-travelers alike go to apply for important documents. They are neither authorized nor employed by the respective agencies and offices, nor are their activities officially condoned. These vagabonds will often offer their services to you, promising to obtain for you, in record time, whatever it is you need, be it boarding passes, visas or just forms. They usually promise to do this for a reasonable price. Although many do in fact succeed in providing you with the requested services in real record time, their activities are often illegal and frowned upon by the government. You will be taking a big risk dealing with them and this could get you into trouble, including jail time. Besides, you cannot be so sure who the person you are contracting with really is. He or she may well be an undercover police officer. By supporting these vagabonds and patronizing their activities, you may end up losing, time, money, and any documents you might have advanced to them. If you plan appropriately, you will often succeed in getting, legitimately, whatever it is you are applying for. Just give yourself more time.

**Security-related information from the US State Department.** The Department of State's Consular Information Sheets are available for every country of the world. They describe unusual entry or currency regulations, unusual health conditions, the crime and security situation, political disturbances, areas of instability, and drug penalties. They also provide addresses and emergency telephone numbers for US. embassies and consulates. In general, the sheets do not give advice. Instead, they describe conditions so travelers can make informed decisions about their trips.

In some dangerous situations, however, the Department of State recommends that Americans defer travel to a country. In such a case, a Travel Warning is issued for the country in addition to its Consular information Sheet.

**Consular Information Sheets** and **Travel Warnings** are available at the 13 regional passport agencies; at U.S. embassies and consulates abroad; or by sending a self-addressed, stamped envelope to: Overseas Citizens Services, Room 4811, Department of State, Washington, DC 20520-4818. They are also available through airline computer reservation systems when you or your travel agent make your international air reservations.

In addition, you can access Consular Information Sheets and Travel Warnings **24-hours a day** from three different electronic systems. To listen to them, call (202) 647-5225 from a touchtone phone. To receive them by fax, dial (202) 647-3000 from a fax machine and follow the prompts that you will hear on the machine's telephone receiver. To view or download the documents check out these state department web addresses: http://travel.state.gov/travel_pubs.html and http://travel.state.gov/travel_pubs.html

**Safety on the Street** Use the same common sense traveling overseas that you would at home. Be especially cautious in, or avoid areas where you are likely to be victimized. These include crowded subways, train stations, elevators, tourist sites, market places, festivals and marginal areas of cities.

(1) Don't use short cuts, narrow alleys or poorly-lit streets. Try not to travel alone at night. (2) Avoid public demonstrations and other civil disturbances. (3) Keep a low profile and avoid loud conversations or arguments. Do not discuss travel plans or other personal matters with strangers. (4) Try to seem purposeful when you move about. Even if you

are lost, act as if you know where you are going. When possible, ask directions only from individuals in authority. (5) Know how to use a pay telephone and have the proper change or token on hand. (6) Learn a few phrases in the local language so you can signal your need for help, the police, or a doctor. (7) Make note of emergency telephone numbers you may need: police, fire, your hotel, and the nearest US. embassy or consulate. (8) If confronted by superior force, don't fight attackers - give up valuables.

**Safety on Public Transport** In countries where there is a pattern of tourists being targeted consider taking the following precautions:

**Taxis.** Only take taxis clearly identified with official markings. Beware of irregular cabs.

**Trains.** Well organized, systematic robbery of passengers on trains along popular tourists routes is a serious problem. It is more common at night and especially on overnight trains. (a) If you see your way blocked by someone and another person is pressing you from behind, move away. This can happen in the corridor of the train or on the platform or station. (b) Do not accept food or drink from strangers. Criminals have been known to drug passengers by offering them food or drink. Criminals may also spray sleeping gas in train compartments. (c) Where possible, lock your compartment. If it cannot be locked securely, take turns with your traveling companions sleeping in shifts. If that is not possible, stay awake. If you must sleep unprotected, tie down your luggage, strap your valuables to you and sleep on top of them as much as possible. (d) Do not be afraid to alert authorities if you feel threatened in any way. Extra police are often assigned to ride trains on routes where crime is a serious problem.

**Buses.** The same type of criminal activity found on trains can be found on public buses on popular tourist routes. For example, tourists have been drugged and robbed while sleeping on buses or in bus stations. In some countries whole bus loads of passengers have been held up and robbed by gangs of bandits.

**Safety When You Drive** When you rent a car, don't go for the exotic; choose cars that are commonly available locally. Where possible, ask that markings that identify it as a rental car be removed. Make certain it is in good repair. If available, choose a car with universal door locks and power windows, features that give the driver better control of access to the car. An air conditioner, when available, is also a safety feature, allowing you to drive with windows closed. Thieves can and do snatch purses through open windows of moving cars.

(a) Keep car doors locked at all times. Wear seat belts. (b) As much as possible, avoid driving at night. (c) Don't leave valuables in the car. If you must carry things with you, keep them out of sight in the trunk. (d) Don't park your car on the street overnight. If the hotel or municipality does not have a parking garage or other secure area, select a well lit area. (e) Never pick up hitchhikers. (f) Don't get out of the car if there are suspicious individuals nearby. Drive away.

**Patterns of Crime Against Motorists** In many places frequented by tourists, including areas of southern Europe, victimization of motorists has been refined to an art. Where it is a problem, U.S. embassies are aware of it and consular officers try to work with local authorities to warn the public about the dangers. In some locations, these efforts at public awareness have paid off, reducing the frequency of incidents. Ask your rental car agency for advice on avoiding robbery. Where it is a problem, they are well aware of it and should tell you how best to protect yourself.

Carjackers and thieves operate at gas stations, parking lots, in city traffic, and along the highway. Be suspicious of anyone who hails you or tries to get your attention when you are in or near your car.

Criminals use ingenious ploys. They may masquerade as good Samaritans, offering help for tires that they claim are flat or that they have made flat. Or they may flag down a motorist, ask for assistance, and then steal the rescuer's luggage or car. Usually they work in groups, one person carrying on the pretense while the others rob you.

Other criminals get your attention with abuse, either trying to drive you off the road, or causing an "accident' by rear-ending you or creating a "fender bender."

In some urban areas, thieves don't waste time on ploys, they simply smash car windows at traffic lights, grab your valuables or your car and get away. In cities around the world, "defensive driving" has come to mean more than avoiding auto accidents; it means keeping an eye out for potentially criminal pedestrians, cyclists, and scooter riders.

**Protection Against Terrorism** Terrorist acts occur at random and unpredictably, making it impossible to protect oneself absolutely. The first and best protection is to avoid travel to unsafe areas where there has been a persistent record of terrorist attacks or kidnapping. The vast majority of foreign states have good records of maintaining public order and protecting residents and visitors within their borders from terrorism.

Most terrorist attacks are the result of long and careful planning. Just as a car-thief will first be attracted to an unlocked car with the key in the ignition, terrorists are looking for defenseless, easily accessible targets who follow predictable patterns. The chances that a tourist, traveling with an unpublished program or itinerary, would be the victim of terrorism are slight - no more than the random possibility of being in the wrong place at the wrong time. In addition, many terrorist groups, seeking publicity for political causes within their own country or region, are not looking for American targets.

Nevertheless, the pointers below may help you avoid becoming a "target of opportunity." They should be considered as adjuncts to the tips listed in the previous sections on how to protect yourself against the far greater likelihood of being a victim of ordinary crime. These precautions may provide some degree of protection, and can serve as practical and psychological deterrents to would-be terrorists.

(1) Schedule direct flights if possible and avoid stops in high-risk airports or areas. Consider other options for travel, such as trains. (2) Be aware of

what you discuss with strangers, or what may be overheard by others. (3) Try to minimize the time spent in the public area of an airport, which is a less protected area. Move quickly from the check-in counter to the secured areas. on **arrival,** leave the airport as soon as possible. (4) As much as possible, avoid luggage tags, dress, and behavior which may identify you as an American. (5) Keep an eye out for suspicious abandoned packages or briefcases. Report them to airport security or other authorities and leave the area promptly. (6) Avoid obvious terrorist targets such as places where Americans and Westerners are known to congregate.

**Travel to High-Risk Areas** If you must travel in an area where there has been a history of terrorist attacks or kidnappings make it a habit to:
(1) Discuss with your family what they would do in case of an emergency, in addition to making sure your affairs are in order before leaving home. (2) Register with the U.S. embassy or consulate upon arrival. (3) Remain friendly, but be cautious about discussing personal matters, your itinerary or program. (4) Leave no personal or business papers in your hotel room. (5) Watch for people following you or "loiterers" observing your comings and goings. (6) Keep a mental note of safe havens, such as police stations, hotels, hospitals. (7) Let someone else know what your travel plans are. Keep them informed if you change your plans. (8) Avoid predictable times and routes of travel, and report any suspicious activity to local police, and the neatest U.S. embassy or consulate. (9) Select your own taxi cabs at random - don't take a cab that is not clearly identified as a taxi. Compare the face of the driver with the one posted on his or her license. (10) If possible, travel with others. (11) Be sure of the identity of visitors before opening the door of your hotel room. Don't meet strangers at unknown or remote locations. (12) Refuse unexpected packages. (13) Formulate a plan of action for what you will do if a bomb explodes or there is gunfire nearby. (14) Check for loose wires or other suspicious activity around your car. (15) Be sure your vehicle is in good operating condition in case you need to resort to high-speed or evasive driving. (16) Drive with car windows closed in crowded streets; bombs can be thrown through open windows. (17) If you are ever in a situation where somebody starts shooting, drop to the floor or get down as low as possible. Don't move until you are sure the danger has passed. Do not attempt to help rescuers and do not pick up a weapon. If

possible, shield yourself behind or under a solid object. If you must move, crawl on your stomach.

**Hijacking/Hostage Situations** While every hostage situation is different and the chance of becoming a hostage is remote, some considerations are important.

The US. government's policy not to negotiate with terrorists is **firm** - to do so would only increase the risk of further hostage-taking. When Americans are abducted overseas, we look to the host government to exercise its responsibility under international law to protect all persons within its territories and to bring about the safe release of hostages. We work closely with these governments from the outset of a hostage-taking incident to ensure that our citizens and other innocent victim are released as quickly and safely as possible.

Normally, the most dangerous phases of a hijacking or hostage situation are the beginning and, if there is a rescue attempt, the end. At the outset, the terrorists typically are tense, high-strung and may behave irrationally. It is extremely important that you remain calm and alert and manage your own behavior.

(1) Avoid resistance, sudden or threatening movements. Do not struggle or try to escape unless you are certain of being successful. (2) Make a concerted effort to relax. Breathe deeply and prepare yourself mentally, physically and emotionally for the possibility of a long ordeal. (3) Try to remain inconspicuous, avoid direct eye contact and the appearance of observing your captors' actions. (4) Avoid alcoholic beverages. Consume little food and drink. (5) Consciously put yourself in a mode of passive cooperation. Talk normally. Do not complain, avoid belligerency, and comply with all orders and instructions. (6) If questioned, keep your answers short. Don't volunteer information or make unnecessary overtures. (7) Don't try to be a hero, endangering yourself and others. (8) Maintain your sense of personal dignity, a gradually increase your requests for personal comforts. Make these requests in a reasonable low-key manner. (9) If you are involved in a lengthier, drawn-out situation, try to establish

a rapport with your captors, avoiding political discussions or other confrontation. (10) Establish a daily program of mental and physical activity. Don't be afraid to ask for anything you need or want - medicines, books, pencils, paper. (10) Eat what they give you, even if it does not look or taste appetizing. A loss of appetite and weight is normal. (11) Think positively; avoid a sense of despair. Rely on your inner resources. Remember that you are valuable commodity to your captors. It is important to them.

**Assistance Abroad** If you plan to stay more than two weeks in one place, if you are in an area experiencing civil unrest or a natural disaster, or if you are planning travel to a remote area, it is advisable to register at the Consular Section of the nearest U.S. embassy or consulate. The will make it easier if someone at home needs to locate you urgently or in the unlikely event that you need to be evacuated in an emergency. It will also facilitate the issuance of new passport should yours be lost or stolen.

Another reason to contact the Consular Section is to obtain updated information on the security situation in a country.

If you are ill or injured, contact the nearest U.S. embassy or consulate for a list of local physicians and medical facilities. If the illness is serious, consular officers can help you find medical assistance from this list and, at your request, will inform your family or friends. If necessary, a consul can assist in the transfer of funds from the United States. Payment of hospital and other medical expenses is your responsibility.

If you become destitute overseas, consular officers can help you get in touch with your family, friends, bank, or employer and inform them how to wire funds to you.

Should you find yourself in legal difficulty, contact a consular officer immediately. Consular officers cannot serve as attorneys, give legal advice, or get you out of jail. What they can do is provide a list of local attorneys who speak English and who may have had experience in representing U.S. citizens. If you are arrested, consular officials will visit you, advise you of your rights under local laws, and ensure that you are held under humane conditions and are treated fairly under local law. A consular officer will also contact your family or friends if you desire. When necessary, consuls can transfer money from home for you and will try to get relief for you, including food and clothing in countries where this is a problem. **If you are detained remember that under international agreements and practice, you have the right to talk to the U.S. consul.** If you are denied this right, be persistent; try to have someone get in touch for you.

<u>Protecting Yourself</u> Sometimes peace of mind can be just a phone call away. If you have any concerns or questions about local conditions or your destination, call the Department of State's Citizens Emergency Center as (202) 647-5225 for 24-hour-a-day recordings of all current travel advisories. You can also obtain travel advisories from U.S. passport agencies, or U.S. Embassies and consulates abroad. The Citizens Emergency Center also provides information on emergency services to U.S. citizens overseas.

## Be Smart!
When you're having a wonderful time in a new environment it's easy to let your guard down. That's why you need to use your common sense and be extra conscious of you actions so you do not become and easy target for crime.

Here are some precautions to take while traveling in a foreign country:

● **Keep a low profile**. This means leaving your valuables, expensive jewelry, and luggage at home. These items might mark you as a wealthy or important American.
● **Avoid dangerous areas.** Don't use short-cuts or walk down narrow alleys or poorly lit streets.
● **Never travel alone after dark.** Always let someone know where you are going, and what time you expect to return, especially at night.
● **Meet visitors in the lobby of your hotel.** Don't give out your room number. Always keep your hotel and car doors locked.
● **Carry belongings in a secure manner.** Women should wear handbags tucked under their arm and hold the strap. Men should put their wallets in

their front trouser pocket or wear a money belt.

● **Don't carry valuables in coat pockets, handbags, or hip pockets** which are particularly susceptible to theft.

● **Avoid using "gypsy" taxis that pick up more that one person per cab.** Use a hotel or airport taxi. If there is no meter, always agree on the fare in advance.

● **Be wary of street vendors.** While one has your attention selling you goods, someone else may be picking your pocket.

● **Book hotel rooms between the second and seventh floors** to prevent easy entrance from the outside, but low enough for fire equipment to reach. Check out the fire safety instructions and the exits.

● **If you have a problem, the local police department** is the best place to go for help.

● **Learn a few important phrases in the local language** so you can signal for fire, the police, the doctor, or the nearest bathroom.

● **Avoid displaying company name or logos** on luggage and tags.

**Do's and Don'ts at the Airport:** Traveling abroad means you'll be spending time in foreign airports, going through customs, exchanging money and waiting for flights. That's why you should take a moment to review these practical tactics.

**DO**

Proceed to boarding gate as soon as possible. Secure belongings.

Keep your distance from unattended luggage.

Keep a low profile, behave quietly and inconspicuously.

Be alert. Survey your surroundings and check out emergency exits.

**DON'T**

Discuss travel plans indiscriminately.

Leave bags unattended, even for a minute.

Carry any bags or packages for strangers or friends unless you are certain of what is inside.

Carry all your money in one place.

**What to Do if there is an Incident:**

● Try to remain calm and inconspicuous. Do not move until the situation is under control.  Be passive, yet remain alert.

● Avoid confrontation.  Do not engage in political discussions  or volunteer information.

● Comply with requests.  If you must surrender personal belongings, do so without a struggle.

● Make any requests you may have in short, simple sentences.

● If there is a rescue attempt, stay as close to the ground as  possible.

● Do not try to be a hero.

**Traveling Abroad with your children:** If you plan to bring your children overseas, it is important that they become familiar with the local laws and customs.  Foreign languages, symbols, and signs can be very confusing to young children.  Be sure to prepare them well in advance for the differences they will encounter.  Here are some common sense issues to discuss with your children before leaving the United States and once you have reached your destinations.

(1). Make sure young children know the name and the address of the place where they are staying. A sample child I.D. a Form/Card has been provided. It should be filled out on both sides by an adult and kept in a safe place on your child at all times. (2). Using a foreign telephone can be confusing to a child. Show your child how to use the telephone, and be sure he or she has enough money to make several calls if needed. (3.) Go over with your child who to call or approach in an emergency situation.  These numbers and addresses should be kept on his or her I.D. card and, if possible, memorized.  Point out a local, uniformed police officer to your child so he ore she will be able to recognize one (4.) Discuss traffic rules with your child. Red lights don't  always necessarily mean stop. (5.) Make sure your child is aware of the dangers of electrical outlets, appliances, and TVs that operate on strong current overseas. (6.) Do not let your child go anywhere alone. Enforce the "Buddy System" and explain the importance of always being aware of his or her surroundings. (7.) In crowded places such as open market, busy streets, and airports, keep your child close by. Always have a designated spot to meet in case you get separated.

## HEALTH MATTERS

**Physician:** Your international travel plans should include consultation with your physician. Your physician may be helpful in responding to your health problems while overseas, but equally important, in counseling you regarding how to maintain good health while abroad. He or she will be in a good position to advise you on what medications to carry, what to eat and drink and what to stay away from. Do not forget a trip to your dentist.

**Vaccination:** Vaccination requirements vary from country to country. some countries may deny you entry or subject you to vaccination at the airport before allowing you to enter. It will be very prudent to have your shots here in the U.S. before traveling. Make sure your shots are properly and officially documented on a yellow colored "International Vaccination Card" or the 'International Vaccination Certificate." For a list of countries and the recommended shots, or for additional diseases you should be aware of contact the Centers for Disease Control at (404) 329-3311. As you go through the vaccination requirements for the various countries you plan to visit, do not overlook discussing with your physician immunization for such diseases as hepatitis, polio, tetanus/diphtheria, typhoid and cholera. For those travelers who have already had these shots, all that may be needed are just booster shots. A number of these shots are still controversial. Your physician, however, should advise you appropriately. Whereas some of the shots you will need may be available free-of-charge with some health plans, in some cases you may be required to pay to get them. Contact your physician or your state or local health office on this matter. Remember, a number of these inoculations may require more than one dose of the shot and therefore, more than one visit. Some shots must be given several weeks apart and some have side-effects that could render you uncomfortable for several days. It is, therefore, important to plan appropriately and give yourself a reasonable amount of time.

**Clinical/Medical:** For those travelers who are particularly concerned about their health and who feel that during their trip abroad they may have to seek some form of medical treatment, carrying along a copy of your medical records stating any special conditions or problems and suggested treatments may be a wise idea. A similar record or log of any type of problems encountered while overseas, including treatment should also be kept. It may be needed for reference by your physician upon return. You may consider investing in a Medical Alert bracelet currently available from the Medical Alert Foundation. See Appendix W.

**Medical Help Overseas:** While it is never a traveler's wish to be injured or ill while traveling overseas, it is a fact of life that travelers abroad do get injured and ill and may require medical attention. Americans traveling abroad may take solace in knowing that there are qualified physicians available world wide who are capable of providing them with the same level of quality treatment as is available at home. In several countries, especially in Europe and in urban centers of most developed countries, quality hospitals and medical facilities do exist. For the American traveler, the other important need may be for qualified physicians who understand and speak English. For your consolation, you may want to take advantage of the services of the several international travel, medical assistance organizations listed in Appendix 1A.

While you contemplate on the topic of medical treatment abroad, you want to be aware of the fact that your medical treatment abroad, especially with private, independent physicians, may not be free-of-charge and you may be required to pay in advance in cash. The cost to you may, also, be high. This is all the more reason it is strongly recommended before you travel abroad, that you take out some form of insurance that will cover all or most of your treatments or medical costs incurred abroad. You may consider shopping around or delaying until you return home those routine, non-life threatening, non-essential, less urgent problems and treatments. It's really up to you.

As part of your pre-travel plans, you may want to find out the quality and status of medical facilities and treatment generally available to you in the country or countries you plan to visit and whether as a foreign traveler, you may have to pay or not. It is always safer to think you may have to pay and make the necessary financial or payment plans. Should there be a need to be hospitalized, university affiliated hospitals may be worth considering.

Besides the quality of treatments, chances are that you may run into American or Western trained doctors who may be fluent in English.

As always, taking the proper precautions through a careful preparation in consultation with your physician will save you a bundle and will make your trip abroad a healthy, safe and enjoyable one. For example, a medical emergency kit with such items as bandages, cotton wool, swabs, and disinfectants, a little extra prescription medication, and extra eyeglasses, may be worth much more than any minor inconvenience of taking them along. Should you decide to carry with you a substantial quantity of needed medication or a controlled or prescription drug, you may want to secure a special letter from your physician stating your care and need. Failure to do so may cause your medications to be taxed or confiscated. Although you may find your medical needs abroad adequately met for the most part, travelers to less developed countries and to rural parts of most countries must always take extra precautions. It is safer to be overly prepared than to be less prepared. Importantly, do not always expect the same level of quality medical treatment and facilities as may exist at home.

**Medical Emergency Kit:** A good emergency medical kit should be an important carry-along item for an international traveler. This is particularly important for those traveling to Less Developed Countries or to rural and remote parts of foreign countries. A timely attendance to a sudden but minor ailment by way of first aid treatment may make a difference between enjoying your vacation, terminating it or finding yourself in a hospital. A good medical kit doesn't have to be bulky or heavy. What is important are the contents. Remember, even in the possession of the best of medical kits, it is always advisable to seek immediate professional medical attention in the event of any form of illness, even more so when you are in a foreign country. Being sick away from home is not something to take lightly, and you should not depend solely on a medical kit. See Appendix X for a sample Emergency Medical Kit.

**Hospitalization While Abroad:** Should there be a need to be hospitalized, university affiliated teaching hospitals may be worth considering. Besides the advantage of quality treatment, the chances are that you may run into

American or Western trained doctors, who may also be fluent in English.

**The Jet Lag Drag:**[IL] Your internal clock runs on a fairly regular schedule. But every time you fly into another time zone, you disrupt your internal rhythms and experience jet lag. (The medical term for jet lag is circadian dysynchronization.) Jet lag causes you to become overwhelmingly tired, groggy, and lightheaded. The following is a list of precautions to take:

* Before you leave, try to prepare your body for the new time zone. For example, if you are going to London, which is five hours ahead of EST, start going to bed one hour early and getting up an hour earlier five days before your departure. By the time you depart, your body will have adjusted.

* A few days before you leave and during your flight, decrease your caffeine intake.

* Although many airline offer free alcoholic beverages, avoid them. You don't need the added impact of a hangover. If you do indulge, drink only wine. The alcohol content is lower in wine than in mixed drinks.

* Eat lightly during your flight. If you eat too heavily, you may feel nauseous.

* Try to sleep during your flight. This will reduce your exhaustion when you arrive.

* Once you land, take a few minutes to stretch. Do not go to your hotel to sleep if it is only 5 p.m. Stay awake as long as possible, try to eat a light meal, and remain active. This will allow your body to adjust more quickly to the new timetable and reduce the effects of jet lag.

**Who Should not Fly?:**[IL] A person who is undergoing severe emotional illness probably is not a good candidate for a long air trip unless absolutely necessary, and then a responsible traveling companion is essential.

If good sense is used and proper consultation is made with a physician, most persons having an illness or a chronic disability, such as diabetes or epilepsy, can tolerate air travel and their disabilities will not be aggravated.

If you should have a disease that occasionally causes loss of consciousness, such as epilepsy or diabetes, carry a card in your wallet identifying the illness.

The Medic-Alert Company has stainless steel bracelets or emblems with engraved serial numbers that have key words such as **DIABETIC** written on them. The serial number enables the attending physician to call collect night or day for more specific information about the patient.

**Medications/Prescription Drugs**: Carry along with you any necessary medications and keep them in their original, labeled container in your hand luggage. Because of strict laws on narcotics, carry a letter from your physician explaining your need for any prescription drugs in your possession. Failure to do this may result in the confiscation of your medication and/or a fine and imprisonment.

**A Trip to Your Doctor:** This is highly recommended for International Travelers, particularly the elderly, the disabled and those with medical problems. To get more out of your visit, you should ask your physician to educate you on a host of health-related issues including the required vaccinations. Obviously you should be equally concerned about preventive measures. Because there are numerous diseases you may contract and numerous related health problems that you may encounter when traveling abroad, it is fair to say that the chances will very much depend on where you are traveling, the time of the year and how much personal health precautions you have taken.

As you discuss these issues with your physician you may want to explore to the extent possible, what measures you can take to prevent and/or treat the following: diarrhea, blisters, sting bites (mosquitoes, dogs, and snakes, etc.), dysentery, ear aches, food poison, infections, (including fungal infections) sun burns, motion sickness, jet lag, hemorrhoids, giardia, exhaustion, tooth aches, rashes, anxiety, insomnia, and foreign objects in the eye. Discuss preventive measures for diseases such as malaria,  yellow fever, hepatitis, typhoid, cholera, rabies, tetanus, AIDS, herpes syphilis, gonorrhea, measles, mumps, rubella, poliomyelities, diphtheria, pertussis, encephalitis, typhus fever, tuberculosis, schistosomiasis, trypanosomiasis (sleeping sickness) and leishmaniasis. As you will immediately notice the list can be quite extensive. The list however only includes the diseases and problems you are most  likely to experience. Keep in mind that all of them may not be relevant or applicable to your destination. You may already be immunized for some of these conditions and can make arrangements to be immunized against others.  You may already be adequately knowledgeable about many of these conditions, but it would not hurt to make extra inquiries to protect yourself.

**Water**:  In some parts of the world, water remains a scare resource. Potable water is scarce and water for general purpose may not be readily available. Do not be alarmed if your hotel does not provide you with adequate water to shower or with hot water at all. This is true even in Europe. Of course, you may get some flimsy apologies and excuses from management, but the absence of water, especially hot water, may be a regular occurrence rather than a sudden problem as they sometimes try to explain. Since your stay will very likely entail a hotel or similar lodging facility, find out from the reservation clerk if there is water available, particularly hot water and if there are any limitations. This is important since there might be some rationing going on in which case, your room may be pre-programmed for just a few minutes of hot waters.

With regard to portable water, your best bet is to take maximum precautions. Discuss with your physician and consider investing in one of the inexpensive, but effective, water filtration gadgets or tablets readily found in drug stores. Not even the hotel clerks can truly guarantee the safety of the drinking water they serve you.

**Buying Prescription and Other Drugs**   Unless for very quick expiring medications, fill all of your prescriptions in the U.S. before you go. Because of the lack of rigid controls on drugs and other pharmaceutical products in certain countries, particularly in developing countries, there have been numerous case of expired and adulterated drugs being sold. This is true even among many of the, supposedly registered and professionally staffed chemists as they are sometimes referred to overseas. The proliferation of street-side drug vendors, unlicensed and non-professional pharmacists adds even more to the risk of endangering your life when you fill your prescriptions overseas.

An additional reason for getting your prescriptions in the U.S. is that you may not be able to find your favorite brand overseas. There is, of course, the likelihood that the nearest pharmacy or drug store may be several miles away and/or with limited operating hours. Finally, do not forget that in several countries, there is an acute shortage of drugs. The drugs you need may, therefore, not be available. If you do find them, they may command exorbitant price tags, perhaps turning out more expensive than the same drugs in the U.S.

It is for these reasons that you should seriously consider carrying along extra medications. This should include   both prescription and non-prescription (over-the-counter) medications. On the other hand, if you must fill all or some part of your medications abroad, do so only at large professionally attended drug stores. Do not forget to request a generic prescription from your physician before you go, since names of drugs abroad may differ from those in the U.S.

**Be Prepared:** If you have allergies or other medical conditions, be sure to take along an ample supply of medication, and keep it in a carry-on bag. Don't make the common mistake of packing all your medications in your suitcase, which can get lost or stolen. Before you go, you may obtain a list of English-speaking doctors for the areas you plan to visit. Contact the International Association for Medical Assistance to Travelers for such a list at (716) 754-4883. [A listing of other Medical Assistance Organizations is provided elsewhere in this book. See the Appendix section.]

# LAW AND ORDER MATTERS

**Adoption**:   For those Americans traveling abroad to adopt children, be aware that several countries prohibit adoptions by foreigners or have laws governing adoption by foreigners.  In some cases, the law requires formal court adoption of the child in the country before the child is permitted to immigrate to the U.S.  Because of scandals over the illegal activities of some adoption agencies and attorneys both in the U.S. and abroad, you should be ready to experience some difficulties.  The more knowledgeable you are about the local laws and requirements, the less burdensome the process.  Americans interested in adopting a child from a particular country should contact the U.S. embassy or consulate in that country. In the U.S., contact the  Department of State's Office of Citizen Consular Services, (202) 647-3712, to obtain information on the adoption process in that country.

**Child Abduction**:   Americans traveling abroad with their foreign spouses and American children should be aware of recent cases  where the foreign spouse has prevented the children from returning to the U.S. In almost every case reported, the U.S. government, through various avenues, has continued its efforts for the safe return of the children.   The results, however, have not always been successful nor hopeful due in part, to the laws and practices of those foreign countries.  Remember, once overseas, you are subject to the laws and practices of the country you are in; United States laws cannot protect you. American women, in particular, should be aware that in some countries, either by law or by custom, a woman and/or her children may be required to get her husbands' permission in order to travel out of  the country.  If you or your children are planning to travel, be aware of the laws and customs of the places you visiting.  It is advisable not to visit or allow your children to visit unless you are confident that you will be permitted to leave. Although this is not a common experience, you may want to give it some thought as there may be a chance of it happening.

**Contraband:** (Prohibited and restricted Items):  Every country has a variety of goods that are prohibited for import or export. Violators may be subjected to heavy fines or imprisonment in addition to the goods being

34

confiscated. Often a list of such products is available with the country's foreign mission (Embassy and Consulate) and Tourist Information Office. To ensure a smooth trip to a foreign country, I suggest requesting such a list. If in doubt, verify the import/export status of whatever object or goods you plan to carry along with you. For example, whereas firearms are generally prohibited by many countries, some countries allow hunting guns and guns used in sporting activities. There might even be restrictions or a need to get a prior permit to import or use such gadgets as computers and radio transmitter-receivers. Products commonly found on the list of import contraband for most countries include drugs (e.g. cocaine, heroin) pornographic materials, firearms and certain wildlife products of endangered species.

Contraband goods for export purposes will often include some of those prohibited for import such as drugs, pornographic materials and wildlife products of endangered species. Other forms of contraband may prohibit the export of certain products by unauthorized or unlicensed exporters; e.g., precious metals and minerals and certain artifacts. In some cases, the contraband may be limited to certain products or to products from certain countries or regions. The United States also prohibits and restricts the importation and exportation of a variety of items.

**Consumer Protection**: One luxury that travelers do have in the U.S. as well as in several developed countries is the existence of strict state and federal government rules, regulations and laws aimed at protecting them and insuring their safety and well being. These rules, regulations and laws covering such common travelers' concerns such as bumping, flight delays or cancellations spell out your rights and privileges and provide you with legal backing for seeking redress if you feel your rights have been violated.

As an international traveler, you should be aware, that once you are outside the United States, you may not get the same level of protection that is available to you in the United States. Although such protection may be provided on paper, it is not effective in many countries, particularly in less developed countries. Nevertheless, as an American traveling abroad you may still be able to take advantage of the protection provided you here at home by dealing with the U.S. offices of the airline or shipping lines since their activities in the U.S. are governed and subjected to U.S. laws.

If you have complaints about an airline or if you feel you have not been treated fairly, you may contact the Customer Relations Manager of the airline. Very often, they will make an effort to deal with your concerns. At times, you may run into very uncooperative representatives or agents. In these instances, you may consider contacting the office of Community and Consumer Affairs, U.S. Department of Transportation; 400 7th Street, S.W., Rm. 10405, Washington D.C. 20590 (202) 366-2220. Of course, your attorney is always at your disposal to take additional steps if necessary.

Before traveling, you may want to familiarize yourself with some of your rights, privileges and responsibilities as an air traveler. The U.S. Department of Transportation booklet entitled <u>Fly Right</u>, is a useful reading for those planning to travel by air.

**Complaints:** As with many travelers and long-haul travelers in particular, there is always a chance for cause to want to complain about one thing or the other. If such a situation should arise it is always advisable to do it immediately on the spot with the appropriate authorities or personnel. Later on, perhaps upon your return, follow up in writing. While you may at times have the urge to threaten and curse out loud, you may find a persistent but polite approach more successful. In the event of damages, missing or lost luggage, a verbal complaint may not be sufficient. (See Lost/Damaged Luggage).

**Criminal Assault:** Any U.S. citizen who is criminally assaulted should report the incident to the local police and to the nearest U.S. embassy or consulate.

**Foreign Laws**: Foreign laws, rules and regulations may be very different from those of the United States, and violators may be subject to different penalties. For a foreigner, these penalties may be even harsher. Tourists who commit illegal acts usually have no special privileges. It is, therefore, advisable before you travel and when you are abroad to learn as much of the country's <u>do's</u> and <u>don'ts</u> as possible, particularly those aspects which often

36

get tourists in trouble with the law. In most cases, the same type of violations that will get you in trouble in the U.S. would more than likely get you in trouble abroad; for example, those relating to drugs, firearms, traffic, public safety, theft and robbery. Remember that while traveling in a foreign country, you are subject to that country's laws, and not U.S. laws. See Appendix 1C for the book entitled Do's and Don'ts: A Country Guide to Cultural and Social Taboos and Etiquette.

**Drunkenness and Drunken Driving**: Public drunkenness and drunken driving is against the law in several countries and should be avoided. These social nuisances often lead to fights, traffic accidents and even death. Arrests and jail terms are common for violators. In some countries, drunken driving invites mandatory jail sentences.

**Restricted Areas**: Travelers abroad should be aware that some countries do have strict regulations prohibiting travel in certain areas or traveling without special permission. Contact the country's embassy or consulate in the U.S. or if you are abroad, contact the U.S. Embassy or the nearest U.S. consulate for a list of such places and what may be required.

**Bribery and Corruption:** This is a phenomenon that exists in every country and which is illegal in every country. In practice, it flourishes in different forms and with different degrees of impunity and tolerance. As you travel from one country to another, you may find yourself confronted with this moral dilemma. Although the effects on you for not abetting or complying may be inconveniencing and time delaying, the consequences to you for bribing or attempting to bribe may be great. You can easily find yourself in jail as a result. For an international traveler, particularly in a foreign country your best bet is "do not attempt to give or accept a bribe." The cost for complying with the law always pays off favorably in the long run.

**Drunks:** You will probably run into them in several places. Be aware not only of their presence, but the likelihood of their nuisance turning into confrontation. Some of these drunks will try to have a chat with you, will touch and fondle you or even spit at you. Abusive and foul language is a

37

common trade mark of drunks and you can deal with them relatively easily by simply ignoring them. The best way to handle them is to just walk away. Any attempt on your part to deal with their harassment is at best, a waste of time.

Do not forget that tricksters, pickpockets and baggage thieves often go about their trade, pretending to be drunks.

**Dealing with foreign law enforcement authorities:** Be smart, be alert and be polite. You need these virtues when dealing with foreign law enforcement personnel, including the police, customs and immigrations. On your trip, you will very likely  make contact with customs and immigration officers. How you present yourself and interact with these officials is important and may very well determine how you start-off your first few hours or day in the foreign country. In dealing with customs and immigrations and all law enforcement officers try to (1) be polite; (2) speak clearly and coherently, particularly in stating the purpose of your trip; (3) do not fraternize or flirt with foreign law enforcement officers. They are not a breed to be trusted with your secrets or jokes. Besides, you may be risking your stay. (c) Stick only to the questions asked you and avoid volunteering information. (d) If you must "declare" what you are carrying, do so and do not leave out any item. Describing the contents of your luggage as "personal items" will be subject to less scrutiny than if the contents are for sale or for business. (e) Avoid carrying any goods that may be considered as contraband or subject to quantity limitations. Most non-prescription drugs are likely to be illegal as are pornographic materials. The quantity of liquor, cigarettes and tobacco products you may bring into a country as duty-free may also be limited. Check with your travel agent for duty-free items and limitations for the countries you plan to visit.

**How to Avoid Legal Difficulties** When you are in a foreign country, you are subject to its laws and are under its protection - not the protection of the U.S. Constitution.

You can be arrested overseas for actions that may be either legal or considered minor infractions in the United States.  Be aware of what is considered criminal in the country where you are. Some of the offenses for which U.S. citizens have been arrested abroad are:

**Drug Violations.** More than 1/3 of U.S. citizens incarcerated abroad are held on drug charges. Some countries do not distinguish between possession and trafficking; many have mandatory sentences - even for a small amount of marijuana or cocaine. Although we know of no U.S. citizens who have been arrested abroad for prescription drugs purchased **in the United States for personal use and carried in original labeled containers,** a number of Americans have been arrested for possessing prescription drugs, particularly tranquilizers and amphetamines, that they purchased legally in certain Asian countries and took to some countries in the Middle East where they are illegal. Other U.S. citizens have been arrested for purchasing prescription drugs abroad in quantities that local authorities suspected were for commercial use. If in doubt about foreign drug laws, ask local authorities or the nearest U.S. embassy or consulate.

**Possession of Firearms.** The places where U.S. citizens most often come into difficulties for illegal possession of firearms are nearby - Mexico, Canada and the Caribbean. Sentences for possession of firearms in Mexico can be up to 30 years.

In general, firearms, even those legally registered in the U.S., cannot be brought into a country unless a permit is first obtained from the embassy or a consulate of that country. (Note: If you take firearms or ammunition to another country, you cannot bring them back into the U.S. unless you register them with U.S. Customs before you leave the U.S.)

**Photography.** In many countries you can be harassed or detained for photographing such things as police and military installations, government buildings, border areas, and transportation facilities. If in doubt, ask permission before taking photographs.

**Purchasing Antiques.** Americans have been arrested for purchasing souvenirs that were, or looked like, antiques and which local customs authorities believed were national treasures. Some of the countries where this has happened were Turkey, Egypt, and Mexico. In countries where antiques are important, document your purchases as reproductions if that is the case, or if they are authentic, secure the necessary export permit (usually from the national museum).

U.S. Citizenship and Residence Abroad U.S. citizens who take up residence abroad or who are contemplating doing so frequently ask whether this will have any effect on their citizenship. Residence abroad, in and of itself, has no effect on U.S. citizenship. However, a person who becomes a U.S. citizen through naturalization and then takes up a permanent residence abroad within 1 year thereafter is subject to possible revocation of naturalization on the grounds that he/she did not intend to reside permanently in the United States when the petition for naturalization was filed. Each particular case is judged on its own merits. Clearly, some persons may have intended to reside in the United States but due to unexpected circumstances, it became necessary for them to take up residence abroad. Revocation of naturalization is the responsibility of the court where the naturalization occurred. The initial steps leading to revocation are taken by the Departments of State and justice. Contact the nearest U.S. embassy or consulate if you have any questions about nationality.

**Loss of Citizenship** Loss of citizenship can occur only as the result of a citizen's voluntarily performing an act of expatriation as set forth in the immigration and Nationality Act with the intent to relinquish citizenship. Such acts most frequently performed include the following:
- Naturalization in a foreign state;
- Taking an oath or making an affirmation of allegiance to a foreign state;
- Service in the armed forces of a foreign state;
- Employment with a foreign government; or
- Taking a formal oath of renunciation of allegiance before a U.S. consular or diplomatic officer.

If you have any question about any aspect of loss of nationality, contact the nearest foreign service post or the Office of Citizens Consular Services, Bureau of Consular Affairs, Room 4817, Department of State, Washington,

D.C. 20520.

**Dual Nationality:** A foreign country might claim you as a citizen of that country if:

- You were born there.
- Your parent or parents are or were citizens of that country.
- You are a naturalized U.S. Citizen but are still considered a citizen under that country's laws.

If you are in any of the above categories, consult the embassy of the country where you are planning to reside or are presently living. While recognizing the existence of dual nationality, the U.S. Government does not encourage it as a matter of policy because of the problems it may cause. Claims of other countries upon dual-national U.S. citizens often place them in situations where their obligations to one country are in conflict with U.S. law. Dual nationality may hamper efforts by the U.S. Government to provide diplomatic and consular protection to individuals overseas. When a U.S. citizen is in the other country of their dual nationality, that country has a predominant claim on the person. If you have any question about dual nationality, contact the nearest foreign service post or the Office of Citizens Consular Services at the address on the previous page.

### Be Alert! Getting to Know Foreign Laws

**Be a Considerate Guest:** Visiting a foreign country exposes you to different customs and different laws. That's why you should familiarize yourself with the local regulations before you go. Don't assume that what is acceptable in the United States is acceptable abroad. For example, some countries are particularly sensitive about photographs. It's best to refrain from taking pictures of police, military installations and personnel, or industrial structures unless you know for certain that it will not offend anyone, or break any laws. Check around to see what is considered appropriate clothing. What's acceptable in the United States may offensive elsewhere. And before you decide to sell personal effects such as clothing, cameras, or jewelry. make sure that the local law permits you to do so.

### Be informed!

On the average, 2700 Americans are arrested abroad each year. About one-third are held on drug charges. **Do Not Get Involved With Illegal Drugs.** The consequences are serious. If arrested, you will be subject to local, not U.S. laws.

<u>Know the Laws about Arrest Laws!</u>: Many countries do not provide a jury trial or accept bail, which means you may endure lengthy pretrial detention.
● Prison conditions overseas can be harsh. Some lack minimal comforts, such as beds, toilets, and wash basins.
● Officials may not speak English.
● Diets are often inadequate. Payment for food and amenities may be expected.
● Inhumane treatment and extortion are possible.
● Depending upon your offense, if convicted of a drug charge, you could face up to 10 years in prison with a minimum of 6 years of hard labor, and stiff fines in some countries. The death penalty is possible in others.

<u>Getting Legal Aid Abroad:</u> If you are arrested, the U.S. Embassy or consulate will do what it can to protect your legitimate interests and ensure you are not discriminated against, but cannot pay your legal fees or get you out of jail. A list of local attorneys can be provided by a U.S. consular officer. However, neither the state Department nor the U.S. consular officer can act as your attorney or assume responsibility for the professional competence of local attorneys.

## MONEY MATTERS

<u>Exchanging Your Currency:</u> As an international traveler, knowing the host country's rules and requirements for exchanging your foreign currency is very important since the rules and requirements are different from country to country. While in some countries, the requirements are less stringent or optional, in other countries, especially Less Developed Countries, they may be quite strict. Obviously, if your interest is to safeguard your funds and stay out of trouble, follow strictly the government's requirements with regard to where to exchange foreign currency. While you might be used to

using banks in the U.S., in many countries you might have the option of carrying out such transactions only at authorized banks, hotels, <u>bureau de change</u> and money changers. In most cases, you will be given a receipt (if not, ask for one) and/or the transaction may be endorsed in your passport. Hold on safely to your receipts and/or endorsement, since they may be requested of you, during departure.

Avoid having to exchange your money with unauthorized dealers or in the "black market" even though their higher rates of exchange are often tempting. With high expected return is always high risk including the risk of getting counterfeit currency, the risk of robbery, and running into problems with the law. Some of these unauthorized dealers may be undercover officers of the law.

**Currency Import/Export Requirements:** As an international traveler, it is important to know that many countries do have restrictions on the import and export of both foreign and local currencies. Be aware, also, of U.S. Government currency requirements. Presently, there is no limit on the amount of money or negotiable instruments which can be brought into or taken out of the United States. However, any amount over $10,000 must be reported to U.S. Customs on Customs Form 4790 when you depart from or enter into the United States.

**(a)    Import of Foreign Currency:** Most countries do not impose restrictions on the import of foreign currency. In several countries, however, there may be additional requirements which often include declaring the amount and/or exchanging your foreign currency only at approved or authorized offices or dealers. Declaration of currency usually takes place at the airport upon arrival. In all exchange transactions, ask for a copy of your receipt and keep it safe. You may need it on departure or in reclaiming or re-converting unused currency. Although not common with most countries, some do prohibit the import of certain amounts of the country's currency. In almost every country where the import of foreign currency is allowed, the usual assumption is that it is legal to export both the currency and the given amount from your country of departure. As you may expect, very large amounts of foreign currency, especially notes, will attract additional attention and questioning.

**(b)    Import of Local Currency**:    Most countries restrict and, in some cases, prohibit the import of local currency by both residents and non-residents, especially the latter.  Where restrictions apply, they often take the form of a ceiling, above which it will be considered illegal or require that such monies be declared and even subject to visual inspection.

**(c)    Export of Local Currency:**    Like the import of local currency, most countries restrict or prohibit the export of local currency.    Where restrictions apply, they often take the form of a ceiling above which it will be considered illegal or they might require that such monies be declared and subject it to visual inspection.  Many countries, especially Less Developed Countries, are very strict with currency movement, particularly the import or export of local currency.  Even where some amount is allowable to non-residents, it is often a very small amount usually limited to local remembrance coins.    Although developed countries are generally more generous with the import and export of local currency, it is a fact that no country will allow a large or unrestricted amount of import or export of its currency.

Because the rules and requirements dealing with the import and export of currency for many countries do change constantly, I suggest you  verify with the country's embassy, consulates, Tourist Information Office or with your travel agents prior to traveling.

**Currency Exchange**: Make it a habit to find out precisely what the rules and regulations are with regard to exchanging your U.S. dollars, travelers checks and other currencies into local currency and vice versa and stick to them. In some countries, re-converting excess local currency back to U.S. dollars or other hard or convertible currency is not easy and may entail a substantial loss to you.  Upon arrival, find out government authorized places for such transactions. Many travelers find themselves in trouble by failing to play by the rules either due to sheer ignorance or taking actions on their part to short cut the regulations and procedures. The outcome for violators could spell disaster for your vacation.  Do not be distracted or deceived by unauthorized entities wanting your U.S. dollars and offering you higher rates. Some of them turn out to be undercover government agents and plain clothes police. Although in many countries a large number of hotels serve as official currency exchange centers, not all of them are authorized. Personally, I restrict my currency transactions to banks. Besides, they usually offer a much better rate as compared to other approved currency exchange centers. Keep in mind that coins are rarely accepted for conversion into local currency and that includes U.S. coins.

**Hard Currencies Only!:** In some poor, developing countries "hungry" for hard currency, non-residents and foreign visitors may be required to make virtually all of their purchases in hard or convertible currency, particularly in dollars. Beware, should your travels include some of these countries. These are the countries with strict rules regarding exchanging foreign currencies. They are also the countries where you might have your money confiscated with the slightest currency violations and where you might find it hard to re-convert your excess local currency to a convertible currency. Your best safeguards are (a) declare all of your currency upon arrival. This is especially important for all countries with currency restrictions. (b) Restrict your activities only to authorized currency exchange places. (c) Keep receipts of all of your currency transactions. (d) Even though the commissions may appear high, only exchange the amount you need to use in the country. To find out what the current rules and regulations are regarding currency transactions, contact that country's embassy or consulate in the U.S. or their tourist bureau in the U.S.

**Cash Machines:** Automatic Teller Machines (ATMs) are becoming very popular overseas, particularly in Western Europe. With your ATM card, you may be able to access the cash machines in the same way and with the same ease as you do in the states. As usual, a personal identification number (PIN) is required. And as in the U.S., you may only access machines at certain ATMs. Two ATM systems with world-wide locations are the CIRRUS and the Plus System. Find out if your ATM is part of these systems. And if they are, find out if they are available in the country and city you plan to visit. It is, also, important to check to see if your card and PIN number can be used at overseas locations. If not, your credit card company may issue a new access code or PIN valid for use overseas. To reach any of the two systems mentioned here, dial 1-800-THE-PLUS or 1-800 4-CIRRUS.

**Foreign (money) Exchange Centers:** As an international traveler, you will have occasion to deal in foreign exchange. This will include: (a) buying travelers's checks, whether foreign currency denominated or denominated in U.S. dollars; (b) buying foreign currency (c) exchanging excess foreign currency for U.S. dollars; (d) cashing foreign drafts and checks including VAT refund checks; (e) wiring money to an account overseas. Some of these financial services can be provided directly by several large U.S. banks. However, a large number of smaller banks can provide a limited number of these services at prices that may not be your best bargain.

Alternatively, you may consider dealing directly with specialized currency exchange firms which provide direct currency exchange and transfer services. You are likely to get better rates from these services. For a listing of companies specialized in providing foreign currency exchange services, see Appendix Y.

In order to save money on currency exchange transactions, you will need to keep abreast of current exchange rates, fees and commissions charged by the various institutions which engage in currency transactions. Exchange rates are subject to constant fluctuations. With such fluctuations your savings will depend on what is happening to the U.S. dollar vis-a-vis the foreign currency. Generally, a stronger (appreciated) dollar, will favor your position in which case you will be able to get more for the same dollar than before the appreciation. Timing, therefore, is as important as shopping around for financial institutions that charge lower commissions and fees. Did you know, that as a member of the Automobile Club of America, you can get American Express Traveler's checks free of commissions, and that you can get Thomas Cook Traveler's Checks free if purchased through any of its travel agencies? Check with your bank and credit card issuer to discover if they provide currency exchange services or any other "freebie" services. A list of dollar-foreign currency exchange rates is often published in the financial section of some local newspapers and in a number of national and international financial newspapers. The <u>Wall Street Journal</u> and the <u>International Herald Tribune</u> are two excellent sources of daily rates.

**Learning to Use Foreign Currencies:** Before you go abroad, familiarize yourself with the foreign currencies you will soon be using. Check out money exchange services here in the U.S. and exchange a few of your dollars for the foreign currencies. Besides the obvious advantage of having a few foreign currency on hand upon arrival, you should make a deliberate effort to understand how they are used. This will save you time and minimize the chances of short-changing yourself or being short-changed. Some travelers wait only start learning how to use a foreign currency upon arrival, but only to quickly find out that it is not as simple as they had previously thought.

**Cash:** Before you go abroad, exchange a small amount of your U.S. dollars into the local currency. This will be very handy and particularly useful in covering taxi fares, handling tips and other incidentals. It, also, assures that you have a ready supply of local currency and will save the cost of breaking larger bills into local currency that you may not need. Furthermore, it will eliminate the need to pay to re-convert currency or can save you the cost of being "forced" to exchange your money with currency exchange centers whose rates, fees and commissions may be much higher than those of banks.

## SHOPPING MATTERS

**Banking, Business and Shopping Hours:** International travelers should be aware that banking, business and shopping hours vary from country to country and within a particular country. Sometimes, the hours of operation may change in response to changes between seasons. The typical differences that are likely to interest an American traveling abroad will include the fact that in some countries business is not transacted during some working days and/or during what we generally consider normal working hours by U.S. criteria. In some of these countries, banks, shops and offices may be closed either voluntarily or by law. In other countries you may find that government offices may be open during the weekend. Another likely observation in some countries is the "two-shift" type of operation where banks, businesses and shops may close at mid-day for lunch, resume one to three hours later and then close finally at night. Other than these striking differences, the others, are merely differences in opening and closing hours. Since as an international traveler, you will inevitably be affected, I have included elsewhere in this book the banking, business and shopping hours of various countries. See Appendix T.

**Value-Added Tax (VAT):**  Most foreign travelers to Western Europe are usually  not knowledgeable about VAT.  This is a sales tax usually imposed on almost all goods sold in Western European countries.  These taxes (ranging from 6% to 33% depending on the country) are usually included in the price of goods and services and are levied on purchasers irrespective of the country of origin.  The good news for the international traveler is that you may be able to get a refund.  You must, however, ask for it and meet the requirements.

To receive a refund, (a) you must shop at stores that are authorized to offer VAT refunds and (b) you must carry your purchases with you when you leave.

If you desire to request a refund of your VAT payments, do not forget to request the VAT form from your salesperson.  The form should be signed by the salesperson.  Upon departure, present the form and your receipt to the customs officers for final endorsement. Upon returning home, you may then mail the form to the store and a refund will be mailed to you.

**Rail Passes:**  For the cost conscious international traveler, passes can be an important money saving investment.  Rail passes in particular, can be a source of a bargain for those travelers who plan to conduct a lot of their travel by train.

While some of the passes are limited to travel within the country, some do allow for travel across countries. The Eurailpass, for example, allows you to travel to all the 17 member European countries.

Rail passes and tourist cards are very popular in Europe. Similar arrangements and opportunities to travel at a discount are also available on other continents. Your travel agent should be able to assist you in this matter. However, you may direct your inquiry to the country's tourist office in the U.S., the country's embassy, the consulate or railroad authority. A list of foreign government tourist offices and embassies in the U.S. is also provided. See Appendices F & B.

Children and older travelers may take advantage of available opportunities. Several countries in Europe offer discounts of up to 50 percent, including rail and other travel passes. It is up to you to ask about the availability when making your reservation or purchasing your ticket or passes. Remember that the definition of "seniors" varies from country to country. While most countries restrict use to those 65 years and older, in some countries the definition might be different.

It is worth noting that despite the convenience of passes and the cost advantage, it may not be beneficial to everyone. The individual traveler should always compare the cost of a pass or tourist card with the total cost of alternative transportation as the latter may turn out to be more convenient and/or cheaper, especially for those contemplating limited travel.

Like rail and bus passes, some airlines sell limited air passes as well as other substantial discounts to older travelers. Contact your travel agent or the airlines.

**Credit Cards, Traveler's Checks and Personal Checks**. Unless your trip abroad will entail only cash expenses, always inquire about the forms of payment widely accepted in the countries you plan to visit. If credit cards and travelers checks are acceptable, find out which ones are acceptable. This is particularly important for a variety of reasons: (a) In some countries, personal checks are not widely used and are looked upon with suspicion, especially a check drawn on a far away foreign bank. (b) In some countries credit cards are not widely used or may only be gaining minimal recognition in a few select places. Even in those select places, not all types of major credit cards are readily acceptable. (c) In some countries travelers checks are not as popular as we may think. They may not be widely used and will not be an acceptable form of payment. Like credit cards, the particular type of traveler's check may determine its acceptability. If you decide to carry traveler's checks, you may consider using American Express or Thomas Cook traveler's checks. Although there are over seven brands of traveler's checks world-wide, American Express and Thomas Cook traveler's checks are perhaps the most widely accepted. Their world-wide network of offices and service centers make them easiest to replace.

It is appropriate to point out that most of the limitations noted above are more prevalent in small developing countries in rural parts of some developed countries, and in small establishments (shops, hotels, etc.). Travelers to large metropolitan cities of most countries who plan to shop in large national boutiques or who plan to stay in large international hotels may hardly notice the limitations mentioned here. Nevertheless, it would not hurt to be quite certain and prepared. Questions regarding what forms of payments are widely acceptable in a particular country should be addressed to that country's embassy, consulate or tourist bureaus in the U.S. Your travel agent, credit card or travelers check company should assist you in this matter.

## CARNET:

### What is an ATA Carnet ?

* Carnet is an international customs document, a merchandise Passport.

* Carnets facilitate **temporary** imports into foreign countries and are **valid for up to one year.**

### What are the advantages of using an ATA Carnet?

* **Reduces costs to the exporter.** Eliminates value-added taxes (VAT), duties and the posting of security normally required at the

time of importation.

* **Simplifies Customs procedures.** Allows a temporary exporter to use a single document for all Customs transactions, make arrangements for many countries in advance and do so at a predetermined cost.

* **Facilitates reentry into the U.S.** Eliminates the need to register goods with Customs at the time of departure.

## What merchandise is covered by the ATA Carnet ?

* **Virtually all goods,** personal and professional, including commercial samples, professional equipment and goods intended for use at trade shows and exhibitions.

* **Ordinary goods** such as computers, tools, cameras, video equipment, industrial machinery, automobiles, gems, jewelry and wearing apparel.

* **Extraordinary items,** for example, Van Gogh Self-portrait, Ringling Brothers tigers, Cessna jets, Paul McCartney's band, World Cup-class yachts, satellites and the New York Philharmonic.

* **Carnets do not cover:** consumable goods (food and agricultural products), disposable items or postal traffic.

## Where can an ATA Carnet be used?

Currently, Carnets can be used in over 44 countries located in Europe, North America, Asia and Africa. Additional countries are added periodically. To learn more about Carnets and how to apply for an ATA Carnet, contact the CARNET Headquarters at

U.S. Council for International Business:
1212 Avenue of the Americans

New York, New York 10036
(212) 354-4480 Fax: (212) 944-0012

* The U.S. Council for International Business was appointed by the Treasury Department in 1968 to manage the ATA Carnet System in the United States. Typically, the Council issues over 10,000 Carnets a year covering goods valued at over one billion dollars.

**Auto Rental/Leasing/Purchases:** Renting or leasing an automobile for use overseas may be a money-saving option, depending on your particular circumstance and travel plans. This might be an option worth considering if you are travelling with a large family or group or plan an extended stay with travel to areas that are not accessible by public transportation. You could make your reservations upon arrival overseas or right here in the U.S. before you go. Booking your reservations in the U.S. can be done by contacting the rental agencies directly or <u>via</u> several of the International Rental and Leasing Agencies. Check your local telephone books (yellow pages) for a listing.

Some travelers invest in used cars overseas and then sell them before returning to the U.S. Others buy cars in the U.S. for overseas delivery and use or make arrangements to purchase new cars overseas which are then sold at the end of the stay abroad or exported to the U.S. Several firms specialize in leasing and purchasing automobiles for overseas delivery. These firms are often knowledgeable about applicable foreign country regulations in these areas. Companies specializing in overseas delivery will also be helpful in assisting you with shipping arrangements. Those travelers who contemplate importing or exporting foreign automobiles and pleasure boats must be well aware of U.S. Government regulations and procedures.

If you plan to rent, lease or drive overseas, you should be aware of the rules and requirements. Some countries have strict age requirements not only for renting or leasing automobiles, but also for driving. Because some of these requirements may differ from the U.S., it is prudent to familiarize yourself with those of the foreign country before you go. Useful information for driving overseas can be obtained from your local automobile association or from the American Automobile Association.

**Tickets/Passes and Reservations**:  Get as much of what you will need for your trip in the United States. These include your tickets, visas, insurance, medications, rail passes and reservations (hotel, airlines plane seat assignment, car rental). You can always re-confirm them, if need be, when overseas. By so doing,  you will save considerable time, energy and inconveniences. You may also save money. You may not be able to imagine these savings and the advantages of taking care of some of these aspects of your travel before you go until you find yourself agonizing over your lack of foresight and foreknowledge. In several countries you may find yourself spending hours, days, weeks and money in order to obtain the same information and services that would have taken just a fraction of the time and cost to obtain in the U.S. In other words, many of the things we take for granted here in the U.S. constitute luxuries in several countries. From transportation to communication, speedy and courteous services, you will be amazed at the contrasts.

Other than for the above reasons, certain discount opportunities such as some railway passes do have stipulations requiring the passes to be purchased in the United States to qualify.

**Warranties**:  Do not rely on them (Warranties and guarantees are not things you should take seriously when overseas.) Carry out your shopping on the assumption that there will be no reason for you to return the items for a refund or exchange. If you request a copy, you will get it, both verbally and in writing, but often they are not worth much. In practice, you will have a hard time recovering on the strength of such warranties. This is not to say you should not ask for them or safeguard them if it is received. With every generalization, there are some exceptions. Your best approach is to examine thoroughly your agreements and purchases before you commit yourself or pay for them.

**Valuables and Registration:**  If you plan to travel with an item that may be subject to import duty by the U.S. Government, you may consider registering it with the U.S. Customs before you go. If you do, retain your copy of the registration. You could have your valuables registered with the U.S. Customs at the airport or you could check with the nearest customs office for a location. A list of U.S. Customs District Offices can be found at your local libraries. Failure to register your valuables and other items of value may subject these items to duties when you return. One way you can eliminate the need to register with the customs at the time of departure is to obtain an ATA Carnet. See the section on Carnet elsewhere in this section for additional information.

**Finding Lodging**: Finding a place to lodge is not usually difficult if you have the money to spend. If you are on a tight budget, you may have to do some comparison shopping, including toning down on the quality of services you expect from lodging facilities. Many large hotels in the U.S. have international subsidiaries or have reciprocal referral agreements which make it easier for international travelers in the U.S. to reserve accommodation overseas. All it may take is just a phone call. A list of international hotel chains and telephone numbers can easily be found at your local library. You can also make arrangements for lodging through your travel agent or room-finding service provided by some international airlines tourist offices, student organizations, youth organizations, youth hostels, YMCAs and YWCAs.

Lastly, you could utilize travel guide and other publications. Many of them list the names and addresses of a variety of foreign hotels, boarding houses, pensions, youth hostels and camps with detailed descriptions and ranking including price information. After the first night, you can always, after the first night, find an alternative cheaper facility. This is usually easier if you are located downtown, within the city, since you could do your search on foot. Do not get discouraged by signs saying "No Vacancy," go ahead an inquire. It is not uncommon to find such signs even when there are vacancies. Occasionally, management forgets to take down the "No-Vacancy" sign. You can save yourself a lot of money if you conduct your own search for lodging than to rely on your travel agent. This is important, since most travel agents/agencies operate largely on commission basis and may not commit the time and interest to finding you a real bargain. Remember, finding overseas accommodations for travelers is not their specialty.

__Lodging__:   A variety of lodging facilities and arrangements are available overseas. They include hotels (different sizes, types, and qualities), bread and breakfast, boarding houses, pensions, villas, apartments, private homes, inns, youth hostels, student hotels, farm houses, camps, parks, road-side shelters, home exchange programs, and the Ys (YMCAs , YWCAs). Addresses and telephone numbers of some of these facilities can be found in many special interest travel guides and from travel agents, foreign tourist offices and foreign embassies.

When making reservations for your lodging, do not forget to discuss meal plans. Meal options vary depending on the type of accommodation arrangements.

Some plans may include breakfast while others may not. Meal plans, alone or as part of a package, may include one, two or three meals a day and may or may not include weekends. Some comparitive-shopping may be a prudent thing to do, particularly if you are looking for substantial savings. However, you do have the choice of taking care of your food needs outside of any formal plan.

Packages that include room and board usually turn out to be cheaper. Before you sign the contract for your room it is important to read the fine print to ensure that what you pay for is what you really want.

__Acceptable Credit Cards__: Not all credit cards are widely accepted overseas. The cards, and with the most world-wide recognition and acceptance are American Express, Visa, MasterCard, Dinners Clubs, and Carte Blanche. If you have other credit cards, you may consider leaving them at home. Department stores and oil companies cards are neither popular not acceptable.

__Air Passes:__  This is another money-saving option, and similar to rail passes. Air passes are particularly useful for those planning to engage in extensive travel within a particular country or region. They often allow for multiple stops and unlimited mileage within the specific limitations of the pass. Air passes are common with European airlines. If you are interested in air passes, contact the respective airlines. Air passes do have their restrictions and may not be a money-saving alternative to every traveler. Your travel plans and the cost of alternative plans will help you determine the suitability of air passes.

**Courier:** If you have what it takes, you could fly free or for a considerably cheaper cost as a courier. Good candidates for courier service are travelers who (1) are not inconvenienced traveling alone (2) are flexible with their travel plans, (3) do not have baggage to check, since as a courier all you may take is your carry-on bag. What the courier companies basically need from you is your checked baggage allowance. Of course, the courier company hopes you will deliver the baggage claim tags and the baggage to their agent on arrival. You can expect the courier company to check you in at the port of departure and have their agent wait for you at the airport or at a designated location overseas. Courier service may be for one-way or round-trip travel. As a courier, you may have to subsidize part of the fare and/or be required to pay a nominal fee for the service depending on supply and demand for couriers. You are expected to make arrangements for your visas and other entry requirements.

If you are interested in flying as a courier, you may want to contact any of the courier companies often listed in the yellow pages of your local telephone book. Contacting these companies or brokers early is important since it may take up to four months to get you going.

**Traveling Standby:** This type of travel can be a source of large savings. To be able to take advantage of this service, you need much flexibility with your travel schedule as well as patience. You must be willing to tolerate disappointments, especially those resulting from your not being able to make a particular flight. As a standby traveler, expect to purchase your standby ticket on a short notice. Beyond that, there is nothing more than engaging in the waiting game at the check-in counters of the airline and praying for a vacant seat on the plane. Once on board, you will enjoy the same privileges as any regular fare passenger. The problem is only with securing a seat on board. As a standby passenger, you will have less luck on weekends, holidays and other peak traveling periods. On the contrary, you may find better luck at night, off peak seasons and during the weekdays. Various airlines, however, have their definition and rules regarding standbys. Standby arrangements may not always exist with every airline. For these reasons, it is advisable to check with the airlines to determine if standby fares are available for your intended destination and what the conditions are.

Alternatively, you may employ the services of companies that specialize in standby tickets. Most of these companies require a registration or service fee. Cruise travelers should and explore standby opportunities with the cruise lines.

**Frequent Flyers:** The frequent flyer mileage program has become a growing phenomenon in the world of travel and it will be unimaginable not to take advantage of it. Previously offered only by the airlines, today credit card companies, automobile rental agencies and big hotels are getting involved by offering frequent flyers and frequent users opportunities for savings towards a future trip. As a frequent flyer, you may qualify for other complementary services offered by the airline such as upgrading to first class and  use of special lounges at the airport. The problem is that most travelers who can benefit because they happen to fly more frequently, do not sign up for these free services and/or do not take the time to register or maintain a good record of the amount of air miles accumulated during their trips. On the other hand, there are many travelers who have accumulated frequent flyer miles (points), but are yet to utilize them. You may loose those points. Read the fine print.  To learn more about frequent flyers and similar programs, contact the respective airlines. Many U.S. and European carriers have frequent flyer programs. In addition, some newsletters and magazines have begun to emerge focusing on the frequent flyer and mileage programs. Check with your local public library.

**Charters:**  Charter flights are becoming very popular with budget-conscious travelers. Substantial savings can be accrued traveling on a chartered carrier. Although charter packages have been around for a long time, they are beginning to add new twists and incentives that appeal to today's sophisticated travelers. If you are considering traveling on a chartered flight either as part of a group or solo, you should be aware of the characteristics and limitations of this form of travel. They include (1) advanced reservations and payment, (2) sacrificing some of your comfort; (3) penalties and forfeiture of some or all of your payment in the event you cancel; (4) possible postponement or cancellation of the trip by the charter operator. Generally, charters do not provide the type of flexibility as do regular flights. Some of the restrictions mentioned above may turn out to be costly when the time lost and inconvenience are factored in. There are rules and regulations governing charter operators, such as those dealing with refund, in the event the operators cancel the charter. None of those regulations will adequately compensate you for a charter trip gone sour. It is advisable to search around carefully for reputable and reliable specialized charter or tour operators and compare cost. As you conduct your research, inquire as to what services are included and what is excluded in the arrangements the terms of the contract. The same level of prudence you apply when dealing with airlines must be applied when dealing with cruise line charters. If you are concerned about the reputation of a charter agency, check with the local Better Business Bureau. You may also check with the American Society of Travel Agent, or the National Association of Cruise only Agents listed in Appendix 1B. A trip cancellation insurance is recommended for travelers on a charted carrier.

**Rebators:**  Rebators and rebator services are a growing phenomena in the travel industry. Rebators operate like travel agents except that they may charge you a fee for their service in exchange for passing on to you some portion or all of the commission traditionally available to travel agents. Depending on the amount of travel you plan to make, the savings could be substantial. Rebators are not necessarily travel agents and are not as organized as travel agents. Find out more about the particular rebator and its charges, and get references before committing your time and money.

**Bucket Shops and Discounted Tickets and Wholesalers:**  With careful researching you may be able to purchase air tickets at a deeper discount from the so called "discount travel agencies" or "bucket-shops" and/or from wholesalers called "consolidators." Some of these "travel agents" are able to buy concessions from airlines, allowing them to offer an unusually sizable amount of discounts. If you are a traveler interested in this type of arrangements you should expect certain restrictions on the tickets including penalties for any deviation from the terms of the contract. Tickets bought from bucket shops and consolidators may carry non-refundable and non-endorsable clauses and may require cash payments. Many reputable agencies will accept alternative means of payment, including credit cards. Most bucket shops are not registered travel agencies as we know them. The same is true of consolidators, most of whom are just wholesalers buying from the airline and selling to travel agencies or to the consumers. Great care and providence must be applied should you chose to use their services. You may consider restricting your dealings with registered discount travel agencies. Do some shopping around, compare costs, risks and terms of the contract before letting your money go and check out the business before you go. A listing of bucket shops and ticket wholesalers can often be found in the travel column of most big national and international dailies and in the advertisement section of most travel magazines and newsletters.

**Travel Clubs/Airline Clubs:** Travelers interested in special treats should consider joining a travel club. Advantages accruing to club members could be wide ranged and does vary from club to club. Privileges often include opportunities for better services at a bargain price. Airline clubs are becoming common with major air carriers and the privileges members enjoy can better be appreciated when you suddenly find yourself hustling and bustling at the check-in counter or looking lost, helpless or tired in the waiting area. During this time, club members are probably relaxing, and being provided with "free" entertainment in a private lounge exclusive to members. Even an opportunity to take showers often exist in such lounges for club members. It is VIP treatment all the way. For the majority of travel clubs, benefits in the form of savings (ticket, hotels, rentals) can be expected, including last minute reservations, some insurance coverage and regular newsletters and toll-free numbers to keep members informed of bargain opportunities. Membership in travel clubs for the most part requires an annual membership fee that could range from $30 to $200. Some clubs charge a one time initiation fee. Lifetime membership opportunities do exist and for a nominal fee, benefits could be extended to spouses. For inquiries on Airline Clubs, contact the respective airlines. A list is provided in Appendix J.

**Cruise Lines and Freighters:** The difference between the two may be more of quality of service and trip completion time than any other factors. These differences are, reflected in the cost. Cruise lines specialize in providing an alternative, more romantic and equally comfortable means of traveling than by air or land, but at a longer time than by air. Freighters, on the other hand, take longer time than cruises liners for the same travel, carry fewer persons and charge considerable less. You may have to be much more flexible with your travel schedule with freighters than with cruise lines. Long waits and frequent schedule changes are not uncommon. Foreign vessels, for the same quality of service, tend to charge less than their U.S. counterparts. Apply the same level of prudence in dealing with cruise lines and freighters as you do in deciding what airline to fly with . Some shopping around and cost comparison are important. Ticket terms and conditions for travel with a sea vessel are different from those on your airline ticket. Read the dotted lines carefully before signing and before letting go your money.

**Things Not to Buy Overseas**: As you plan to go shopping overseas beware! You may buy things, but may not be able to import them into the United States. There are numerous commodities, items of seemingly common and harmless use, that are prohibited entry by the U.S. Government. These items range from certain birds, pets and wildlife and products made from them, to plants and animals. These are in addition to many contraband items considered dangerous and a threat to security. The latter may include unlicensed firearms, illegal drugs and pornographic materials. For a listing of prohibited items commonly considered by travelers, see the U.S Customs publications listed in Appendix 1C. Beside your concern for U.S. Government requirements, and lists of prohibited items, do not forget the requirement and lists of the host country. Every country has a list of items you can neither bring in nor take out. If you are not sure, always check with that country's customs office.

**Beware of Street-Side Vendors**:  Like in the United States, you will find them in almost every country, particularly in the large urban centers. You will find them trading in items ranging from ornaments, jewelry, radios and stereo sets to cameras and watches. While some of the articles they sell may be legitimately acquired, some may not. Many turn out to be stolen goods. It is advisable to stay away from these street-side vendors. While their prices may be unusually, attractive and tempting, their activity may be illegal, and their products fake and defective, and with no guarantees. There is also the danger that you may be dealing with an undercover police officer or being set-up for a robbery. Make things easy for yourself. Avoid buying or dealing with street vendors whether they are registered or not.

**Shopping Abroad**: It is not always the case that you will find a better deal abroad. Those items you plan to buy may well turn out to be more expensive than at home. If you plan to buy any thing abroad, it is advisable to develop a list of those items including their U.S. prices. While you comparison shop abroad, you should consider the taxes and duties that will be assessed on those items. You may have to pay the  cost of transporting them to the U.S. You should consider the exchange rate of the dollar vis-a-vis that country's currency.

If your shopping abroad includes, shopping for articles of clothing and precious stones, you should be aware that there are significant differences between American size, and the size in other parts of the world. To assist you, a guide has been provided in Appendix L. Similarly, you should be careful as you shop around for precious stones. You may already be aware that fakes are common. This is true irrespective of the country of purchase.

## DRIVING MATTERS

**Driving Abroad**:   Depending on the country you are visiting, driving abroad could be both exciting and safe or could be scary and risky. Whereas the road conditions and road infrastructure in many of the Developed Countries and some urban centers of Less Developed Countries are safe, good and properly maintained, the same may not be true for most of the developing countries. Travelers to European countries should expect about the same conditions as in the U.S. However, if you are traveling to a Less Developed Country, you must anticipate such conditions as narrower roads, untarred roads, muddy or dusty roads, poorly lighted roads, loose animals and livestock, poor or nonexistent shoulders, few road signs or traffic lights as well as a limited number of restaurants, motels, gas stations or auto-repair shops. If you plan to drive, it is advisable to familiarize yourself with the route. As always, avoid excessive speed and, if possible, avoid driving at night. In some countries local driving signals are prevalent. Familiarizing yourself with these signals will add to the pleasure of your driving.

In addition, you may want to familiarize yourself with driving automobiles with manual (stick shift) transmission. Unlike in the U.S. where automatic transmissions and power accessories are plentiful, you will find more cars with manual transmissions in the rest of the world. Do not be surprised if that automatic shift car you reserved with your rental agency is not available and you are offered instead, a car with stick shift.

Be aware that in some countries, European countries included, you may find car with steering wheels on the right side of the car, and you might be required to drive on the left hand side of the road. Like in the U.S., you must be properly licensed to drive and the car must be insured. Although some countries will accept a U.S driver's license, others may require that you have an International Driver's Permit. See Appendix G for information on how to obtain an International Driver's Permit. For those planning to use their U.S. automobiles abroad, remember you may be required to obtain a vehicle import permit. Your U.S. automobile insurance plan and coverage may or may not be acceptable. Some countries may require that you have an International Green Insurance card or obtain such coverage from a local insurance company. Needless to say, it is important to adhere to local traffic laws. Speeding and drunk driving may land you in jail in addition to a financial penalty.

**Vehicle Precaution:** If you plan to drive during your trip abroad, you should take safety precautions. Foreign travelers often become favored prey to local muggers and thieves. Incidentally, the same can be said of foreigners who visit the U.S. Incident, ranging from car break-ins to car jackings, including physical assaults on the occupiers, have been reported by American travelers. The motives for these incidents vary and the resultant impacts have varied. Sometimes have been fatal. You can minimize the chances of becoming a victim by taking, the following precautions:

- Drive the more common kinds of locally available cars; if there are not many American cars in use, don't insist on an American model.

- Make sure the car is in good repair.

- Keep car doors locked at all times.

- Wear seatbelts.

- Don't park your car on the street overnight if the hotel has a garage or secure area. If you must park it on the street, select a well-lit area.

- Don't leave valuables in the car.

- Never pick up hitchhikers.

- Don't get out of the car if there are suspicious individuals nearby. Drive away.

- If you are renting or leasing a car, request one with a local tag as opposed to one with an international tag or clearly marked tourist tag. This way your car will not stand out.

- If you must stop to ask for directions, do so at a gas station or in a relatively populated and well lit area. In other words, avoid isolated areas when requesting services.

- If you are bumped, particularly repeatedly, do not stop to check if you consider the area too isolated  or if you are suspicious of the motive. You might well be right. Instead, drive to a safe, populated area.

- Although it may sound cruel, beware of situations that may look like an accident scene. Some are staged just to attract your attention and sympathy. You could end up becoming a victim of an assault. This also includes stopping to render help to a supposedly needy and helpless traveler or pedestrian, especially in very isolated spots. There are other ways besides stopping, that you may be able to render help. If you must react to your need to help, drive to a safe area and place an emergency call on behalf of the accident or stranded victim. Remember, you are in a foreign country and environment and may not totally understand how things work.

**Automobile Accessories:**  If you plan to drive abroad, be aware that in several countries and regions certain accessories are standard and are required in cars. Traffic police may stop you to check for these items. They include an emergency first-aid kit and, in some places, a jack a spare tire and an emergency reflective triangular plate. Operating an automobile not equipped with these accessories may result in delays and/or fines. It is prudent, if you are going to drive overseas to find out the practices and requirements of that country. Your local Automobile Association should be able to assist you.

## MATTERS OF ETIQUETTE

**Personal Appearance:**  While relatively few travelers ever get bothered or delayed just for their personal appearance, a tattered and weird appearance may attract an unwelcome attention and may subject you to avoidable scrutiny and or questioning by foreign immigration and security officers. A clean, smart and unsuspecting appearance and demeanor on your part as a foreigner in a foreign land may save you embarrassment and unnecessary delays.

**Dress Code:** Some countries, especially those in the Middle East and Moslem countries, expect foreigners to adhere to their dress codes. These codes may relate to and may be restricted to certain places, such as places of worship or to women, men or children. For example, some countries require women to have their hair covered when in public or covered when in places of worship, while some prohibit wearing of shorts and miniskirts in public or sleeveless garments. In many other countries, such rules may not exist. Check with your travel agent, the respective foreign embassy or the tourist office for the appropriate dress code in their country.

**Tipping:** We, in America, are fond of and used to tipping in hotels, restaurants, saloons and almost every time someone renders us some form of assistance. If you are planning a trip abroad, you may want to know that although the "rules" and expectations are the same for most countries, the amounts may be different. In some countries, tipping may not be expected and may be officially prohibited.

Different countries have different rules and expectations regarding tipping and gratuities. In some countries, the practice is expected and clearly defined. In some others, this may not be the case. For the International traveler to be confused in terms of whether to tip or not, how much to tip, when, or to whom is understandable. Since this could be a potential source of embarrassment, you should try to familiarize yourself with what the rules are in the country you plan to travel to. To assist you, a country by country guide to tipping has been provided in Appendix O. It is not comprehensive, but at least acquaints you with the country's official position as well as the expectations on tipping, particularly in hotels, restaurants, taxis and saloons. You may, also, contact that country's embassy, consulate or tourist bureau for advice. Your travel agent may also be of help.

Should you decide to tip wherever such practice is allowed, do restrict your gratuities to services actually rendered. Do not forget that there are really no hard and fast rules as to how much you must tip. In other words, do not expect to be thrown in jail for not tipping. Generally, a tip should reflect what you believe is "reasonable" and what you can afford. Sometimes, a handsome expression of appreciation may make a difference in the quality of service you may subsequently receive. A poor tip may be insulting and may even be worse than not giving at all. Finally, do not forget that your bill may already include expected tips. The one way of knowing in most cases is to inquire.

**Taboos**:  Travelers to foreign countries have often been embarrassed, humiliated and even isolated as a result of their inadvertently stumbling into actions and words considered as taboos.  To many travelers, this could be very uncomfortable and could sour an otherwise exciting trip.  Breaching a taboo in some societies could invite trouble and mean spirited treatment.  It behooves the prospective foreign traveler to learn as much as possible about the cultural and social **do's** and **don'ts**.  See Appendix 1C for the book series entitled *Do's and Don'ts: A Country Guide to Cultural and Social Taboos and Etiquette*.

**International Protocol Pointers**:[RI]  Whether traveling internationally for business or pleasure, here are some useful tips:

- Don't "over-gesture" with your hands; it can be offensive.

- Avoid American jargon and idioms.

- Don't refuse food; taste a little of everything.

- Don't over schedule.

- In Arab countries, don't openly admire things.

- Arrange for your own translator. Relying on someone else's translator could be a mistake.

- Gift-giving is an art and a science. Study the science and perfect the art. Giving a clock in China is a bad idea.

- You may be expected to sing after a dinner in either Japan or Korea.

■  Contact the State Department for travel advisories before embarking.

■  Don't photograph religious statues.

**Attitude**:  Success with your trip abroad may depend on your attitude and degree of tolerance as well as on how much flexibility you built into it. What will become clear to you is the strangeness of the environment which is not dramatically different from a trip to another city back home. You can break these feelings and thoughts by maintaining a positive attitude complete with unreserved tolerance and great flexibility and by toning down your expectations. After all, this a foreign country, not really home. The folks you see could have come from some part of the United States with their weird looks, funny accents and "wild and crazy" attire.

I must caution that in parts of some countries you might travel to, smiles may be rare and the faces you see may not be inviting. Do not take these looks so seriously or pre-judge them as to feel, "Oh! I have come to the wrong place." Behind these sad looking and unpolished faces are truly peaceful and loving hearts just waiting to know and understand more about you. Even if you were to run into one or two of these faces with the "wrong heart" during your very first encounters, try not to jump to a quick generalization of how hostile and unfriendly the country and its people are or get out of town with the next available plane. You may be cutting short what could have turned out to be a wonderful and exciting learning experience.

Receiving unfriendly treatment is not an unusual experience for foreign travelers. You will more than likely experience this at one time or another during your overseas trips. This is not very different from the same incident you might experience in your city of residence in the U.S. While overseas, it is advisable to view these isolated incidents with more smiles than something else. Unless you have done something particularly offensive, you may be sure that what you experience and the faces you see are nothing more than expressions of momentary misunderstanding. They may also be expressions of shyness, inability to communicate appropriately or of

67

curiosity just waiting to be broken. And guess what will break it, **YOUR SMILE,** a product of your **ATTITUDE,** your willingness to be truly adventurous, tolerant, understanding and, above all, appreciative of cultural diversity.

**Searches and Seizures:**  As you travel abroad and  around the world, you will find a variety of practices which could be frustrating, time wasting and perhaps uncalled for. Some of these practices will include road blocks, spot-checks, searches and seizures. Like many other travelers, you would hope not to become a target. While such a feeling is OK, do anticipate them and when confronted by these circumstances, it is in  your best interest to cooperate. You will lose less time if you remain calm and speak out politely as opposed to acting confrontational, questioning the officer's authority or showing signs of anger and disapproval. Law enforcement officers expect to be obeyed and respected. This is true in the U.S. and equally true of foreign law enforcement officers you will come across during your trip abroad.

Spot-checks are common in airports, but they could happen anywhere. A spot-check may just call for you to show or provide the officer with certain documents they normally will expect of you. Other times, they might lead to an elaborate search of your person and your luggage. Female travelers should not expect much privacy as some foreign law enforcement officers can be especially malicious and "dirty."

Do not be surprised if in the process, an officer tells you that an item in your possession is a contraband and, therefore, will be confiscated. This is true even for items that are not prohibited. In other words, you may be unfortunate to come across an unscrupulous official who, in reality, would like to have your item, but figures the easiest way to get it is to tell you that it is prohibited. When confronted with this type of situation, stay calm and polite. However, you can do one of two things. (1)  Consider it a gift and let him or her have the item, particularly if you can do without it. This may be all that the person wanted and letting it go will likely be the end of the search or inspection. (2) Alternatively, request to speak to the boss. Chances are that the officer may refuse to grant your request, but may turn around and let you keep your item. This may turn out to be the case, particularly if the original motive was suspect. On the other hand, you may have your request to see the higher in command, who may over rule the junior officer or who may  reiterate the facts of the law to you.

As for road blocks, expect much more of these in developing countries of Africa, South America and in communist and police states. Routine road blocks often require checking of travel documents (passports, visas, inoculation certificate for required shots, purchase receipts) and if your are a citizen, your tax receipts and voting registration card. In some road blocks, officers may inspect your travel luggage.

**Filing (standing) On Line**:  As civilized and rational as this practice may be and as common as we find it practiced here in the U.S., you may not always find it so in some countries. Corruption, lawlessness, favoritism and nepotism abound in many parts of the world and you might find yourself a "victim." Many times, it is so blatant and overt as to make you really mad. Well, stay calm, that is all the more reason I am letting you know well in advance. It is advisable in such situations not to emulate  them. Educate them instead, but do so politely and with integrity. Point out to the individual and attending official your disapproval. Very likely, yours may be the only open incident you will witness before you are attended to. In most instances, the cost to you is time. With proper planning, you will emerge, having your needs met.

## MATTERS OF COMMON SENSE,
## GOOD JUDGEMENT & GOOD HABIT

**Getting Help:**  Abundant help and information are available to Americans traveling abroad.   In addition to the enormous amount of information covered in this book, you could get general as well as country and region-specific travel information from the U.S. State Department, from the country's embassy, consulates and tourist offices in the U.S. and from travel agencies, consultants and advisors.  Your local public library and bookstores should not be left out.  While abroad, the American Embassy and consulates will be your most important places to seek all forms of assistance.

**Shortages, High Prices and Other Problems**:  Consumer goods, gas and food are in short supply in some countries and prices for these commodities may be high by U.S. standards.  Shortages of hotel accommodations also exist, so confirm reservations well in advance.  Some countries, especially Africa, experience disruptions in electricity and water supply or in services such as mail and telecommunications.  Be informed and be patient.

**Political/Public Gathering**:  Always stay away from political gathering places and avoid public demonstrations. Americans have been arrested when local authorities have thought that they were participating in civil demonstrations.  Remember, public gatherings are usually surrounded by security persons. It is also prudent to avoid engaging in political discussions or making public political statements or announcements as this may get you arrested.  If you are detained or arrested for these or any other reason(s), ask to speak with a U.S. Consular Officer.

**In Your Person**:  As a foreign visitor and for safety purposes, always carry with you your traveling papers,  such as  your passport with visa, tourist card and any other documentation that you may be required to carry.

**Duty Free Import Allowances**:  In almost every country, foreign travelers are allowed to import, duty free, some quantity of products up to a specified value for personal use. Expect to pay extra for any  quantity or value over what is specified. Some of the commonest products include liquor, spirit, alcohol, beer, wine, cigars, cigarettes, perfume and cologne.  The quantity of these products allowable as duty-free varies from one country to the other and changes from time to time for some countries.   In fact, in some countries, the amount allowable may be determined by your country of departure.  Other familiar products that may be considered duty free depending on the quantity, value, intended purpose and country of origin will include such gadgets as cameras, tape recorders, video machines, tapes, sports equipment, TVs, faxes and radio transmitters. Travelers planning to carry along some of these products should contact the country's embassy or consulates or your travel agent prior to traveling for a more current list of requirements.

Business travelers who plan to move certain items and gadgets back and forth should consider getting an ATA CARNET. This document which is described elsewhere in this book will save you money and aggravation. Returning U.S. residents and U.S importers should also familiarize themselves with the list of duty-free imports as well as other import requirements. Imports which are ordinarily subject to duty may be duty-free under the (Generalized System of Preferences (GSP) program because you are importing it from one of the beneficiary countries.

**What To Take With You**: There is always that urge to carry along as much as we can carry and often more than we will need. My advice is to travel lightly and do not carry anything you would hate to lose. Unnecessary credit cards and expensive jewelry should be left at home.

**Money Belt**: Use a money belt or concealed pouch for your passport, cash and other valuables.

**At the Pool or Beach**: Do not leave your belongings on the beach while swimming. Keep your passport and other valuables in a hotel safe.

**On Public Transport:** Be vigilant in bus and train stations and on public transport. Do not accept beverages from other passengers. There have been reports of tourists being drugged and robbed while they slept.

**Sightseeing (getting around) on Foot:** Avoid dark and isolated alleys, crowds and marginal areas. These are areas where you can easily be robbed and assaulted. Be aware that women and small children as well as men can be pickpockets or purse snatchers. Do not stop if you are approached on the street by strangers, including street vendors and beggars. Whenever possible do not travel alone. Avoid traveling at night. Keep your billfold in an inner front pocket; carry your purse tucked securely under your arm and wear the shoulder strap of your camera or bag across your chest. To guard against thieves on motorcycles, walk away from the curb and carry your purse away from the street.

71

**Dealing with Merchants:**  Always avoid disputes with merchants as this may often lead to undesirable outcomes.  Haggling over prices is common with most small independently owned shops.  However, in some it may be insulting and unwelcome.  Learning as much as you can about the modus operandi in foreign market places will be very valuable.  Avoiding disputes requires you to be a careful and informed shopper.  Make sure the goods you buy are in good condition, since efforts to exchange or return the them may be unsuccessful and may lead to disputes.  As always, get a receipt for your transactions.

**Green Backs:**  The U.S. dollar notes are as popular in several countries as U.S. tourists.  You will find the U.S. dollar notes are readily accepted for transactions by local merchants.  While the temptation will always be there, be aware of local legal requirements concerning import and use of foreign currency as this may get you into avoidable trouble.  Equally important is to be aware of how you flash your dollar notes as this may attract the attention of thieves.  As an American, you are always associated with the dollar and there is the tendency to think that you are carrying some U.S. dollars.

**Photography:**  Be cautious when taking pictures.  Some countries prohibit taking photographs of some buildings, places and events; e.g., airports, police stations, military locations, oil installations, harbors, mines, and bridges.  Taking a photo of demonstrations or civil disturbances is usually prohibited.  Violators have often had their films and/or cameras confiscated and at times have been beaten or detained.  A safe rule is to ask when in doubt as to whether you can take a picture or not.  Before including individuals in the picture find out if it is OK with them.  Some persons detest being photographed and may require some form of token compensation.  Be courteous.  Ask first or negotiate first.

**Travel Agencies/Agents:**  Travel Agencies and Agents can be very useful in providing answers to most of the common questions and concerns of foreign travelers and should be included as important information sources.  As in any profession or trade, all travel agencies or agents do not possess the same degree of expertise or experience.  It is important that you shop around for a reliable, reputable and competent one with experience in foreign travels. Such agencies or agents must be committed to assisting you to have a successful and enjoyable trip by providing you with advice, answers and other relevant information about the countries you plan to visit. Travel agencies that are interested only in selling you a ticket, should be avoided. A real helpful agency ought to be willing and able to provide you with not only the "best deal" cost-wise, but also with current information on such issues as relates to hotel reservations, car rentals, visas, passports, travel conditions in the country you are visiting and even some cultural **do's** and **don'ts**. While no formula exists for identifying the type of travel agencies mentioned here, you may want to deal primarily with those that are members of the American Society of Travel Agents (ASTA). Members usually will have the (ASTA) sign or seal clearly affixed to a visible place in the office. The strict membership requirements give their members an edge over non-members. I must caution that membership in ASTA or the lack of it, is not a guarantee that the agency you choose will deliver. Shop around. Ask your traveled colleagues, friends and neighbors for some references. Interested in travel agents who are members of the Institute of Certified Travel Agents (ICTA)? These agents, upon certification, carry the title of Certified Travel Counselor (CTC). For additional information about these organizations, including members that may be in your area, write or call the American Society of Travel Agents (ASTA), 1101 King St., Alexandria, Virginia 22314. Tel: (703) 739-2782. Or the Institute of Certified Travel Agents (IGA), 148 Linden Street, Wellesley, Massachusetts 02181. Tel: (617) 237-0280.

**Visa Services:** (See Travel Counselors)

**Travel Counselors/Travel Planners/Travel Advisors:** (Also, see Travel Agencies). Travelers who are planning an extensive trip or a trip for the first time may consider using the services of a travel counselor, a travel advisor or travel planner for a fee. Although a good travel agency should be able to provide you with valuable counseling and advice regarding your trip, you may find the services of a travel counselor more specialized, timely, personable and comprehensive. A good travel counselor should be able to advise you on every topic and every concern that you may have regarding your trip including scheduling. Some of your concerns may require the counselor to do some research and this means time and money. The more planning and research you do before contacting a counselor, the less costly for you and the less painful the outcome of poor consultation.

When researching a travel agency, it is advisable to engage the services of only those travel counselors who specialize in the country or region of the world you plan to visit or in certain aspects of travel such as a ski-vacation, budget-tours, business travels, group and luxury travels. They are often more helpful than the general practitioners. Consider using professionally certified travel counselors such as those certified by the Institute of Certified Travel Agents (ICTA), a U.S. based nonprofit educational organization. Upon certification, their members carry the insignia and title of "Certified Travel Counselor (CTC). Look for the ICTA and CTC logos. Although the eligibility requirements for members of these organization give them an edge over non-certified agents, being counseled by a member may not necessarily guarantee the best results; so shop around. Be careful and be selective. For information on ICTA certified travel counselors in your area, check your local telephone directory or write or call the Institute of Certified Travel Agents, 148 Linden Street, Wellesley, Massachusetts 02181. Tel: (617) 237-0280).

**Tickets:** It is advisable to spend a few minutes making some sense out of your tickets, preferably right on the spot where they are being issued. You should be able to reconcile the information contained in your ticket with your travel plans. Many travelers have found, much to their disappointment, that the ticket they are carrying is deficient. Sometimes the ticket may contain schedules and clauses that are different and restricting and that may be expensive to rectify once you commence your trip. Double checking your ticket could save you money and time. In checking your ticket, take special note of the name of the airlines you will be traveling. The names of the airlines are usually identified by their respective two-letter codes. See the Appendix K for these codes as well as the list of foreign and international airlines operating in the U.S. Your ticket check should also include reconciling the dates and times of departure and arrival, your class of ticket, the validity of your ticket and of the flight(s). Also check for the correct validation stamp or signature of the issuer. Don't forget to read all other information on the front and back of the ticket. You might find additional useful information.

**Hold onto Your U.S. Passport**[IL]: A U.S. passport can cause you trouble in some regions of the world. But there are ways to get around that if you meet certain requirements. Children and sometimes grandchildren of immigrants can obtain passports from the country of their parents' birth. In many countries, once you obtain a second passport, you are required to have a dual citizenship.

This is not as easy as it sounds. You must be careful not to unintentionally renounce your U.S. citizenship. The U.S. State Department recommends the following precautions:

* Do not accept a government job from an adopted government.
* Do not serve in another country's military.
* Do not suggest to friends or anyone else that you intend to renounce your U.S. citizenship.
* Write a statement of intent to retain your U.S. citizenship and send it to a U.S. Embassy or consulate.
* File U.S. income tax forms.
* Vote in U.S. elections.
* Use your U.S. passport.

**Passport Scam**[IL]: In the classifieds, you'll see advertisements for private passport companies. Some of these advertisements are legitimate; others are not. Check the advertisement carefully. Does it list a telephone number? Does it list a complete address, not just a post office box somewhere in Malaysia? Does it list some ridiculously low or exorbitantly high amount of money? Does it ask for the money right away?

If the advertisement doesn't list a telephone number and doesn't have a legitimate-looking address, chances are the company is a hoax. If you are told to hand over the money right away, forget it. You'll never see your money again, especially if the sum the company is asking for is less than the cost of obtaining a passport from a passport agency. Valid companies usually charge you twice as much as a passport agency for their services.

Call the company and ask for more information. If you are turned down, drop the entire proposition. A legitimate company would be happy to send you more information.

If you must have your passport within a week or less, some countries can help you get a passport quickly and easily. (A list of private visa and passport services is provided in a Appendix E).

**Choosing Your Flight:** For trans-Atlantic passages, find out if your flight is direct or nonstop. Nonstop flights have no layovers or plane changes, but direct flights may stop four or five times en route, even though you don't have to change planes. The stops can be a strain, especially, on pets.

Most airlines allow a limited number of pets per flight, so make arrangements early. Your pet will be issued its own ticket and you will be billed for excess baggage.

Even if you have a boarding pass, you are not guaranteed a seat until you are given a seat assignment. To avoid last-minute decisions to bump you because of your pet, try to get a seat assignment as soon as possible. (Usually you can get a seat assignment nearly a year before the flight, even if boarding passes are not available more than 30 days before the flight). If you are unable to get your seat assignment in advance, allow extra time to board with your pet.

**Tips on Shipping Pets:**[IL]

* Ship your pet in a large, sturdy crate with a leak-proof bottom. Print on it your name and address as well as your pet's name and destination.

* A health certificate and a rabies inoculation are

recommended along with distemper and hepatitis inoculations.

* Exercise pets well the day before the shipment.

* Feed the pet a light meal six hours before shipping.

* Don't give water to pets within two hours of shipping except on a very hot day. Provide a water dish for attendant's use.

* If the trip will be longer than 24 hours, provide food.

**Advanced Notice:** To avoid any last minute disappointments or delays at the airport, it is essential to give advance notice to the airline for the following luggage:

■ Dangerous articles or articles subject to special conditions (see following paragraphs)
■ Animals
■ Heavy luggage (exceeding 32kg)
■ Fragile objects
■ Wheelchairs
■ Bicycles
■ Surfboards, delta gliders
■ Baby baskets including accessories
■ Voluminous luggage

**Records/Receipts:** Make it a habit to keep all receipts of purchases and other financial transactions during your trip abroad. Arranging the receipts by country would facilitate your dealings with a host of law enforcement authorities abroad and at home, including the airlines in the event of loss or damage. The receipts you keep may very well prevent you from getting into trouble with the law or may determine whether or not you will return home with those souvenirs you purchased abroad.

**Surrendering Your Passport**: While the importance of safeguarding your passport must be emphasized, do not panic if your hotel or designated tour guide should request to keep it during the period you are in their service. Although not a common practice in most countries of the world, you may encounter this practice in some Communist countries, developing countries, Middle East countries and in certain countries of the former Soviet Union.

In all cases, however, ask for an explanation, including when and under what conditions it will be returned to you. If you plan to travel to any of the regions cited above, you may want to contact the embassy, consulate, or tourist bureau of those regions here in the U.S. before leaving to find out if such practices are in effect. The U.S. Embassy in the country you plan to visit should, be able to advise you in this matter. You are better off getting the information here in the U.S. before departure.

Remember your passport will almost always be needed when cashing travelers checks and personal checks. You may want to carry out all necessary foreign exchange transactions before parting with your passport.

**Extra Photographs:** Carry with you additional passport-size photographs just in case. Six to eight will be adequate. It is not unusual to be confronted with situations requiring passport-size photographs. For example requests for certain types of permits and licenses or for extension of stay may require passport-size photographs. Having some handy will save you both time and money. Unlike in the U.S. where the requirements are less stringent, passport-size photographs you plan to use overseas should show both ears, not just one ear.

**Safe guarding your Camera Film:** As an international traveler, you and your luggage will go through one or more airport x-Ray machines. This is a part of the security measures that are being taken worldwide. Some airline authorities have claimed that their X-ray machines will not damage camera films passing through them. This claim has been disputed as some trusting passengers continue to notice the effects of X-ray exposure on their prints. Taking extra precautions to safeguard your films, including those inside the camera. Imagine spending all that money, time and effort in taking the pictures just to lose them. One suggestion would be to politely ask the X-Ray operator or attending officer to pass the film through by hand rather than through the machine. Make sure you do not open the film as this will expose and render it useless. Let it stay in its original container or wrapped in a plastic bag. Do the same with your camera if it has film in it.

As you consider taking photographs overseas, you may want to carry adequate film. Film is generally less expensive in the U.S. If you must buy your film overseas, expect to pay up to three times what it would cost in the U.S.

**Visa Vigilance: 14 tips to take the hassle out of traveling on a visa:** Following are some useful tips to help you avoid problems when traveling to countries that require a visa:

- Don't travel on a passport that has less than six months validity. Countries that automatically extend visas for six months at a time will not give you a visa otherwise.

- Keep at least two clear pages in your passport. Many foreign consulates require both a left-and- a right-hand page for their visas. Whatever the expiration date. Renew your passport if you are running short of clear pages.

- It is sometimes possible to get a second passport to travel on while your other is tied up with visa applications.

- U.S. expatriates should avoid getting or renewing passports in their countries of residence. Foreign consulates frequently run time-consuming checks on visa applications from people with passports issued overseas.

- Apply in good time for all the visas you'll require for a trip. Don't rely on picking up a visa at the other end, even if it is possible.

- Be aware that certain countries impose a time limit from the date of issue (typically three months) for using the visa. This is inclusive of the length of your stay.

- Whenever possible, apply for a visa at the foreign consulate nearest your home. You are always liable to be called for an interview.

- It is best to apply in person. You can often iron out problems on the spot and check to be sure that the visa has been issued properly before you leave the building.

- Keep in mind that visa authorities are looking for evidence of financial support and your clear intention to leave their country. Always remember this.

- Know in advance whether you need a tourist or a business visa. If in doubt, ask. In some countries, there is a crucial difference in formalities.

- Ask if an international vaccination certificate is required with your visa application.

- Be sure you get a double or multiple-entry visa to certain countries such as India or Saudi Arabia. If you are on a business trip, you may need to return suddenly. This is impossible with a single-entry visa.

- Check to see if you need an exit visa, especially for African countries, Belize and Brazil.

- If you're going to Israel, consider using a second passport or request that your visa and entry stamp be put on a separate sheet of paper. This can help avoid problems in the future when traveling to other countries.

**Protection Plans**:   As part of your overall travel insurance, do take advantage of any available services to minimize costly mistakes in planning your overseas trip. This will include ensuring that the travel planners, counselors, agents, agencies and tour operators you are dealing with are competent, reputable and registered with their respective professional associations. In this regard, you may want to contact the Institute of Certified Travel Agents at (617)237-0280, the American Society of Travel Agents at (703) 739-2782 and the United States Tour Operators Association at (212) 944-5727. Some tour operators are part of ASTA Tour Protection Agreement which protects clients from unscrupulous tour operators. Consider limiting your tour arrangements to these companies. To verify who is part of this plan and who is not, contact ASTA. A listing of other Associations you may seek assistance from before, during and after your trip abroad is provided in Appendix 1A.

**What to carry or pack:** This is a subject that is not limited to international travelers. Most seasoned travelers face the same issue. You are not alone if you are concerned. While it will be up to you to decide what is important to you, here are a few pointers and some things you must give careful consideration to: (a) You are only entitled to a certain number of free check-in luggages and each luggage limited to a specified weight, beyond which you will be required to pay for the excess. (b) Traveling light is the ideal way to go. In doing so, you should not sacrifice the convenience of having what you really need. Remember, you are going to a foreign country and perhaps to a location where even the most essential commodities and services might not be available or may be quite expensive. Does this mean stuffing you baggage with everything imaginable? Not necessarily. Traveling light after all has a lot of advantages. Besides cost considerations, it is less aggravating, less stressful and could be time-saving. It allows you the freedom you need to react quickly, walk faster, and keep an eye on your belongings. It also gives you an edge for consideration when bargaining with hotels, airlines and taxis. If your luggage small enough to qualify as a carry-on or hand luggage, you can kiss luggage insurance good bye.

All said and done, the real questions you should ask yourself as you consider any particular item for packing are: (1) Do I really need it? Will I use it?, (2) If yes, to question 1, is the item cheaper and readily available where I am going. If a lighter but durable form of the item is available,

81

take it. If the item is versatile with multiple uses, you have a must-take item for the trip. To facilitate your packing and to ensure that nothing important is left behind, a comprehensive final checklist has been provided to you elsewhere in this book. Research indicates that many travelers do not get around to using many of the things that they carry with them. Do not take what you cannot afford to lose.

Finally, your packing plan should include consideration for airline requirements. Some airlines restrict certain items in the cabin or in carry-on bags. There are the more familiar and obvious items generally prohibited by all airlines. These are listed elsewhere in this book. There are also, the not so familiar or obvious items such as battery-powered equipment, scissors and knives. The rules vary from airline to airline. It is always advisable to check with the airlines.

**Get The Name.** As you make your plans to travel, you will have to deal with different individuals, including travel agents, travel counselors, ticket agents, airline personnel, hotel and automobile rental reservation clerks. Because the information they provide may determine how your trip turns out, it is prudent that you make a log of the person(s) you speak to including the day and time. In the event of any mix-up, this will provide you with some basis to establish your case. It makes your story credible. Whenever possible, request a written confirmation of your reservations and any important agreements made between you and the other party.

**Inventory:** Maintain an inventory of your luggage and have the list in a separate place. A list of what is contained in each piece of luggage would be very useful for identification and to establish a claim in the event of a loss. Similarly, keep a log of all purchases made including the prices paid for each item. Also, note whether the form of payment, is in local or hard currency.

**Jokes:** Avoid careless remarks, particularly around airport premises or on the plane. They could disrupt your trip and send you to jail. Statements about bombs, grenades, terrorists and terrorism, drugs and hijacking are usually sensitive to most travelers and law enforcement authorities. Some persons, particularly law enforcement officers, take it seriously even when you consider it to be only a joke. The consequences can be painful and could ruin your trip.

**Checking and Boarding**:  Do it on time. You have spent weeks, perhaps months preparing for your trip; do not mess it up by being tardy. Tardiness could cause you to loose money, especially if you are traveling on a restricted ticket. Allow yourself ample time on the day of your trip. Get to the airport at least two hours before the scheduled departure. Arriving early will allow you time to check your luggage and get a seat assignment if you have not already done so.

In some countries, particularly developing countries, the time required to check-in and to go through immigration, customs and security formalities can be enormous and so is the risk of missing your flight and other scheduled connections. Don't be surprised if no one seem to care. You can minimize this risk by giving yourself ample time. There are numerous experiences of travelers who make it to their destination only to find out that their luggage did not because they checked in late. Similarly, there are instances where the luggage makes it through to the destination, but the owners missed the flight because they were late in boarding.

**Unnecessary IDs:**  Before taking off on your trip, carefully go through your wallet and examine your identification cards (IDs).  Remove those IDs you will not need, particularly those that could implicate and/or complicate your travels abroad. Implicating or "killer" Is are those Is that you do not need abroad and that may invite intense questioning by law enforcement officers. Included in this category are Federal, State and local government job Is. Is that indicate your title and position should also be left at home, more so if you work in a "sensitive" industry, such as weapon manufacturing, nuclear laboratories, security and investigating agencies and law enforcement. Avoid using such titles as president, chairperson or director. Instead, use common and simple titles such as Mr. Miss or Mrs., or  Reverend. Always keep a low profile when traveling abroad.

**Stop-Over Flights:**  Always isnist on a direct flight unless a stop-over is absolutely necessary. By so doing, you will minimize the risk of flying as well as save time. You also avoid such inconveniences as having to subject yourself to security checks. Although transit travelers rarely go through this, it is not an uncommon practice in some countries.

**Your Ticket:**  Make it a habit to check your ticket and reservation confirmation slips once you receive them. Many of the tickets have caveats and other details you must be clearly aware of before you go. You may ruin your entire trip or loose money and time due to  information on your tickets and reservation slip that you overlooked. Immediate and careful examination will give you ample time to correct mistakes as well as request clarifications. Inquire about the meaning of any unfamiliar codes used and any restrictions. Importantly, cross-check the information on the tickets with your intended itinerary.

**Places and Gestures to Avoid:**  As safety concerns will be paramount in your mind during your trip abroad, you ought to be careful of what you do and how and where you do it. There are places that will certainly open you up to interrogation and other actions that may invite jail term for you even though a citizen doing the same thing may go "scott-free".

1. A partial list of places you should avoid include:
(a) military facilities, (b) facilities that manufacture military or security products, (c) places where protests or political rallies are being staged

2. A partial list of actions to avoid include:
(a) Burning or defacing the national flag, (b) Sitting down (in public) when the National Anthem is being played and when everyone else is standing up, or not taking off your hat or head gear in the same instance, when everybody else is doing so. (c) Making negative or derogatory remarks about the head of state, the military or the country and government as a whole, (d) Participating in rallies, riots, protests and strikes, (e) Taking photographs of military installations, (f) Taking photographs in the airport, or of the airport, (g) Taking photographs of communication facilities, (h) Defecating or urinating in public even though you may find the latter

common with local inhabitants, (i) Fraternizing or flirting with local law enforcement authorities, (j) Engaging in political discussions, (k) Engaging in discussions about, or where such words as explosives, bombs, grenades, revolt, over throw, coup and the like are used, (l) Carrying in public SPY, CIA, FBI and/or reading books that may be perceived as a source for sensitive information and for dangerous ideas, (m) Drunkenness and public nuisance, (n) drunken driving, (o) Cursing.

Equal rights and freedom of speech and expression may be inalienable rights of U.S., citizens, in the United States and central to the constitution of the U.S. but may be hardly so in many countries abroad. Being careless and not watching what you say and do or how and where you say and do things, may be an invitation for trouble abroad. It does not take much to stay out of these given areas, but first you must be aware of them.

## MATTERS HERE AND THERE

**Photocopy:**   Make 1-2 sets of photocopies of all of your documents including your passport, tickets, credit cards, travelers checks, drivers' license and prescriptions.  Leave one or two sets with your family or friends at home and carry one set with you in a separate place from the originals.

**Purchases:**  Keep all original receipts of purchases.  You may need them to satisfy U.S. Customs requirements or in the event your luggage is lost or stolen.

**Contents:**   Make an inventory of the contents of your check-in luggage before you leave.  Such a list  may become useful in the event they are lost or stolen.

**Addresses:**  Make sure you have all the addresses and telephone numbers you may need while abroad, including those of your friends and relatives at home and abroad, your physician, the nearest U.S. Embassy or consulate and the U.S. State Department.

**Scheduling:** Make sure you schedule to get your passport, visas and vaccinations on time. An early start will save you a lot of heartaches. Similarly, do arrive at the airport on time, at least two hours early and check in as early as you can. This way you will minimize the chances of being "bumped". It will also allow you time to make alternative plans in the event of a cancellation.

**Research:** No amount of information is too much for someone traveling to a foreign country, especially those dealing with the customs and laws of the foreign country, the people, the climate, transportation, food, etc. Learn as much as you can about the country from your local library, the U.S. Department of Tourism, the U.S. Department of State, the country's embassy, consulates and tourist offices, travel agencies and agents. While you are abroad, brochures and newspapers often available in the large hotels and newsstands may be very helpful information sources.

**Itinerary:** A copy of your itinerary should be left with your family or friends at home. This will be handy in the event of an emergency. Travelers very concerned about their health may also leave a copy with their physician just in case.

**Electricity:** Electricity requirements vary from one country to another. In other words, appliances specifically designed for usage in the U.S. may not operate in some other countries without risking damage to the appliance or even loss of life. For example, whereas U.S. appliances use 110 volts and 60 cycle, several countries require 220 volts and 50 cycles. Such appliances will be inappropriate and may not function. To avoid this problem and still be able to use your 110 volt, 60 cycle American appliance, you will need a converter and an adapter plug. If your appliance is equipped with dual-voltage capability, all you may have to do is to flip the switch accordingly. Even in the case of a dual-voltage appliance, you may still need an adapter plug with the right type of prong to fit into the wall outlet. Check your local department store or electronic shop for a converter and adapter. You may want to get a "universal adapter plug" since it has the advantage of having different size plugs which can be used when traveling to countries with different requirements. As in all cases with electrical appliances and devices, please read carefully the instructions before using them. If unsure, ask someone. Your hotel management will be of help. See appendix Q for country by country electricity requirements.

**Telephoning:** Whereas the privilege of telephones are taken for granted in the U.S., you must know that it is a luxury, especially in less developed countries. In other words, In many countries, telephone facilities may not exist for some cities. If they do exist, they may not function efficiently. In other cases, telephones may be hard to find or may be expensive. Considerable patience may be required on your part. You may have to explore alternative methods of sending messages, including telegrams, cablegrams, faxes or telex. While abroad you may save yourself a lot of worry by placing your overseas calls from a post office or from coin-operated phones as opposed to your hotel room. You may even benefit through exchange rate differentials and billing procedures if you use your credit card, calling card or call collect.

**Addressing Mail:** In addressing mail to or from abroad, it is important to print as clearly as possible. This will minimize the chances of your mail not getting to its destination.

**Writing Dates:** Whereas in the U. S. the month of the year is written before the day of the month, e.g. January 10, 1999, (1/10/99), in several countries it is customary when writing dates to write the day followed by the month and the year, e.g. 10 January 1999 (10/1/99).

**Weather**: As an international traveler, weather conditions in the countries you plan to visit should be an important consideration both as a guide to the type of clothing that you carry along and to your ability to have fun. Because weather and climatic conditions vary around the world, it is advisable to include this as part of your pre-trip plan and to verify what the conditions may be during the period of your intended travel. Summer, winter, spring and fall as commonly used to describe seasons in the U.S. are not commonly used in many parts of the world. In some parts, you may find people referring to "dry' and "rainy" seasons. You may find many people totally lacking in knowledge about names we are so used to in the U.S.

Incidentally, there are important differences as well as similarities in characteristics between rainy and dry seasons and the seasons in the U.S.

**Lost/Damaged Luggage:** Losing luggage or finding your luggage damaged is a common experience among travelers, long and short haul travelers alike. Should you find your luggage missing or damaged, immediately contact the appropriate personnel at the baggage area or at the lost luggage office to file your complaint. With airlines, you may have to complete a report form. With missing luggage, insist on filing a written report (keep a copy) as this may become useful in the event your luggage is not found and you decide to seek legal recourse or compensation. Do not give up or release your luggage check ticket.

With regard to both lost or damaged luggage, you have the right to seek and receive some compensation. Rarely are you compensated fully. This right, however, does not extend to luggage misplaced elsewhere in the airport due to your negligence. In such cases, immediately contact the airport police the Lost Property office or the Information desk for assistance.

**Information Desk:** Information Desks, which are readily available and visible in almost every air and sea port as well as bus and train station, are an immediate source of assistance and information ranging from locating post offices, police offices, banks, restrooms and dining places to finding connecting flights, taxi, bus, rail and limousine services. Information desks at most large hotels are very useful in providing you with additional information on a variety of subjects that will help make your trip more enjoyable. Use them!

**Foreign Jails:** While it is never any traveler's wish to end up in a foreign prison, it is a possibility and some travelers have had this experience. For would-be visitors, do not expect anything close to the condition of U.S. penal institutions. For most countries, especially Less Developed Countries, it is worse. Reports of jail conditions have ranged from physical abuse and torture to sexual assault of prisoners and outright deprivation of any rights or privileges. There have been reports of prisoners and those awaiting trial not being properly fed, of poor lighting or no lights at all, and of poor sleeping conditions and toilet facilities. In many cases, you may have to sleep on a bare, dusty or muddy floor. It is to your best interest as a foreign traveler to make every effort to avoid having to face foreign jail experiences.

**Minors and Traveling Restrictions**: For those travelers who may be traveling with minors, be aware that the definition of minor and the age of majority vary from country to country and that many countries do impose restrictions on minor children who travel alone with only one parent or with someone who is not their parent. In many cases, some form of documentation or written authorization for travel from the absent parent or legal guardian may be required. Check with your travel agent or with the country's embassy or consulate for requirements.

**Hotel Bills:** Many countries consider it a fraud if you fail to pay your hotel bill or pay for other services rendered. Those accused may be subject to arrest and conviction with stiff fines and jail sentences. Keep track of your expenditures and your resources. As usual, travel with sufficient funds including a little extra for a few days subsistence in case you are stranded.

**Weights and Measures:** Most international travelers engage in some form of shopping while abroad. For these travelers, understanding the type of weights and measures used in the country will be beneficial at least in insuring that you do not end up buying something that may be cheaper in the U.S. The types and standards of weights and measures vary from country to country. Whereas most countries use the metric system or are in the process of converting to metrication, several countries still use the imperial system or other local systems. In others, one or more of these systems of weights and measures are used. Even for those countries that have officially adopted either the metric or the imperial system, it is not uncommon to find transactions still being carried out using a different system. Understanding these differences will facilitate your shopping and may save you money. A list of countries and the type of system officially being used is provided in Appendix N. Also provided are conversion factor and tables of equivalent weights and measures in both metric and Imperial forms. See Appendices N and M.

**Visa and Passport Services:**  If you plan to travel abroad and do not have the time to process your application for a visa or passport, there are businesses out there whose primary service is to assist you in obtaining them.  You can find additional listings of these businesses in your local telephone directory under the heading "Visa Services."  A listing of some of the private visa and passport services has also been included in this book. See Appendix E.

**Clothing:**  If you are traveling abroad and you plan to go shopping for clothing, be aware that clothing such as shirts, pants, gowns, suits and shoes, may not carry the same size labels.  Some countries employ labeling forms quite different from those used on U.S. made clothing.  A table comparing the U.S. and two other labeling systems has been included elsewhere in this book.  See Appendix L.

**Comfort Hints on Flights:**  It is amazing how much we value comfort and strive to achieve it on flights, especially on long flights. The act of flying can be discomforting, especially over time zones.  However, as a frequent flyer and a long-haul traveler, you may take a few steps to minimize the source of discomfort, making your trip less tiring and annoying.  Among other factors, discomfort often results from inadequate leg room and noise. By properly choosing your seat, you may be able to reduce the level of discomfort.  Aisle seats provide more legroom than window seats. Seats directly behind the emergency exit doors provide even more additional legroom.  Aisle seats are more convenient for those travelers who may have to use the restroom frequently.

As for the noise, because most engines are situated at the back, the closer you are seated towards the front the lesser the noise effect. Besides, you are more likely to find excited and rowdy holiday groups toward the rear spectrum of the plane.  Sitting just behind first class, may be your best choice unless you are a first class passenger. You may also minimize the noise effect by sitting away from the toilet facilities. You may not have much pre-planning opportunity to reduce the effect of noisy neighbors.  A little politeness and a smile may do the trick.

You can  minimize some of the discomforting feelings by being selective with what you eat and drink as well as what you wear.  It is advisable to minimize the intake of alcoholic and fizzy, carbonated drinks. Instead, drink non-alcoholic liquids such as water and fruit juices. It is advisable to wear loose-fitting clothes and shoes. The feet tend to swell on long flights. Unless your shoes are sufficiently loose, you may find it difficult to put them back on.

Finally, you may consider periodically rotating your feet, ankles, and neck as an exercise or you may treat yourself to some sleep.

**The Best Seat on the Plane:**[RI]  Of course, the best seats on a plane are in first-class. In terms of safety, experts agree that the midsection of the plan, close to the wings, is safest in case of disaster. Being close to an exit door should increase your chances for survival.

Should you specify an aisle, window or center seat?  The advantages of the aisle seat are:

1.     It's easier to exit the plane.

2.     Your shoulders and arms have more space.

3.     You can see other passengers and have a more roomy feeling.

A problem with the aisle seat is that you might repeatedly get your side brushed or toes run over by the beverage cart if you don't stay out of the way of flight attendants.

The center seat has no advantages except when you are sitting next to someone you know. The window seat allows a view of the sky and ground which can help if you tend to feel claustrophobic in flight.

The closer you are to the front, the less time you will wait in line to deplane. Engine noise will also be less pronounced toward the front. The first row after the coach bulkhead gives you a ride up front plus more storage space. On smoking flights, a seat toward the front means you are away from smoke.

All of the major airlines, except for Southwest, offer seat selection at least 30 days in advance. The sooner you choose your seat, the better the seat you'll get. Once you get on the plane, you may request a seat reassignment.

Seats over the wing provide the smoothest ride; those in the back, the bumpiest.

**Special Diets:**  One of the advantages of today's international traveler is the airlines' or cruise lines' willingness to provide special diets.  Whether you prefer vegetarian, fat-free, salt-free, infant, diabetic, Muslim or Jewish (Kosher and Kedassia) meals, there is a growing number of international airlines & cruise lines that will make an effort to get them for you.  First class passengers may find their request for special meals more easily fulfilled.  As with all special services, it is advisable to place your order with the airline or cruise lines well in advance. Not all airlines provide the wide range of special meals noted here. Whereas the larger carriers are often good with providing this type of service, you may not have many choices with the smaller ones and with carriers of many Less Developed Countries.  As a precaution, it is always a good idea to eat something before embarking on your flight or cruise and to take along a few of your favorite snacks.

**Baggage Identification:**  Security concerns in many countries have led to a variety of practices and procedures in several international airports. One of these practices is a Baggage identification by owner-passengers prior to embarkation. In some countries, especially in Africa, you may be required to identify your baggage. Usually upon physical identification, your baggage is immediately loaded onto a carriage or directly into the plane. Unidentified baggage is not loaded. In which case, you may arrive at your destination unaccompanied by your baggage. The worst of it is that such baggage left behind may end up being misplaced, tampered with and/or lost. To avoid this, take some time to verify with the airline or airport authority if such practices or procedures are in effect and if so, when and where.

**How to take the Kids:**[IL] Yes, you can travel with your children and still enjoy the trip. The key is planning. Following are some tips:

\* Rent a car. Although public transportation is reliable and inexpensive particularly in Europe, your children's schedules may not match those of the trains and buses. With your own car, you can come and go as you want and you can carry around everything the children need.

\* Take your own car seat. Some car rental agencies also rent car seats, but most won't guarantee that one will be available when you pick up the car.

\* Contact the tourist bureau for the country you're planning to visit for help in choosing your accommodations. Tourist bureaus (listed in Appendix F of this book.) can tell you which hotels, pensions and apartments welcome children and are equipped with cribs, playrooms and babysitting services.

\* Choose an airline that welcomes children. Ask if you can bring a car seat for your child to sit in during the flight. Ask if children's meals are available and if training tables are provided.

\* Pack a backpack carrier, a stroller and an attachable high chair. Take along your own baby wipes (those sold in Europe are heavier, rougher and oilier than those sold in the United States), but buy disposable diapers on the road.

Do you need a helping hand in planning and arranging travels with your children? If you do you may consider using the services of this organization: Travel With Your Children (TWYCH), 80, Eighth Ave., New York, NY. (212) 206-0688.

**Babies - On Board:**   Many reputable international airlines do carry on board a stock of baby food, diapers and useful accessories for the care of your baby. Some also provide baby baskets for babies no more than 27 inches in length. Because of the limited number of these baskets, it is advisable to give the airline an advance notice and to be on the safe side, to carry along some food for your baby. It is not unusual to run into international flights that do not provide any of these services.

**Reduced Fares For Children:**   International airlines generally charge lower fares for children. However the rates charged may vary from airline to airline. Some airlines will charge only 10 percent of the full fare for children under 2 years who do not require a seat of their own provided that they are accompanied by an adult. For each additional infant traveling with the same adult, 50 percent of the corresponding fare is charged. These amounts are reduced to 10 percent per child if there are two accompanying adults.

Most international airlines charge children between two and 12 years of age, 50 percent of the adult fare. In this case the children are entitled to seats of their own. Depending on the time, the country, the airline and the conditions, other opportunities for reduced fare for children and/or their traveling family members may be available. Check with your travel agent or the airline.

**Emergency:**   Telephone codes used in summoning for help during emergencies vary from country to country. Most of us are used to dialing **911** during emergencies. While this may be the code for many parts of the U.S. it may not be valid for other countries of the world. Travelers abroad should inquire and familiarize themselves with the correct emergency dialing code upon arrival at their hotel. Children accompanying parents should be included in this learning exercise. A country by country list of emergency numbers is provided in Appendix Z.

**Minors Traveling Unaccompanied/Accompanied:**   Be aware that International Airlines may not fly children under five years who are unaccompanied. Some airlines, with experienced hostesses are willing to assist with the care of the child. Depending on the airline, this additional service may or may not require extra cost of a full adult fare.

For many International Airlines, children between five and 12 years of age may travel unaccompanied provided certain conditions are met. The most common conditions are that (1) the unaccompanied child be brought to the airport of embarkation and met at the airport of destination; (2) the parents or legal guardians sign a written authorization. This consent form is usually available at any of the airline offices; (3) overnight stays en route can only be included if the parents or legal guardian provides an adult to accompany the child from arrival until departure the following day. Depending on the airline, two or more flights on the same day may be permitted.

For children between five and 12 years accompanied by a hostess, a full adult fare is often charged for the child and another full adult fare if a personal hostess is provided at a cost. Quite often, no extra fare is charged if the personal hostess is an employee of the airline.

For children over 12 years accompanied by hostess, a full adult fare is often charged in addition to a percentage (about 50 percent) of the regular adult fare if the airline uses one of its own hostesses.

In all cases for children over 5 years accompanied by an independent, non-airline personal hostess, a full adult fare is often charged to cover the hostess.

Because the rules and conditions vary from one airline to another, it is advisable to contact the airlines prior to your departure date to find out more about their policy, cost, and conditions relating to traveling by minors. You may be surprised to find out that the age limits differ from those discussed here.

Do remember to check visa requirements. Depending on the country or countries the child is traveling to, visas may be required for both the child and the paid independent personal hostess.

**Liability and Insurance:**   As an international traveler, remember that the luggage you carry on the plane is not insured by the airline against loss or damage during air transportation. Under certain conditions, the liability of the airline is limited in value and this liability is based in principle on weight and not on the value of the contents. This is all the more reason that it is advisable to have your luggage insured.

**Transport of Animals:**   The transport of animal is a normal service for most international airlines. Doing it does, however, require advance notice. Usually, domestic animals are carried in the cargo hold. The holds for animals are often pressurized, well ventilated and maintained at a comfortable temperature.

Some airlines, allow small domestic animals to travel in the cabinet. Others, by contrast, do not allow transportation of animals in the cabin.

This procedure is often subject to certain conditions. For most airlines, only a number of animals are allowed per class. Furthermore, the animals whether in the cabin or in the cargo hold are required to be carried and must stay in a cage or container that meets certain specifications. For those travelers who do not have a suitable cage, you may want to contact the airline. Some of them do stock a limited number of these cabin for sale to their clients.

**Regulations on Animal Transportation:** As an international traveler, you should bear in mind that some countries do not permit either the import or the transit of animals. In certain countries, it is required that animals first spend some time in quarantine. This mandated period may last for a few days, several weeks or months and at a cost that may be considerably high. Most airlines will not fly pregnant animals or those under two months of age. International airlines are generally willing to provide their customers with relevant information regarding the official and veterinary regulations in force at the place of embarkation, transit points and destination. Regulations for the transportation of animals may vary from airline to airline.

**Animal Transportation - Rates:**  The excess luggage tariff is often charged for the transportation of the animal. This tariff is based on the combined weight of the animal and the container. The excess tariff rate applies irrespective of whether or not you carry the full luggage allowance. If your pet flies as cargo, special cargo rates may apply. In this case, it is important to remember that checking in and picking up of your animal may be carried out in the cargo building, rather than in the passenger terminal. Airlines generally transport guide dogs for blind or deaf passengers free of charge.

**Storing Your Pet on Board:**  Some airlines will allow you to bring your pet on board with you and to store it in a compartment under your seat. However, most airlines require that you use an approved airline carrier for your pet during the flight, which is stowed in the airplanes's cargo hold. You can get one of these carriers secondhand.

Your veterinarian can help your pet endure the flight by prescribing a tranquilizer.  You should arrange for it to have water during the flight.  One trick is to freeze water in the bowl that attaches to the carrier.  That way you will avoid drips while transporting the carrier.

**Traveling with Pets:**[IL]  Veterinarians advise against traveling with your pet. But some dogs and cats become so miserable when their owners are away that they literally starve themselves. If you are moving across the ocean, you probably will want to take your pet with you.  As long as your pet has had its shots, it can travel with you freely throughout Europe-with the exception of Britain, Ireland and Norway which have quarantine systems because their areas are rabies-free.  The only restriction usually is that you possess a yellow international vaccination certificate for your pet.

Most airlines will make arrangements for your pet-unless it is a boa constrictor, a ferret or a bird. Birds are particularly unwelcome on airlines because they carry diseases.

In addition to the vaccination certificate, most European countries require a health certificate for any animal taken across borders.  The certificate must be filled out by a veterinarian a limited number of days before you arrive in the country. You may be required to obtain a second certificate once inside Europe if you plan to cross additional border-checks with the consulates of the country you are visiting.

**Expectant Mothers:** With the approval of the physician, most airlines generally allow expectant mothers to fly until a specified period of their pregnancy. This period varies from airline to airline. For a flight after this time, you may be denied boarding for obvious reasons. Check with your airline after consulting with your physician.

**Group Travel Versus Solo:** There are advantages and disadvantages to both group and solo traveling. These advantages and disadvantages not withstanding, an international traveler with adequate planning can always expect to have a perfectly enjoyable, exciting and successful trip abroad. Whether one plans to travel as part of a group or solo is a matter of choice and personal preference, many times determined by such variables as cost, age, foreign travel experience, language, privacy, flexibility, timing, health conditions and familiarity with the foreign country.

By and large, traveling as part of a group can add to the overall security of your trip and will facilitate some of the procedural requirements that accompany traveling to a foreign country. Group travelers often attract and get faster attention, sometimes resulting in savings of time and/or money. Because your group travel may involve a tour guide, you probably will have the advantage of sampling the best sites in town on the usual congested schedule. As a member of a tour group, you must be ready to sacrifice your need for complete privacy, flexibility and independence for a schedule that may not allow them. Ultimately, it is you who must provide the verdict as to the success of your trip abroad.

**Facilities:** Many of the services and gadgets that are customary in the U.S. are conspicuously missing or inadequate in many parts of the world. This is particularly true in developing countries, but also occurs in rural areas and in some developed countries. Such amenities as a regular supply of heat, hot water or air conditioning are rare in public as well as in private facilities.

98

In some areas even hotels lack these services. Medical services are often inadequate and transportation and telecommunications are often inefficient. Computers, color television sets and other modern gadgets remain luxury items in many parts of the world and are not readily available. Even services as routine as dry cleaning may prove to be a challenge.

Essentially, you must be aware that many foreign countries are not as advanced, developed, rich, cultured and "blessed" as the U.S. and its citizens. Shortages abound and poverty and primitive technology are very much alive in several parts of the world. As an international traveler, you can avoid the failures, losses, disappointments and frustrations experienced by many overseas travelers through careful pre-travel research and planning. The more knowledgeable you are about the people, their culture and the level of development in the country you plan to visit, the better your chances of having an exciting and successful overseas trip.

**Hotel Phone Calls:**   Placing phone calls from your hotel room may be convenient but it may also cost you considerably. Before you make that call, check with the hotel desk clerk or phone operator to ascertain charges for local, long distance and overseas calls. Surcharges of up to 200 percent% are not unusual.

There are various options and approaches you can use to reduce the cost of hotel phone calls. If you must make your call from the hotel: (a) Find out if the hotel has low rate calling periods. If they do, place your calls during those times. (b) Remember that most hotels have pay phones at the lobby. If those phones are  programmed to handle long distance or international calls, use them. (c) Find out if the hotel has calling card facilities. By placing your calls with a calling card, you may end up paying in U.S. dollars when you return home. (d) Alternatively, make that first time sacrifice and use a call-back approach. This allows you to provide your number to your calling party while asking the other party to call you back. (e) Explore collect calls if it is available. Some of these approaches may only defer payments for your calls, but most will save you money.

Another option that will help to reduce telephone costs is to place your calls at the designated central telephone stations found at most airports and in some train stations. Specially marked public telephones which allow you to use your calling cards are springing up in several large cities overseas. Because you will need a calling card to access this service, you may want to request one by signing up with one of the major long distance carriers in the U.S. before you depart.

**Receiving Mail overseas:** Central Post Offices in several large cities do provide facilities that allow foreign travelers to receive mail while overseas. <u>Poste Restante</u> is a general delivery service which allows mail to be sent to someone overseas to the care of a particular post office. The mail is then held for pick up by the owner. Proper identification such as a passport is often required. Important points to remember about this facility are: (1) They may not be available in every country. It is important to use the exact address and phone number (2) Your letter may be held only for a limited time period and can only be picked up during designated hours. (3) You may be charged a nominal fee for this service. (4) It is advisable for the sender to make an appropriate note on the envelope; for example, "Hold until Dec. 31, 1999." Additionally, it is advisable to call the post office before going to pick up your mail. In this way, you will be sure the post office is open and that your letter is ready for pick-up.

You could also apply this same approach with mail sent to hotels. If appropriate, have the sender place a note on the envelope: for example, "Mail for a guest; Hold until Dec. 31, 1999." Another alternative would be to use the services of the American Express Company. Customers of American Express including American Express Cardholders may have their letters sent to The American Express Office nearest their destination. This service is provided free of charge. Some restrictions may apply, as it is important to inquire about these services before you leave. Decide on which services you wish to use and make appropriate inquiries.

**Making Business Contacts overseas:** This can be taxing for businesses seeking new overseas markets for their products and sources for their raw materials. Business contacts in some countries become even more difficult for women. U.S. businesses in need of assistance in this area or in any activity relating to international trade may contact the U.S. International Trade Commission in the Department of Commerce. This agency will provide you with advice, references and resources on a variety of issues in international business including sources of financial assistance for U.S. exporters. They also provide information on the domestic markets including local business customs and practices. A listing of the Department of Commerce District Offices and the International Trade Information can be found at your local public library. Other sources that should be explored are: (1) the commercial section of the country's embassy or consulate in the U.S., (2) the U.S. Chamber of Commerce. A growing number of companies now have a Chamber of Commerce in the U.S., (3) International Trade offices of City and State Governments, (4) Commercial attaches of American Embassies and Consulates Overseas and (5) International Business Clubs and Organization in the U.S.

**Overseas Employment:** Before considering employment overseas, you should familiarize yourself with the Internal Revenue Service rules regarding income earned abroad. Several rules and tests apply including the "foreign residence test" and the "physical presence test." You may avoid future confrontations with the IRS by checking the current rules and regulations. Check your local telephone directory for the IRS office nearest you.

As you embark on your search for employment overseas, be cautious of the growing number of unscrupulous agents and agencies with bogus claims. Many of these so called "overseas employment agencies" are not reliable, but are out to con you out of your money. It is advisable to think hard and long before committing any monies to them. Alternatively, you should consider applying for overseas jobs directly with the overseas employer. A number of international newspapers and magazines as well as foreign magazines circulated in the U.S. carry job announcements. Other sources of information regarding overseas jobs may be obtained from the respective foreign embassies and consulates in the U.S. (See Appendix B).

An offer of a job overseas does not exempt you from the rules and regulations governing employment of foreigners in a particular country nor are you exempted from the necessary permits, including entry and exit visas,

101

and other requirements of that country. Check with the respective embassies and consulates.

**Discount Travel Opportunities:** You can save a lot of money as I have on your trips and still enjoy the same treats as everyone else. This is true whether in the U.S. or abroad if only you know what it takes. And what does it take? It takes flexibility and willingness on your part to give up some comfort and conveniences. The more knowledgeable you are about these opportunities, the greater the potential for large savings. Unfortunately, some of the opportunities for bargain fares carry risks and penalties which may end up being costly in both time and money. Hence, it is important to shop around for the least restrictive bargain opportunities. As you begin exploring opportunities for discount fares, you may want to bear these generalized observations in mind:

(a) Tickets for flights during peak seasons cost more than those for during off seasons. This is also true for prices charged by hotels, theaters, etc. Summers are usually considered peak seasons as opposed to winters. Airlines and cruise lines have actual months signaling the start and end of the various seasons. It is important to remember that the actual dates may vary from carrier to carrier and for travel to or from some parts of the world. It is advisable to shop around and to check with the various carriers.

(b) Tickets for travel during early morning or night hours tend to be cheaper. Although this may not be true for international carriers, you may find such bargains with domestic flights.

(c) Tickets for weekday and holiday travel tend to be more expensive than on weekends and non-holiday periods.

(d) Depending on the class of ticket you buy, you may pay more or less and still not notice any significant difference in services provided the different classes of passengers. In the case of travel by air, depending on the airline, you will find as many as four classes of fares. These are, in descending order of cost beginning with the most expensive, first class, business class, coach class (sometimes called tourist or economy) and excursion or discount fares. There is also the "super first class" as one may categorize the fare on the Concord. Most international airlines offer the four basic fares. In some, the number of fare classes may be less. You may find slight variations between airlines in their definitions of these classes. It is not unusual to find some airlines selling different types of coach or economy tickets. From time to time new packages with new terms are added to the usual economy and excursion classes of fares. In recent years, these have included the advance purchase excursion (APEX) fare and the Youth fare. These are all potentially bargain opportunities for international travelers. Exploring some of these special fares may be worth the effort.

(e) Standby fares are considerably lower than regular fares, and are potential money-savers for those who qualify. Standby opportunities are described elsewhere in this book.

(f) Tickets for low-fare travel on generic airlines such as Virgin Atlantic, Icelandair and several other small carriers, are generally much cheaper than tickets bought for travel with any of the large carriers.

Alternatively, you could save handsomely on your overseas trip by employing the services of charter operators, ticket rebators, air couriers and bucket shops and consolidators. The services provided by these groups are explained elsewhere in this book.

As you explore the various avenues to save on your trip expect some restrictions and learn to consider them before making any financial commitments. Read all fine print. Some of the common conditions will include one or more of the following clauses: (a) advance reservation, (b) advance payment, (c) short notification of the traveler, (d) reconfirmation of reservation, (e) non-refundable payments, (f) no cancellations (except documented real emergency), (g) minimum and/or maximum stay (h) weekend sleep-overs (i) some stopovers/connections, (j) right to cancel on the part of the service provider.

You also have the option of reserving a flight or cruise without making immediate payment. You can make reservations with more than one carrier up to six months in advance. However, you may be required to pay and get your ticket within a few weeks of the actual travel date. I must caution that carriers generally do not appreciate multiple reservations for the same traveler since this ties up opportunities for others. Avoid booking your reservations with the airline and making a duplicate booking with a travel agency. Most airlines, once they notice the duplication, will cancel both and toss out your name.

**Vegetarians**: Surely, you are not left out. Most international airlines will honor your request for a special vegetarian diet. The only requirement is that you give them advance notice. Such notice is better done when booking your reservation and again when re-confirming your flight. Do not be surprised if you suddenly find out while on board, that they forgot to keep their word. You can expect apologies when this happens, although that won't be of much help. It may not be a bad idea to carry along some food or snacks just in case. International airlines generally do a better job of meeting your dietary needs than do local or domestic airlines. In fact, do not expect much in this area from domestic airlines. So be prepared.

Similar to international flights, you may not have difficulties getting a decent vegetarian meal in the big, well-known hotels where salad bars are equally popular. Travelers with alternative room and board arrangements should expect to be on their own with regard to feasting on a good vegetarian meal. There are obviously ways that you can make up for these deficiencies, such as a trip to the local food market. This is an alternative that I will not recommend for an international traveler. You do not have to lodge in an expensive, big-time hotel to eat in their restaurants. Finally, do not be surprised if your host/hostess does not understand what a vegetarian meal is or perhaps find it strange. To assist you in your travel plan, you may employ the assistance of the North American Vegetarian Society at P.O. Box 72, Dolgeville, NY. 13329 (518) 568-7970.

**Emergencies and Restricted Reservations**: We do not always expect them, but they do happen. I mean emergencies. Sometimes the losses go beyond the actual emergency to include  broken vacations or trips and financial losses from restricted tickets. Airlines and other carriers and service providers are aware of such possibilities. It does not always have to translate to a total loss. Irrespective of the type of restrictions and penalties contained in your reservations and tickets, with proper and verifiable documentation, you may be able to recover. Proper documentation would include a note from your doctor in the case of illness, a copy of a newspaper release or an obituary notice in the case of death of a family member. Any convincing and verifiable document will help. If you are lucky you may not only be able to get some credit or refund, but you may even qualify for a discount such as the special bereavement fare offered by some airlines. Although these opportunities exist to minimize your loss in the event of an emergency, do not interpret this as an obligation on the part of the other party unless specifically included in the contract. For the most part, it is a favor being rendered to you and how you approach the other party is important.

**Limitations To Airline Compensation For Lost Luggage:**   Contrary to what some travelers think, airlines are not obligated to pay you an unlimited sum in compensation for lost or damaged luggage. The limit to an airline's obligation is clearly stated on the back of your ticket. Read it carefully. Even with all of your receipts in tact, you will be entitled to no more than what is stated. How much you get depends largely on the weight of your luggage as indicated on your ticket when you checked in and the contents after being subject to depreciation and any insurance on the luggage. The value of the contents is not the primary determining criteria. For lost or damaged items, airlines may reimburse each passenger a maximum of $12.50 per pound on domestic flights and $9.07 per pound for each piece of checked baggage on an International flight. The maximum reimbursement for unchecked baggage on an International flight is $400. If the contents of your luggage(s) are valued at over $800 dollars, you might want to get additional insurance. A list of Travel Insurance providers is provided in Appendices V and W.

Alternatively, consider traveling light, and leaving at home those items you cannot afford to lose. Expensive items such as jewelry, furs and cameras should be left at home. Otherwise, you should consider having them insured. Adding a floater to your existing policy may be all that is necessary.

In the event your luggage is damaged, you should request a replacement baggage to carry you through the rest of your trip. Many airlines, particularly European Airlines, will often honor your request on the spot. Others may prefer to refer you elsewhere to have your luggage replaced or repaired. You may be requested to have your luggage repaired and to submit the bill for reimbursement. Because time is of essence to you, insist on immediate replacement. Document the loss or damage to the airline authorities in writing. Hold on to your copy of the report and to your ticket. Remember not to surrender your luggage tag unless you are provided with a signed letter stating that they are in possession of your luggage tag.

**Bumped:** If you are bumped by an airline and because of overbooking denied boarding you may have recourse. Depending upon whether you are voluntarily or involuntarily bumped, you may be entitled to compensation by the airline. The mere fact that you are booked and have a ticket for the flight does not automatically qualify you to fly, nor does it entitle you to compensation if you are bumped. Failure to confirm or re-confirm your flight within the time required (usually 72 hours) or to arrive and check-in on time as stipulated on your ticket, may result in forfeiture of your right to fly and to a seat on the plane.

**Re-Confirming Flights**: The general rule with international airline tickets and reservations is that you re-confirm your flight within 72 hours. This can be done in person or over the phone. Do not take this for granted. You stand to loose your original reservation and seat on the plane, if you fail to confirm. Many airlines take it seriously and will waste no time selling your seat. When you re-confirm your flight, request your confirmation number and the name of the airline personnel attending to you.

**Canceled/Delayed Flights**: Flight delays and cancellations are not unusual and can be frustrating. This is the reason some travelers carry flight cancellation insurance coverage. The reasons for delays and cancellations vary and may or may not entitle you to compensation, let alone to special considerations. It is very unlikely that you can do much about it. In the instance of a protracted delay or cancellation, most airlines will provide the travelers with alternative options and services including meals and lodging at no extra expense to the traveler. Sometimes, you may have to request these services. The rules governing flight delays and cancellations vary from country to country and among the various airlines. Unless your carrier is a U.S. based airline, you may be just wasting your time. Flight delays and cancellations are more prevalent in developing countries. Do not expect an explanation or an apology since none may be forthcoming. Nevertheless, do ask and request a substitute arrangement. If you have a suggestion on how you can be helped, make it. You may get what you ask for especially if your request is reasonable.

**Baggage Storage Facilities:** Do not leave your luggage unattended or in the care of a stranger. Most international airports are equipped with baggage storage facilities where, for a small fee, you can store your baggages. Although many of these facilities operate 24 hours a day, seven days a week, there are variations from airport to airport. In some of these facilities, you can leave your baggage with them for a maximum of up to several days. Obviously you do not want to leave your luggage in these places for too long. Take your valuables with you including your passport, tickets, credit cards and travelers checks. Make sure that the luggage left behind has locks and your identification tag. Collect a receipt, and keep it safe. If you lose your receipt you may find it difficult to re-claim your luggage. In addition to storage facilities at the airports, lockers can be found in train stations of large cities. Some of your excess luggage can be safely stored in these lockers for a short period of time. Lockers found in Western Europe are safer than those in countries in Africa, South America and Asia.

**Hotel Reservation from the Airport:** For those who like to brave it by not making advance hotel reservations, you may want to know that at most international airports, there are often specially marked telephones directly hooked up to the major hotels in the city. There is often no cost to you to use these phones. All you have to do is lift up the phone and a hotel reservation clerk will be on the line to assist you. Most of these hotels also operate free transportation to and from the airport. If you cannot locate any of these phones, inquire at the information desk located in every airport.

**Camping Carnet:** If you plan to camp overseas, the international camping carnet could save you money. You can apply for a copy from the National Campers and Hikers Association at 7172 Transit Rd. Buffalo NY 14221 tel. (716) 634-5433.

**U.S. Embassies Abroad and Holidays:** U.S. Embassies and consulates abroad observe a number of holidays and are closed during those holidays. For the most part, they observe both U.S. holidays and public holidays of the host country. For a listing of commercial holidays contact the country's consulate, embassy or tourist office located in the US. See Appendices B & F.

**What the U.S. Embassies and Consulates Can and Cannot Do**: The U.S. embassies and consulates abroad provide a number of services to Americans. While you may be tempted to seek their assistance, embassies and consulates do not engage in travel agency functions. Approaching them for assistance, to change your itinerary or re-issue your ticket may yield you very little positive results. Certainly embassies and consulates will not be able to assist you in such things as recovering your lost or damaged luggage or cashing your. Although they may direct you to assistance elsewhere, they are much more concerned with emergency and life threatening issues affecting you and other American citizens.

**Catching Local (domestic) Flights and Other Transportation**: Do not expect to find orderliness and timeliness when taking domestic flights in many countries, particularly in developing countries. Delays are rampant. Planes are often overbooked and you may have to engage in some hustling if you really want to travel from one point to another. This is also true for other means of transportation. After all of this, do not be surprised to find someone occupying your seat because it has been assigned to more than one person. It seems like a tradition in some environments. In these environments, I usually put on my sneakers and travel light.

**Authentication Services:** Foreigners engaged in official business transactions are occasionally required to submit authenticated (not notarized) documents. These documents which require an official seal include birth certificate, marriage license, school transcripts and divorce papers. If you must submit documents to foreign governments, agencies or institutions, find out if notarized copies are acceptable or if they must be officially authenticated. To have your documents authenticated call or write: Authentication Service Foreign Affairs Center, Bureau of Administration, United States Department of state, 2201 C. St. NW Rm. 2815, Washington, D.C. 20520 tel: (202) 647-7735.

**Time Zone Differential:** Just as there is time variation between cities in the U.S., depending on where you live, such variations, also, exist between countries. In the U.S. we have five time zones: Pacific, Mountain, Central, Eastern, and Atlantic. Los Angeles, California is in the Pacific, Montana is in the Mountain zone, Texas and Illinois, are in the Central zone, New York and Washington D.C. are in the Eastern zone, and Maine is in the Atlantic time zone. When it is 12 noon in New York, it is 11 a.m. in Chicago because it is 1 hour behind Eastern Standard Time, and it is 9 a.m. in Los Angeles because Los Angeles is 3 hours behind Eastern Standard Time. Since these variations exist between countries, you should be aware of them . They will invariably affect your flight time and schedule of appointments. Familiarize yourself with the time zone differential and make appropriate adjustments.

**Place of Worship:** Finding a place to worship while overseas is as simple as just asking. Your hotel desk clerk should be able to help you locate the nearest place of worship. Alternatively, the tourist information center or local phone book will do the same. As you journey around remember that you may not necessarily find a denomination of your first choice. Just as some countries may be predominantly Christian so too are others dominated by non-Christian faith, such as Islam. In many countries, you will find a mixture of minority and majority religious denominations and places of worship scattered here and there. There are also non-denominational houses of worship. The more flexible you are, the greater the chance of finding a place of worship close to where you are staying. If your preference is for an English speaking place of worship, you may not be able to find one. You can still enjoy the activities and recite your prayers even where the local language is used in services.

**Meal on Flight**:  Between international flights and domestic flights expect a wide range in the quality of services provided. This is particularly true with meals. Meals on domestic flights are relatively poorer. When overseas, it would be advisable to eat before boarding or to carry snacks with you. Do not be surprised if no foods is served on journeys of reasonable distance. I have had to deal with this on more than one occasion during my trips in some African countries.

**Travel Luggages: Specifications and Allowances**:  As you go shopping for luggage and carry-on bags, you should be aware that airlines do have specifications. Any luggage exceeding the required dimensions for check-in and carry-on  may be refused. Generally, the linear dimensions for check-in-luggage ranges between 45 and 62 inches (i.e. length and width and height). Luggage with sizes no more than 21 x 16 x 48" or 23 x 13 x 9" are ideal. Carry-on pieces cannot exceed 45 inches in total linear dimension and must fit in the overhead compartment or underneath the seat.

Most international airlines allow two pieces of check-in luggage and one carry-on piece per passenger. Each piece of check-in luggage be 70 lbs or less. Some airlines give first-class passengers allowances of up to 80 lbs and limit the allowance to economy class passengers to only 50 lbs. If you must carry more than two pieces of check-in luggage expect to pay extra. For heavier or larger luggage, the airline may refuse to carry them or may levy additional charges. It is better not to count on the latter.

Specifications vary from carrier to carrier. You are, therefore, better off checking with the carrier you intend to use. Specifications may differ from those on domestic travels within a particular country, and you may be required to pay extra. Again, check with the airline for guidelines on luggage requirements on domestic flights.

**Language Barrier**:  Unless English is the language of conversation in the country you plan to visit or you are quite fluent in the language of your host country, you will, occasionally ponder how much easier your trip would have turned out if only you understood the language. Well, you are not alone in this territory. Depending on the length and purpose of your trip, you could do something about it. Some travelers enroll in language courses offered by a number of national and local organizations and schools. Others engage in home study and self-tutoring, with the help of TVs, videos, phrase books and cassette tapes. You could do any of these. I suggest that you familiarize yourself with a few conversational words and phrases of your host country. You will be amazed at the difference they will add to your trip. Check with your local colleges and libraries for basic language course offerings. Your local yellow pages also have resources such as names and addresses of foreign language institutes. Wouldn't you like to say "Thank you" to that cab driver, door man or waiter who just rendered you a magnificent service and in a language he or she understands? A country by country listing of official and other major languages is provided in Appendix U.

**Front Desk Service**:   Not sure of something, lost, confused or forgotten something? Ask the clerk at the front desk. Every hotel overseas will certainly have an information desk with a clerk ready to assist you. In most cases, these clerks will have answers to many of your  questions regarding your host  country. If they do not have answers, they will gladly direct you to the appropriate places to get answers. Front desk personnel may even have postage stamps to sell to you. Do not hesitate to approach them  on any matters of concern to you. While at the front desk, look around for other items of information. Hotel lobbies are often stuffed with local newspapers, maps, and other publications that you will find useful as you explore your new environment.

**Stray Animals**:   Afraid of animals; take precautions. In several parts of the world, particularly rural communities of developing and some developed countries, animals, from dogs and cats to pigs, goat, sheep and cows, roam about freely. Do not be surprised also to find yourself riding in a commercial vehicle next to these animals or to find them wandering around your place of residence. For the local inhabitants, these animals are not hostile nor a threat to them. My advice is not to cuddle them or try to play with them. The last thing you want is a bite from an animal you may perceive as friendly. Remember that rabies exist in many developing countries. Beware!

**Airport Facilities:**  Airports provide a variety of facilities aimed at providing safety and comfort to the traveler, and an increasing number of international airports are taking added steps to provide for the special needs of babies, young children and the disabled.

Most international airports are now equipped with special rooms where babies can be fed and changed, and some have short-term nursery and play facilities for young children.

Disabled travelers can also take advantage of various free services available to them.  A disabled traveler is entitled to ask for an escort both in the aircraft and in the airport.  Deaf passengers can request  written announcements from the ground staff.  Blind persons are entitled to take their guide dogs, but your dog may not be exempt from both the home and host country quarantine laws.

It is worth remembering, however, that to take advantage of special airport facilities, you have to request them since most of them may only be available on demand.  You are always better off making your requests early, especially for those facilities with limited availability or supplies.

For travelers to Less Developed Countries, especially African countries, you may want to keep in mind that the conditions of most of their international airports are comparatively poor and inadequate; hence, some of the services noted above may not be available.  It is not uncommon to find unavailable such facilities as clean toilets  with tissue and paper towels. Based on this experience, I have made it a habit of carrying a few rolls of toilet paper with me whenever I am traveling.

# A FINAL CHECKLIST
## FORGET-ME-NOTS
**- - - -**

- ☐ Addresses book.
- ☐ Addresses.
- ☐ Adhesive tape.
- ☐ Alarm clock.
- ☐ Alcohol pads
- ☐ Alcohol.
- ☐ Antacid.
- ☐ Anti-acid tablets
- ☐ Anti-diarrhea medication.
- ☐ Antibiotics.
- ☐ Aspirin.
- ☐ Athletes Foot medication.
- ☐ Auto repair kit
- ☐ Band Aids
- ☐ Bandage.
- ☐ Battery charger
- ☐ Belt.
- ☐ Binoculars/telescope
- ☐ Birth Certificate (copy)
- ☐ Birth Control Pills.
- ☐ Blank Personal Checks.
- ☐ Blood pressure kit
- ☐ Blouses
- ☐ Bottle Opener.
- ☐ Bra.
- ☐ Buttons (assorted).
- ☐ Calculator (pocket).
- ☐ Calling Card, telephone.
- ☐ Camera.
- ☐ Can Opener.
- ☐ Card (playing).
- ☐ Cash.
- ☐ Chapstick.
- ☐ Clothes line
- ☐ Coat (trench).
- ☐ Coat (overcoat).

- ☐ Coats.
- ☐ Cold tablets.
- ☐ Cologne.
- ☐ Comb.
- ☐ Compass.
- ☐ Condoms.
- ☐ cone remover.
- ☐ Contact lenses.
- ☐ Contact lens cleaning
  solution.
- ☐ Converter
- ☐ cotton swab.
- ☐ Credit Cards.
- ☐ Cufflinks.
- ☐ Curling Iron.
- ☐ Currency (Foreign)
- ☐ Currency (U.S).
- ☐ Customs registration
  Certificate
- ☐ Decongestant.
- ☐ Dental Floss.
- ☐ Dentures.
- ☐ Deodorant.
- ☐ Diary.
- ☐ Dress.
- ☐ Driver's License.
- ☐ Ear plugs.
- ☐ Ear drops
- ☐ Electric adapters and plugs.
- ☐ Emergency Kit.
- ☐ Envelopes.
- ☐ Extra batteries.
- ☐ Extra bag (collapsible).
- ☐ Extra Prescriptions.
- ☐ Eye drops.
- ☐ Films (camera).

113

☐ Flashlight.
☐ Flask.
☐ Foreign Language dictionary.
☐ Fur.
☐ Gifts (presents).
☐ Gloves.
☐ Glue
☐ Golf clubs.
☐ Guide books.
☐ Hair Conditioner.
☐ Hair Dryers.
☐ Hair Remover.
☐ Hair blower
☐ Hair Spray.
☐ Hair shaving blades
☐ Hairbrush.
☐ Hand luggage.
☐ Hangers.
☐ Hat.
☐ Head gear.
☐ Hearing aid.
☐ Hemorrhoidal cream.
☐ Hostel Card.
☐ Hydrocortisone cream.
☐ Immunizations.
☐ Insect Repellant.
☐ Insulin needles
☐ Insurance ID cards.
☐ Insurance claim forms.
☐ International Driver's Permit.
☐ International Vaccination certificate
☐ Iron.
☐ Jewelry.
☐ Knife.
☐ Language dictionary.
☐ Lint remover.
☐ Lipsticks.
☐ log book (diary).
☐ Lotion (suntan).
☐ Lotion (facial).
☐ Lotion (body).
☐ luggage keys (and extra set,

put elsewhere).
☐ Luggage carts.
☐ Luggage (to be checked in).
☐ Magnifying glasses.
☐ Makeup Kit.
☐ Maps.
☐ Medic Alert bracelet.
☐ Medical/clinical records.
☐ Medication (prescription and non-prescription).
☐ Mirror (pocket-size).
☐ Money belt.
☐ Nail Polish.
☐ Neck Ties.
☐ Needle.
☐ Night Gown.
☐ Pajamas.
☐ Panties.
☐ Pants.
☐ Passport.
☐ Pen.
☐ Perfume.
☐ Personal checks.
☐ Photos:(passport-size).
☐ Phrase Book..
☐ Plastic bags.
☐ Plastic utensils
☐ Polish Remover.
☐ Prescription glasses( reading).
☐ Q-tips.
☐ Rain Coat.
☐ Raincoat
☐ Razor.
☐ Reading glasses carrying cases.
☐ Reservation slips.
☐ Rollers (hair).
☐ Safety pins.
☐ Sandals.
☐ Sanitary pads.
☐ Sanitary napkins.
☐ Scarves.

**114**

- ☐ Scissors (small).
- ☐ Sewing Kit
- ☐ Shampoo.
- ☐ Shaving cream/powder.
- ☐ Shaving blades.
- ☐ Shirts (dress).
- ☐ Shoe Polish.
- ☐ Shoe brush
- ☐ Shoe laces.
- ☐ Shoes.
- ☐ Shower cap.
- ☐ Ski-equipments.
- ☐ Ski-jacket.
- ☐ Skirt.
- ☐ Skis.
- ☐ Slacks.
- ☐ Sleeping bag.
- ☐ Sleeping pills.
- ☐ Slip (waist).
- ☐ Snacks, favorite.
- ☐ Sneakers.
- ☐ Soap (bathing).
- ☐ Soap (laundry).
- ☐ Socks.
- ☐ Souvenirs
- ☐ Spare glasses.
- ☐ Stain remover.
- ☐ Stockings
- ☐ Suit (bathing).
- ☐ Suit.
- ☐ Sun Glasses.
- ☐ T-shirts.
- ☐ Tape recorder
- ☐ Tape recorder
- ☐ Tape measure
- ☐ Tape (fiberglass).
- ☐ Thermal wear.
- ☐ Thermometer.
- ☐ Thread (assorted).
- ☐ Timetables
- ☐ Toilet tissue
- ☐ Toothbrush.
- ☐ Toothpaste.

- ☐ Toothpicks
- ☐ Tourist card.
- ☐ Towel.
- ☐ Tranquilizers
- ☐ Transformer
- ☐ Traveler's checks.
- ☐ Tweezers.
- ☐ Umbrella
- ☐ Underwear.
- ☐ Vaccination Card.
- ☐ Visas.
- ☐ Vitamins
- ☐ Walkman radio/cassette.
- ☐ Wallet.
- ☐ Washcloth.
- ☐ Watch.
- ☐ Water pills.
- ☐ Water heater
- ☐ Whistle
- ☐ Windbreaker.
- ☐ Writing pads.
- ☐ Zip lock plastic bags

**HAVE YOU**

- ☐ A copy of your medical report?

- ☐ Checked your credit card and bank account balances?

- ☐ Checked medications for clear labelling?

- ☐ Checked the dress code for the countries you are visiting?

- ☐ Checked currency requirements of host country?

- ☐ Checked medication for clear

**115**

☐ labelling?

☐ Checked your insurance coverage?

☐ Consulted with your physician?

☐ Consulted with your dentist?

☐ Discussed with your loved ones, key code words to use in case of an emergency?

☐ Familiarized yourself with a few conversational phrases of your host country?

☐ Had your shots?

☐ Jotted down addresses and phone number of the nearest U.S. embassy or consulate?

☐ Jotted down addresses and telephone numbers of overseas offices of traveler's checks issuing companies, in case of a refund or lost or stolen checks?

☐ left a copy of your itinerary with relatives, friends?

☐ Made arrangements for money to be transferred to you in case of an emergency?

☐ Made a final telephone call to your host/hostess?

☐ Obtained a Carnet?

☐ Obtained a copy of your medical report?

☐ Obtained your ATM Card?

☐ Obtained your telephone dialing card?

☐ Picked up your prescriptions?

☐ Picked up letters of authorization/explanation from your doctor regarding drugs you are be carrying?

☐ Picked up a dialing card from your long distance telephone carrier?

☐ Picked up your travelers checks?

☐ Picked up your passport?

☐ Picked up your tickets?

☐ Placed tags on all of your luggage?

☐ Re-confirmed your flight/ reservations?

☐ Registered your valuables with the U.S. Customs?

☐ Requested your special diet with the airline/cruise line?

☐ Updated your insurance?

☐ Written down important, addresses, telephone and fax numbers?

**116**

# APPENDIX A

## U.S. EMBASSIES AND CONSULATES ABROAD

Note: APO/FPO addresses may only be used for mail originating in the United States. When you use an APO/FPO address, do not include the local street address.

### ALBANIA
Tirana (E), Rruga Labinoti 103, Room 2921; PSC 59,Box 100 (A), APO AE 29624; Tel 355-42-32875,33520;FAX355-42-32222

### ALGERIA
Algiers (E), 4 Chemin Cheikh Bachir El-Ibrahimi; B.P. Box 549 (Alger-Gare) 16000; Tel [213] (2) 601 -425/255/186;FAX [213] (2) 603979

Oran (C),14 Square de Bamako; Tel [213](6)334509and 335499

### ANGOLA
The United States maintains a liaison office in Luanda accredited to the Joint Political Military Commission that oversees implementation of the Angola Peace Accords. This office does not perform any commercial or consular services. The United States does not maintain diplomatic relations with the Government of the People's Republic of Angola.

Luanda (LO), Predio BPA, 11 Andar, Luanda; Mail international: CP 6484, Luanda, Angola. Pouch: USLC Luanda, Dept. of State, Washington, D.C; 20521-2550 Tel [244] (2) 39.02-42

### ANGUILLA
St. Johns (E), FPO Miami 34054; Tel (809) 462 -3505/06 FAX (809) 462-3516

### ANTIGUA AND BARBUDA
St. Johns (E), FPO AA 34054-0001; Tel (809) 462-3505/06; FAX (809) 462-3516

### ARGENTINA
Buenos Aires (E), 4300 Colombia, 1425; Unit 4334 APO AA 34034; Tel [54] (1) 774-7611/8811/9911

### ARMENIA
Yerevan (E), 18 General Bagramian Street; Tel (7) (8852) 15-11-22

### AUSTRALIA
Canberra (E), Moonah Pl., Canberra, A.C.T. 2600; APO AP 96549; Tel [61] (6) 270-5000; FAX [61](6) 270-5970

Melbourne (CG), 553 St. Kilda Road Melbourne, Victoria 3004; UNIT 11011, APO 96551-0002; Tel [61] (3) 526-5900; FAX [61](3)510-4646

Sydney (CG), 36th Fl., Electricity House, Corner of Park and Elizabeth Sts., Sydney N.S.W. 2000; UNIT 11026, APO AP 96554-0002; Tel [61] (2) 261-9200; FAX FCS 261-8148

Perth (CG), 13th Fl., 16 St. Georges Terr.; P.O. Box 6044, East Perth, WA 6004; UNIT 11021; APO AP 96553-0002; Tel [61] (9) 221-1177; FAX [61](9)325-3569

**Brisbane (C),** 383 Wickham Ter., Brisbane, Queensland 4000; UNIT 11018, APO AP 96553-0002; Tel [61] (7) 839-8955

**AUSTRIA**
**Vienna (E),** Boltzmanngasse 16, A-1091, Vienna; APO AE 09222; Tel [43](222) 31-55-11; FAX [43](222)310-0682; Consular Section: Garten-baupromenade 2, 4th Floor, 1010 Vienna; Tel 1431 (222) 51451

**Salzburg (CG),** Giselakai 51, A-5020 Salzburg; Tel [43] (662) 28-6-01

**AZERBAIJAN**
**BAKU (E),** The Embassy is currently located in the Hotel Intourist, 77 Prospekt Neftyanikov, Tel 7-8922-92-63-06

**BAHAMAS**
**Nassau (E),** Mosmar Bldg., Queen St.; P.O. Box N-8197; Tel [809) 322-1181 and 328-2206; FAX (809)328-7838

**BAHRAIN**
**Manama (E),** Bldg. No. 979, Road No. 3119, Block/Area 331 ZINJ: P.O. Box 26431; FPO AE 09834 -6210; Switchboard Tel [973]273-300; FAX [973]272-594

**BANGLADESH**
**Dhaka (E),** Diplomatic Enclave, Madani Ave., Baridhara, G.P.O. Box 323 Dhaka 1212; Tel, [880](2) 884700-22; FAX [880] (2)883648

**BARBADOS**
**Bridgetown (E),** P.O. Box 302; Box B, FPO AA 34054; Tel [809] 436-4950 thru 7; FAX (809)429-5246; Canadian Imperial Bank of Commerce Bldg., Broad Street, Bridgetown, Barbados

**BELARUS**
**MINSK (E),** 46 Starovilenskaya, Tel. (7) (0172) 34-76-42

**BELGIUM**
**Brussels (E),** 27 Boulevard du Regent; B-1000 Brussels; APO AE 09724; Tel [32](2)513-3830; FAX [32](2)511-2725

**Antwerp (CG),** Rubens Center, Nationalestraat 5, B -2000 Antwerp; APO AE 09724; Tel [32](03)225-0071; FAX (3)234-3698

**BELIZE**
**Belize City (E),** Gabourel Lane and Hutson St.; P.O. Box 286; Tel [501](2)77161; FAX [501](2)30802

**BENIN**
**Cotonou (E),** Rue Caporal Anani Bernard; B.P. 2012; Tel [229]30-06-50; FAX [229] 30-19-74

**BERMUDA**
**Hamilton (CG),** Crown Hill, 16 Middle Road, Devonshire; P.O. Box HM325, Hamilton HMBX; AMCON FPO AE 09727-1002; Tel (809) 295-1342; FAX (809)295-1592

**BOLIVIA**
**La Paz (E),** Banco Popular Del Peru Bldg., Corner of Calles Mercado and Colon; P.O. Box 425 La Paz; APO AA 34032; Tel [591] (2) 350251, 350120; FAX [591](2)359875

**BOTSWANA**
**Gaborone (E),** P.O. Box 90; Tel [267]353-982; FAX [267]356-947

**BRITISH VIRGIN ISLANDS**
**St. Johns (E),** FPO Miami 34054; Tel (809) 462-3505/06; FAX (809) 462-3516

**BRAZIL**
**Brasilia (E),** Avenida das Nacoes, Lote 3; APO AA 34030; Tel [55] (61) 321-7272; FAX [55](61)225-9136

Rio de Janeiro (CG), Avenida Presidente Wilson, 147; APO AA 34030; Tel 1551 (21) 292-7117;

Sao Paulo (CG), Rua Padre Joao Manoel, 933, 01411; P.O. Box 8063; APO AA 34030; Tel [55] (11) 881-6511

Porto Alegre (C), Rua Coronel Genuino, 421 (9th Fl.); APO AA 34030; Tel [55] (512) 26-4288/4697

Recife (C), Rua Goncalves Maia, 163; APO AA 34030; Tel [55] (81) 221-1412/ 13; FAX (81) 231-1906*

**BRUNEI**
Bandar Seri Begawan (E), Third Floor-Teck Guan Plaza, Jalan Sultan; American Embassy Box B, APO AP 96440; Tel [673] (2) 229-670; FAX [673] (2) 225-293

**BULGARIA**
Sofia (E), 1 A. Stamboliski Blvd.; APO AE 09213-5740; Tel [359] (2)88-48-01 to 05

**BURKINA FASO**
Ouagadougou (E), 01 B.P. 35; Tel [226] 30-67-23/24/25, [226]33-34-22; FAX [226] 31-23-68

**BURMA**
Rangoon (E), 581 Merchant St. (GPO Box 521);AMEMBASSY,Box B, APO AP 96546; Tel [95] (1) 82055)

**BURUNDI**
Bujumbura (E), B.P. 1720, Avenue des Etats-Unis; Tel [257] (222) 454; FAX [257] (222) 926*

**CAMEROON**
Yaounde (E), Rue Nachtigal; B.P. 817; Tel [237] 234014; Telex 8223KN; FAX [237] 230753

Douala (C), 21 Avenue du General De Gaulle; B.P. 4006; Tel [237] (42) 0688, (42) 5331, (42) 3434; FAX [237] (42) 7790

**CANADA**
Ottawa, Ontario (E), 100 Wellington St., K1P 5T1; P.O. Box 5000, Ogdensburg, NY 13669-0430; Tel (613) 248-25256, 25106, 25271, and 25170; FAX (613) 233-8511

Calgary, Alberta (CG), Suite 1050, 615 Macleod Trail, S.E., Calgary, Alberta, Canada T2G 4T8; Tel (403) 265-2116 or 266-8962; FAX (403) 264-6630

Halifax, Nova Scotia (CG), Suite 910, Cogswell Tower, Scotia Sq., Halifax, NS, Canada B3J 3K1; Tel (902) 429-2480; FAX (902)423-6861

Montreal, Quebec (CG), P.O. Box 65, Postal Station Desjardins, H5B 1G1; P.O. Box 847, Champlain, NY 12919-0847; Tel (514) 398-9695; FAX (514) 398-0973

Quebec, Quebec (CG), 2 Place Terrasse Dufferin, C.P. 939, G1R 4T9; P.O. Box 1547 Champlain, NY 12919-1547; Tel (418) 692-2095; FAX (418)692-4640

Toronto, Ontario (CG), 360 University Ave., M5G 1S4; P.O. Box 135, Lewiston, NY 14092-0135;Tel (416) 595-1700; FAX (416)595-0051

Vancouver, British Columbia (CG), 1075 West Georgia St., V6E 4E9; P.O. Box 5002, Point Roberts, WA 98281-5002; Tel (604) 685-4311; FAX (604)685-5285

**REPUBLIC OF CAPE VERDE**
Praia (E), Rua Hoji Ya Henda 81; C.P. 201; Tel [238] 61-43-63 or 61-42-53

**CENTRAL AFRICAN REPUBLIC**
Bangui (E), Avenue President Dacko; B.P.

924; Tel 61-02-00, 61-25-78, 61-43-33; FAX [190](236)61-44-94

**CHAD**
N'Djamena (E), Ave. Felix Eboue; B.P. 413; Tel 1235) (51) 62-18, 40-09

**CHILE**
Santiago (E), Codina Bldg., 1343 Agustinas; APO AA 34033; Tel [56] (2) 710133/90 and 710326/75; FAX[56](2)699-1141

**CHINA***
Beijing (E), Xiu Shui Bei Jie 3; 100600, PRC Box 50; FPO AP 96521-0002; Tel [86] (1) 532-3831; FAX [86](1)532-3178

Guanghzou (CC), Dong Fang Hotel, Liu Hua Road; Box 100, FPO AP 96521-0002; Tel [86](20) 669900 (ext. 1000)

Shanghai (CG), 1469 Huai Hai Middle Rd.; Box 200031; FPO AP 96521-0002; Tel 1861 (21) 433-6880; FAX 433-4122

Shenyang (CG), 40 Lane 4, Section 5, Sanjing St., Heping District; Box 45, FPO AP 96521-0002; Tel [86] (24) 290000; FAX 290074

Chengdu (CG), Jinjiang Hotel, 180 Renmin Rd., Chengdu, Sichuan, Box 85, FPO AP 96521-0002; Tel. [86](28) 582222, ext. 131, 135, 138, 141, 130, respectively; FAX [86](28)583-520,583-792

**COLOMBIA**
Bogota (E), Calle 38, No. 8-61; P.O. Box A.A. 3831; APO AA 34038; Tel [57] (1) 285-1300/1688; FAX [571]288-5687

Barranquilla (C), Calle 77 Carrera 68, Centro Comercial Mayorista; P.O. Box A.A. 51565; APO AA 34038; Tel [57] (58) 45-7088/7560; FAX [57] (58)459464

**COMOROS**
Moroni (E), Boite Postale 1318; Tel 73-22-03, 73-29-22

**PEOPLE'S REPUBLIC OF THE CONGO**
Brazzaville (E), Avenue Amilcar Cabral; B.P. 1015; Box C, APO AE 09828; Tel (242) 83-20-70; FAX [242] 83-63-38

**COSTA RICA**
San Jose (E), Pavas, San Jose; APO AA 34020; Tel [506] 20-39-39; FAX (506)20-2305

**COTE D'IVOIRE**
(formerly Ivory Coast)
Abidjan (E), 5 Rue Jesse Owens; 01 B.P. 1712; Tel: 12251 21-09-79 or 2146-72 FAX [225]21-09-79

**CUBA**
Havana (USINT), Swiss Embassy, Calzada entre L Y M, Vedado; 2d Class Mailing Address: USINT c/o International Purchasing Group, 2052 NW 93rd Ave., Miami, FL 33172; Tel 32-0551, 32-0543

**CYPRUS**
Nicosia (E), Therissos St. and Dositheos St.; FPO AE 09836; Tel [357] (2)4651511; FAX [357](2)459-571

**CZECHOSLOVAKIA**
Prague (E), (Int'l) Trziste 15, 125 48 Prague 1; (APO) AMEM, Box 5630 APO AE 09213-5630; Tel [42](2) 536641/9; FAX [42] (2)532-457

Bratislava (C), Hviezdostavovo NAM. 4, Bratislava, Tel [42](7)330861,AMEM B Box 5630, APO AE 09213-5630

**DENMARK**
Copenhagen (E), Dag Hammarskjolds Alle 24; 2100 Copenhagen O or APO AE 09170; Tel [45] (31) 42-31 -44; FAX [45] (35)43-0223

**120**

**REPUBLIC OF DJIBOUTI**
Djibouti (E), Plateau du Serpent, Blvd.
Marechal Joffre; B.P. 185; Tel [253]
35-39-95; FAX [253]35-39-40

**DOMINICA**
Bridgetown (E), P.O. Box 302; Box B, FPO
Miami 34054; Tel [809] 436-4950 thru 7;
FAX (809) 429-5246;

**DOMINICAN REPUBLIC**
Santo Domingo (E), Corner of Calle Cesar
Nicolas Penson & Calle Leopoldo Navarro;
UNIT 5500, APO AA 34041-0008; Tel
(809)5412171

**ECUADOR**
Quito (E), Avenida 12 de Octubre y Avenida
Patria; P.O. Box 538; APO AA 34039-3420;
Tel [593] (2) 562-890; FAX [593](2)502-052

Guayaquil (CG), 9 de Octubre y Garcia
Moreno; APO AA 34039; Tel [593] (4)
323-570; FAX [593](4)325-286

**EGYPT (ARAB REPUBLIC OF)**
Cairo (E), Lazougi St., Garden City; APO
AE 09839-4900; Tel [20] (2) 355-7371; FAX
[20] (2) 355-7375

Alexandria (CG), 110 Horreya Avenue;
APO AE 09839-4904; Tel [203] 482-1911;
FAX [203] 483-8830

**EL SALVADOR**
San Salvador (E), 25 Avenida Notre
No > 1230;, Unit 3116, APO AA 34023; Tel
[503] 26-7100; FAX [503] (26)589

**EQUATORIAL GUINEA**
Malabo (E), Calle de Los Ministros; P.O.
Box 597; Tel Direct Dial [240] (9)
2185,2406,2507; FAX [240] (9)
2164

**ESTONIA**
Tallinn (E), Kentmanni 20, EE 0001; Tel
014-2) 455-313)

**ETHIOPIA**
Addis Abada (E), Entoto St.; P.O. BOX
1014; TEL[251] (1) 550-666; FAX [251]
(1)551-166

**FIJI**
Suva (E), 31 Loftus St.; P.O. Box 218; Tel
[679] 314-466; FAX [679] 300-081

**FINLAND**

Helsinki (E), Itainen Puistotie 14A, SF-
00140; APO AE 09723; Tel [358] (0)
171931; FAX [358] (0)174681

**FRANCE**
Paris (E), 2 Avenue Gabriel, 75382 Paris
Cedex 08; APO AE 09777; Tel [33] (1)
42-96-12-02, 42-61-80-75; FAX
[33(1)42-66-97-83

Bordeaux (CG), 22 Cours du Marechal
Foch, 33080 Bordeaux Cedex; Apo AE
09777; Tel [33] (56) 52-65-95; FAX
[33](56)51-60-42

Lyon (CG), 7 Quai General Sarrail; 69454
Lyon CEDEX 3; Tel [33] (78) 246-849;

Marseille (CG), 12 Boulevard Paul Peytral,
13286 Marseille Cedex; APO AE 09777; Tel
[33](91) 549-200; FAX [33] (91)550947

Strasbourg (CG), 15 Ave. D'Alsace; 67082
Strasbourg CEDEX or APO AE 09777; Tel
[33] [88] 35-31-04

**FRENCH GUIANA**
Martinique (CG), 14 Rue Blenac; B.P. 561,
Fort-de -France 97206; Tel [596] 63-13-03;
FAX [596]60-20-80

## GABON
**Libreville (E),** Blvd, de la Mer; B.P. 4000; Tel [241] 762003/4, 743492;

## THE GAMBIA
**Banjul (E),** Fajara, Kairaba Ave; P.M.B. No. 19, Banjul; Tel [220] 92856, 92858, 91970, 91971

## GEORGIA
**Tbilisi (E),** 25 Atoneli Street, Tel (7) (8832) 98-99-67 or (7) (8832) 98-99-68

## FEDERAL REPUBLIC OF GERMANY
**Bonn (E),** Deichmanns Aue, 5300 Bonn 2; APO AE 09080; Tel [49] (228) 3391; FAX [49](228)339-2663

**Berlin (BO),** Neustaedtische Kirchstrasse 4-5, 0-1080 Berlin; APO AE 09235-5500; Tel (372) 220-2741; Consular Section: Clayallee 170, D-1000 Berlin 33 (Dahlem); APO NY 09742; Tel [49] (30) 8324087

**U.S. Commercial Office (Dusseldorf),** Emmanuel-Leutze-Str. 1B; 4000 Duesseldorf 11; Tel 0211-596790

**Frankfurt Am Main (CG),** Siesmayerstrasse 21, 6000 Frankfurt; APO AE 09213; Tel [49] (69) 7535-0; FAX [49](69)748-938

**Hamburg (CG),** Alsterufer 27/28, 2000 Hamburg 36; APO AE 09215-0002; Tel [49] (40) 411710,

**Munich (CG),** Koeniginstrasse 5, 8000 Muenchen 22; APO AE 09108; Tel [49] (89) 28881; FAX [49](89)283-047-5163

**Stuttgart (CG),** Urbanstrasse 7, 7000 Stuttgart; APO AE 09154; Tel [49] (711)21450; FAX [49](711)649-4786

## GHANA
**Accra (E),** Ring Road East; P.O. Box 194;

Tel Chancery [233](21)775348/9,775297/8; FAX [233](21)776008

## GREECE
**Athens (E),** 91 Vasilissis Sophias Blvd., 10160 Athens or APO AE 09842; Tel [30](1)721-2951 or 721-8401; FAX [30](1)646-3450

**Thessaloniki (CG),** 59 Leoforos Nikis, GR-546-22 Thessaloniki; APO AE 09844; Tel [30] (31) 266-121

## GRENADA
**St. George's (E),** P.O. Box 54, St. George's, Grenada, W.I.; Tel (809) 444-1173/8; FAX (809) 444-4820

## GUADELOUPE
**Martinique (CG),** 14 Rue Blenac; B.P. 561, Fort-de -France 97206; Tel [596] 63-13-03; FAX [596]60-20-80

## GUATEMALA
**Guatemala City (E),** 7-01 Avenida de la Reforma, Zone 10; APO AA 34024; Tel [502] (2) 31-15-41; FAX [502](2)318885

## GUINEA
**Conakry (E),** 2d Blvd. and 9th Ave.; B.P. 603; Tel (224) 44-15-20 thru 24

## GUINEA-BAAS
**Baas (E),** Avenida Domingos Ramos; 1067 Baas Codex, Baas, Guinea-Baas; Tel [245] 20-1139, 20 -1145, 20-1113; FAX [245] 20-1159

## GUYANA
**Georgetown (E),** 31 Main St.; Tel [592] (2) 54900-9; FAX [592](2)58497

## HAITI
**Port-Au-Prince (E),** Harry Truman Blvd., P.O. Box 1761; Tel [509]22-0354,22-0368,

22-0200,22-0612;FAX [509] 23-9007

**THE HOLY SEE**
**Vatican City (E),** Villino Pacelli, Via Aurelia
294, 00165 Rome; APO AE 09624; Tel [396]
639-0558; FAX [396] 638-0159

**HONDURAS**
**Tegucigalpa (E),** Avenido La Paz; APO AA
34022; Tel [504] 32-3120; FAX [504]32-0027

**HONG KONG**
**Hong Kong (CG),** 26 Garden Rd.; Box 30,
FPO AP 96522-0002; Tel [852] 239-011;
FAX [852] 845-1598

**HUNGARY**
**Budapest (E),** V. Szabadsag Ter 12; Am
Embassy; APO AE 09213-5270; Tel [36] (1)
112-6450

**ICELAND**
**Reykjavik (E),** Laufasvegur 21 Box 40; FPO
AE 09728 -0340; Tel [354] (1) 29100; FAX
[354](1)29139

**INDIA**
**New Delhi (E),** Shanti Path, Chanakyapuri
110021; Tel [91] (11) 600651; FAX
[91](11)687-2028,687-2391

**Bombay (CG),** Lincoln House, 78 Bhulabhai
Desai Rd. 400026; Tel [91] (022) 822-3611;
FAX [91](22)822-0350

**Calcutta (CG),** 5/1 Ho Chi Minh Sarani,
Calcutta 700071; Tel [91] (033) 22-3611
through 22-3615, 22-2335 through 22-2337;

**Madras (CG),** Mount Rd. 600006;
Tel [91] (44) 473-040/477-542

**INDONESIA**
**Jakarta (E),** Medan Merdeka Selatan 5; APO
AP 96520; Tel [62] (21) 360-360

**Medan (CG),** Jalan Imam Bonjol 13; APO
AP 96520; Tel [62] (61) 329700

**Surabaya (CG),** Jalan Raya Dr. Sutomo 33;
APO AP 96520; Tel [62] (31) 69287/8;

**IRAQ**
**Baghdad (E),** Opp. For. Ministry Club
(Masbah Quarter); P.O. Box 2447 Alwiyah,
Baghdad, Iraq; Tel [964] (1) 719-6138/9,
7181840, 719-3791

**IRELAND**
**Dublin (E),** 42 Elgin Rd., Ballsbridge; Tel
Dublin [353] (1) 688777; FAX
[353](1)689-946

**ISRAEL**
**Tel Aviv (E),** 71 Hayarkon St.; APO AE
09830; Tel [972] (3) 654338; FAX 19721 (3)
663449

**ITALY**
**Rome (E),** Via Veneto 119/A, 00187-Rome;
APO AE 09624; Tel [39] (6) 46741; FAX
[39](6)4674-2356

**Genoa (CC),** Banca d'America e d'Italia
Bldg., Piazza Portello 6, 16124 GENOA; Tel
[39] (10) 282-741 thru 4; FAX
[39](10)290027

**Milan (CG),** Via Principe Amedeo, 2/10,
20121 Milano; c/o U.S. Embassy, Box M;
APO AE 09624; Tel [39] (2) 2900-45-59;
FAX [39] (2) 29-00-11-65.

**Naples (CG),** Piazza della Repubblica 80122
Naples; Box 18, FPO AE 09619-0002; Tel
[39](81)761-4303; FAX [39](81) 761-1869;

**Palermo (CC),** Via Vaccarini 1, 90143; APO
AE 09624 (c/o Am Embassy Rome-P); Tel
[39](91)343-532; FAX [39](91)343-546

**Florence (CG),** Lungarno Amerigo Vespucci,

123

38, 50123 Firenze; APO AE 09613; Tel [39] (55) 239-8276/7/8/9, 217-605; FAX [39](55)284-088

**IVORY COAST-See Cote d'Ivoire**

**JAMAICA**
**Kingston (E),** Jamaica Mutual Life Center, 2 Oxford Rd., 3d Fl.; Tel (809) 929-4850; FAX (809) 926-6743

**JAPAN**
**Tokyo (E),** 10-1, Akasaka 1-chome, Minato-ku (107); APO San Fran 96503; Tel [81] (3) 3224-5480; FAX [81](3)35821-0496;

**Naha, Okinawa (CG),** 2564 Nishihara, Urasoe City, Okinawa 90121; Box 840, FPO AP 96372-0840; Tel [81] (98) 876-4211; FAX [81](98)876-4243

**Osaka-Kobe (CG),** 11-5, Nishitenma 2-chome, Kita- Ku, Osaka 530; UNIT 45004, BOX 239; APO AP 96337-0002; FAX [81](6)361-5397

**Sapporo (CG),** Kita 1-Jo Nishi 28-chome, Chuo-ku, Sapporo 064; APO AP 96337-0003; Tel[81](11)641 -1115/7; FAX [81](11)643-1283

**Fukuoka (C),** 5-26 Ohori 2-chome, Chuo-ku, Fukuoka-810 or Box 10, APO AP 96337-0001; Tel [81] (92) 751-9331/4; FAX [81](92)713-9222

**JERUSALEM**
**Jerusalem (CG),** 18 Agron Rd., Jerusalem 94190; P.O. Box 290; APO AE 09830; Tel [972] (2) 253288 (via Israel); Consular and Cultural Sections; 27 Nablus Rd.; Tel [972] (2) 253288 (both offices via Israel).

**JORDAN**
**Amman (E), Jabel Amman;** P.O. Box 354 or APO AE 09892-0200; Tel [962](6)

644-371

**KAZAKHSTAN**
**Alma-Ata (E),** 551 Seyfalline St. Tel. (7) (3272) 63-13-75

**KENYA**
**Nairobi (E),** Moi/Haile Selassie Ave.; P.O. Box 30137; APO AE 09831; Tel [254] (2) 334141; CPU STU-III 334122; FAX [254](2)340838

**Mombasa (C),** Palli House, Nyerere Avenue; P.O. Box 88079; Tel [254] (11) 315101

**KOREA**
**Seoul (E),** 82 Sejong-Ro; Chongro-ku; APO AP 96205 -0001; Tel [82] (2) 732-2601 thru 18; FAX [82](2) 738-8845

**Pusan (C),** 24 2-Ka, Dacchung Dong, Chung-ku; Tel 23-7791

**KUWAIT**
**Kuwait (E),** P.O. Box 77 SAFAT, 13001 SAFAT, Kuwait; APO AE 09880; Tel [965] 242-4151 thru 9 FAX [965]240-7368

**KYRGYZSTAN**
**Bishkek (E),** Erkindik Prospekt #66, Tel. (7) (3312) 222-693

**LAOS**
**Vientiane (E),** Rue Bartholonie; B.P. 114; Mail to: Box V, APO AP 96546; Tel 2220, 2357, 2384

**LATVIA**
**Riga (E),** Raina Boulevard 7, 226050; Tel (013-2) 210-005 or (013-2) 210-006

**LEBANON**
**Beirut (E),** Antelias, P.O. Box 70-840, Beirut or Box B, FPO AE 09836-0002; Tel [961] 417774, 415802/3, 402200, 403300

**124**

**LESOTHO**
Maseru (E), P.O. Box 333, Maseru 100
Lesotho; Tel [266] 312-666; FAX [266]
310-116

**LIBERIA**
Monrovia (E), APO AE 09813; 111 United
Nations Dr.; P.O. Box 98; Tel [231] 22299.

**LITHUANIA**
VILNIUS (E), 6 Akmenu Street, Tel. (012-2)
223-031

**LUXEMBOURG**
Luxembourg (E), 22 Blvd.
Emmanuel-Servais, 2535 Luxembourg; APO
AE 09132-5380; Tel [352] 460123; FAX
[352] 46 14 01

**MADAGASCAR**
Antananarivo (E), 14 and 16 Rue Rainitovo,
Antsahavola; B.P. 620; Tel 212-57, 209-56,
200-89, 207-18; FAX 261-234-539

**MALAWI**
Lilongwe (E), P.O. Box 30016; Tel [265]
730-166; FAX [265]732-282

**MALAYSIA**
Kuala Lumpur (E), 376 Jalan Tun Razak;
50400 Kuala Lumpur; P.O. Box No. 10035,
50700 Kuala Lumpur; Tel [60] (3) 248-9011;
FAX [60](3)242-2207

**MALI**
Bamako (E), Rue Rochester NY and Rue
Mohamed V.; B.P. 34; Tel [223] 225470;
FAX [223]223712

**MALTA**
Valletta (E), 2d Fl., Development House, St.
Anne St., Floriana, Malta; P.O. Box 535,
Valletta; Tel [356] 240424/425,
243216/217/653,223654; FAX Same

**MARSHALL ISLANDS**

Majuro (E), P.O. Box 680, Republic of the
Marshall Islands 96960-4380; Tel 692-4011

Martinique (CG), 14 Rue Blenac; B.P. 561,
Fort-de -France 97206; Tel [596] 63-13-03;
912315 MR; FAX [596]60-20-80

**MAURITANIA**
Nouakchott (E), B.P. 222; Tel [222] (2)
252-660 or 252-663 (Oper. Asst. only); FAX
[222](2)1592

**MAURITIUS**
Port Louis (E), Rogers House (4th Fl.), John
Kennedy St.; Tel [230]208-9763 thru 7; FAX
[230] 208-9534

**MEXICO**
Mexico City, D.F. (E), Paseo de la Reforma
305, Colonia Cuauhtemoc, 06500 Mexico,
D.F.; Mail: P.O. Box 3087, Laredo, TX
78044-3087; Tel [52](5)211-0042; FAX [52]
(5)511-9980

U.S. Travel and Tourism Office, Plaza
Comermex, M. Avila Camacho 1-402, 11560
Mexico, D.F.; Tel [52] (5) 520-2101; FAX
520-1194

Ciudad Juarez (CG), Chihuahua Avenue
Lopez Mateos 924N; Mail: Box 10545, El
Paso, TX 7999-0545; Tel [52] (16) 134048;
FAX [52](16) 90-56

Guadalajara (CG), JAL; Progreso 175;
Mail: Box 3088, Laredo, TX 78044-3088; Tel
[52] (36) 25-2998, 25-2700; FAX
[52](36)26-6549

Monterrey (CG), Nuevo Leon; Avenida
Constitucion 411 Poniente 64000 Monterrey,
N.L.; Mail: Box 3098, Laredo, TX
78044-3098; Tel [52] (83) 45-2120 FAX
[52](83)42-0177

Tijuana (CG), B.C.N.; Tapachula 96; Mail:

P.O. Box 439039, San Diego, CA 92143-9039; Tel [52] (66) 81-7400; FAX [52] (66) 81-8016

**Hermosillo (C)**, Son; Monterrey 141: Mail: Box 3598, Laredo, TX 78044-3598; Tel [52] (62) 172375; FAX [52] (62)172578

**Matamoros (C)**, Tamaulipas; Ave. Primera 2002; Mail: Box 633; Brownsville, TX 78522-0633; Tel [52] (891) 6-72-70/1/2; FAX [52] (891) 3-80-48

**Mazatlan (C)**, Sinaloa; Circunvalacion 120, Centro; Mail: Box 2708, Laredo, TX 78044-2708; Tel [52] (69) 85 -22-05; FAX [52](69) 82-1454

**Merida (C)**, Yucatan.; Paseo Montejo 453; Mail: Box 3087, Laredo, TX 78044-3087; Tel [52] (99)25-5011; FAX [52] (99)25-6219

**Nuevo Laredo (C)**, Tamps.; Calle Allende 3330, Col. Jardin; 88260 Nuevo Laredo, Tamps; Mail: Drawer 3089, Laredo, TX 78044-3089; Tel [52] (871) 4-0696, 4 -0512; FAX [52] (871)4-0696 x128

**MICRONESIA**
**Kolonia (E)**, P.O. Box 1286, Pohnpei, Federated States of Micronesia 96941; Tel 691-320-2187

**MOLDOVA**
**Chisinau (E)**, Strada Alexei Mateevici, #103; Tel -0422-233-494 or 233-698

**PEOPLE'S REPUBLIC OF MONGOLIA**
**Ulaanbaatar (E)**, c/o American Embassy Beijing; FPO AP 9621-0002 Tel. 29095 and 29639

**MONTSERRAT**
**St. Johns (E)**, FPO Miami 34054; Tel (809) 462- 3505/06; FAX (809) 462-3516

**MOROCCO**
**Rabat (E)**, 2 Ave. de Marrakech; P.O. Box 120; APO AE 09718; Tel [212] (7) 76-22-65; FAX [212] (7) 76 -56-61

**Casablanca (CG)**, 8 Blvd. Moulay Youssef; APO AE 09718 (CAS); Tel [212] (2)2645-50; FAX [212] (2) 20-41-27

**MOZAMBIQUE**
**Maputo (E)**, Avenida Kenneth Kaunda 193; P.O. Box 783; Tel 258](1)49-27-97, 49-01-67,49-03-50

**NAMIBIA**
**Windhoek (E)**, Ausplan Building, 14 Lossen St.; P.O Box 9890, Windhoek 9000, Namibia; Tel. [264](61)221-601 222-675, 222-680; FAX [264](61)229-792

**NEPAL**
**Kathmandu (E)**, Pani Pokhari; Tel [977] (1)411179,412718,411601,411604,411613, 413890; FAX [977](1)419963

**NETHERLANDS**
**The Hague (E)**, Lange Voorhout 102; APO AE 09715; Tel [31] (70) 3624911; FAX [31](70)361-4688

**Amsterdam (CG)**, Museumplein 19; APO AE 09715; Tel [31] (20) 664-5661; FAX CG [31] (20) 676-1761; FAX FCS [31](20)675-2856

**NETHERLANDS ANTILLES**
**Curacao (CG)**, St. Anna Blvd. 19; P.O. Box 158, Willemstad, Curacao; Tel [599] (9) 613066; FAX [599](9)616489

**NEW ZEALAND**
**Wellington (E)**, 29 Fitzherbert Ter., Thorndon, Wellington; P.O. Box 1190, Wellington; FPO AP 96531 -1001; Tel [64] (4) 722-068; FAX [64] (4) 712-380

**Auckland (CG),** 4th Fl., Yorkshire General Bldg.; CNR Shortland and O'Connell Sts., Auckland; Private Bag, Auckland; FPO AP 96531-1099; Tel [64] (9) 303-2724; FAX [64](9)366-0870

**NICARAGUA**
**Managua (E),** Km. 4-1/2 Carretera Sur.; APO AA 34021; Tel [505] (2) 666010, 666013, 666015-18, 666026-27, 666032-34; FAX[505](2)666046

**NIGER**
**Niamey (E),** Rue Des Ambassades; B.P. 11201; Tel [227] 72-26-61 thru 4

**NIGERIA**
**Lagos (E),** 2 Eleke Crescent; P.O. Box 554; Tel [234] (1) 610097; FAX [234](1) 635397, FAX Consular Section [234](1)612218

**Kaduna (CG),** 2 Maska Road, P.O. Box 170; Tel [234] (62) 201070, 201071, 201072;

**NORWAY**
**Oslo (E),** Drammensveien 18, 0244 Oslo 2, or APO AE 09707; Tel [47] (2) 44-85-50; FAX [47](2)43-07-77

**OMAN**
**Muscat (E),** P.O. Box 50202 Madinat Qaboos; Tel [968] 698-989 FAX [968] 604-316

**PAKISTAN**
**Islamabad (E),** Diplomatic Enclave, Ramna 5; P.O. Box 1048, APO AE 09812-2000; Tel [92] (51) 826161 thru 79; FAX [92](51)822004

**Karachi** (CG), 8 Abdullah Haroon Rd., APO AE 09814-2400; Tel [92](21) 518180 thru 9; FAX [92](21) 513089

**Lahore (CG),** 50 Zafar Ali Rd., Gulberg 5; APO AE 09812-2216; Tel [92] (42) 870221 thru 5; FAX: [92] (42) 872911

**Peshawar (C),** 11 Hospital Road; APO AE 09812-2217 Tel [92] (521) 79801, 79802, 79803; FAX 92-521-76-712

**REPUBLIC OF PALAU**
**Koror (USLO),** P.O. Box 6028, Republic of Palau 96940; Tel. 160-680-920/990

**PANAMA**
**Panama City (E),** Apartado 6959, Panama 5, Rep. de Panama; Box E, APO AA 34002; Tel [507] 27-1777; FAX [507]03-9470

**PAPUA NEW GUINEA**
**Port Moresby (E),** Armit St.; P,O. Box 1492; Tel [675]211-455/594/654;FAX [675] 213-423

**PARAGUAY**
**Asuncion (E),** 1776 Mariscal Lopez Ave.; Casilla Postal 402; APO AA 34036-0001;Tel [595] (21) 213-715; FAX [595](21)213-728

**PERU**
**Lima (E),** Corner Avenidas Inca Carcilaso de la Vega & Espana; P.O. Box 1991, Lima Unit 3822; APO AA 34031; Tel [51] (14) 338-000; FAX [51] (14) 316682; Consular Section: Grimaldo Del
Solar 346, Miraflores Lima 18; Tel [51] (14) 44-3621

**PHILIPPINES**
**Manila (E),** 1201 Roxas Blvd.; APO AP 96440; Tel [63] (2) 521-7116; FAX [63] (2) 522-4361

Extension Makati; Tel [63] (2) 818-6674;

**Cebu (C),** 3d R., PCI Bank, Gorordo Avenue, Lahug; APO San Fran 96528; Tel [63] (32) 211-101; FAX [63] (32) 5-20-20

**POLAND**

**Warsaw (E),** Aleje Ujazdowskie 29/31; AmEmbassy Warsaw, Box 5010 c/o AmConGen (WAW); APO AE 09213-5010; Tel [48] (2) 628-3041 through 48; FAX [48] (2) 628-9326

**US Trade Center (Warsaw),** Ulica Wiejska 20; Tel [48] (22) 21-45-15; FAX [48] (22) 216327

**Krakow (CG),** Ulica Stolarska 9, 31043 Krakow; c/o AmConCen (KRK); APO AE 09213-5140; Tel [48] (12) 229764, 221400, 226040, 227793; FAX [48](12)218292

**Poznan (C),** Ulica Chopina 4; c/o AmConCen (POZ); APO AE 09213-5050; Tel [48] (61) 529586, 529587, 529874; FAX [48](61)530053

**PORTUGAL**
**Lisbon (E),** Avenida das Forcas Armadas, 1600 Lisbon; APO AE 09726; Tel [351] (1) 726-6600,726-6659, 726-8670, 726-8880; FAX [351](1)726-9109

**Oporto (C),** Rua Julio Dinis 826, 3d Floor, 4000 Oporto; Tel [351] (2) 63094 and 690008; FAX [351](2)6002737

**Ponta Delgada,** Sao Miguel, Azores (C), Avenida D. Henrique; APO AE 09720-0002; Tel [351] (96) 22216/7; FAX [351](96)27216

**QATAR**
**Doha (E),** 149 Ali Bin Ahmed St., Farig Bin Omran (opp. TV station); P.O. Box 2399; Tel (0974) 864701/2/3; AMEMB DH; FAX (0974) 861669

**ROMANIA**
**Bucharest (E),** Strada Tudor Arghezi 7-9, or AmConCen (Buch), APO AE 09213-5260; Tel [40] (O)10-40-40

**RUSSIA**

**Moscow (E),**Novinsky Bulvar, or APO AE 09721; Tel [7] (095) 252-2450 through 59; FAX [7] (095) 255-9965

**St.Petersburg (CG),** Ulitsa, Petra Lavrova St. 15; Box L, APO AE 09723; Tel [7] (812) 274-8235

**RWANDA**
**Kigali (E),** Blvd. de la Revolution, B.P. 28; Tel [250] 75601/2/3; FAX [250]72128;

**ST. LUCIA**
**Bridgetown (E),** P.O. Box 302; Box B, FPO Miami 34054; Tel [809] 436-4950 thru 7;

**ST. MARTIN**
**Martinique (CG),** 14 Rue Blenac; B.P. 561, Fort-de -France 97206; Tel [596] 63-13-03; FAX [596]60-20-80

**ST. VINCENT**
**Bridgetown (E),** P.O. Box 302; Box B, FPO Miami 34054; Tel [809] 436-4950 thru 7; FAX (809)429-5246;

**SAUDI ARABIA**
**Riyadh (E),** Collector Road M, Riyadh Diplomatic Quarter; APO AE 09803-1307; International Mail: P.O. Box 9041, Riyadh 11413; Tel [966] (1) 488-3800;

**Dhahran (CG),** Between Aramco Hqrs and Dhahrar Int'l Airport; P.O. Box 81, Dhahran Airport 31932 or APO AE 09858-6803; Tel [966] (3) 891-3200; FAX [966](3)891-3296;

**Jeddah (CG),** Palestine Rd., Ruwais; P.O. Box 149, Jeddah 21411 or APO AE 009811-2112; Tel [966] (2) 667-0080; FAX 669-3074

**SENEGAL**
**Dakar (E),** B.P. 49, Avenue Jean XXIII; Tel [221] 23-42 -96 or 23-34-24; FAX [221]22-29-91

**SEYCHELLES**
Victoria (E), Box 148; APO AE 09815-2501 or Victoria House, Box 251, Victoria, Mahe, Seychelles; Tel (248) 25256

**SIERRA LEONE**
Freetown (E), Corner Walpole and Siaka Stevens St. Tel [232](22) 26481

**SINGAPORE**
Singapore (E), 30 Hill St.; Singapore 0617; FPO AP 96534; Tel [65] 338-0251; FAX [65] 338-4550

**SOLOMON ISLANDS**
Honiara (E), Mud Alley; P.O. Box 561; Tel (677) 23890; FAX (677) 23488

**SOUTH AFRICA**
Pretoria (E), Thibault House, 225 Pretorius St.; Tel [27] (12) 284266; FAX [27](12) 21-92-78

Cape Town (CG), Broadway Industries Center, Heerengracht, Foreshore; Tel [27] (21) 214-280/7; FAX [27](21) 25-4151

Durban (CG), Durban Bay House, 29th Fl., 333 Smith St., Durban 4001; Tel [27] (31) 304-4737/8; FAX [27](31)301-8206

Johannesburg (CG), 11th Fl., Kine Center, Commissioner and Kruis Sts.; P.O. Box 2155; Tel [27] (11) 331-1681

**SPAIN**
Madrid (E), Serrano 75, 28006 Madrid, or APO AE 09642; Tel [34] (1) 577-4000; FAX [34](1) 577-5735

Barcelona (CG), Via Layetana 33; APO AE 09646; Tel [34] (3) 319-9550; FAX [34](3)319-7543

Bilboa (C), Avenida Lehenda Kari Agirre, 11-3, 48014 Bilbao; APO AE 09646; Tel

[34](4) 475-8300; FAX [34](4)476-1240

**SRI LANKA**
Colombo (E), 210 Galle Rd., Colombo 3; P.O. Box 106; Tel [94] (1) 448007; FAX [94]

**SUDAN**
Khartoum (E), Sharia Ali Abdul Latif; P.O. Box 699; APO AE 09829; Tel 74700, 74611;

**SURINAME**
Paramaribo (E), Dr. Sophie Redmondstraat 129; P.O. Box 1821; Tel [597] 72900,77881,76459

**SWAZILAND**
Mbabane (E), Central Bank Bldg., Warner Street; P.O. Box 199; Tel: [268] 46441/5; FAX [268] 45959;

**SWEDEN**
Stockholm (E), Strandvagen 101, S115 89 Stockholm; Tel [46] (8) 783-5300; FAX [46](8)661-1964

**SWITZERLAND**
Bern (E), Jubilaeumstrasse 93, 3005 Bern; Tel [41] (31)437-011; FAX [41](31)437-344

Geneva (BO), Botanic Building, 1-3 Avenue de la Paix, 1202 Geneva; Tel [41] (22) 738-7613, 738-5095; FAX 799-0880

Zurich (CG) Zollikerstrasse 141, 8008 Zurich; Tel [41] (1) 552566; FAX [41](1) 383-9814

**SYRIA**
Damascus (E), Abu Rumaneh, Al Mansur St. No. 2; P.O. Box 29; Tel [963] (11) 333052, 332557, 330416, 332814, 332315, 714108, 337178, 333232;

**TAIWAN**
Unofficial commercial and other relations

with the people of Taiwan are conducted through an unofficial instrumentality, the American Institute in Taiwan, which has offices in Taipei and Kaohsiung. AIT Taipei operates an American Trade Center, located at the Taipei World Trade Center. The addresses of these offices are:

**American Institute in Taiwan,** #7 Lane 134, Hsin Yi Road Section 3 Taipei, Taiwan; Tel [886] (2) 709-2000; FAX [886](2)702-7675

**American Trade Center,** Room 3207 International Trade Building, Taipei World Trade Center, 333Keelung Road Section 1, Taipei 10548, Taiwan; Tel [886](2)720-1550;757-7162

**American Institute in Taiwan,** 3d Fl., 42 Chung Cheng 3d Rd, Kaohsiung, Taiwan; Tel [886](7)224-0154/7; FAX [886](7)223-8237

## TAJIKISTAN
**Dushanbe (E),** Temporarily located on 4th floor of Hotel Independence (formerly known as Hotel October), 105a Rudaki Prospect; Tel [7] (3772) 24-82-33

## TANZANIA
**Dar Es Salaam (E),** 36 Laibon Rd. (off Bagamoyo Rd.); P.O. Box 9123; Tel [255] (51) 375014

## THAILAND
**Bangkok (E),** 95 Wireless Rd.; APO AP 96546; Tel [66] (2) 252-504019; FAX [66] (2) 254-2990

**Chiang Mai (CG),** Vidhayanond Rd.; Box C; APO AP 96546; Tel [66] (53) 252-629/30; FAX [66](53)252-633

**Songkhla (C),** 9 Sadao Rd.; Box S; APO AP 96546; Tel [66](2)311-589/90; FAX [66](74)324-409

**Udorn (C),** 35/6 Supakitjanya Rd.; Box UD; APO AP 96546; Tel [66] (42) 244-270/1; FAX [66](42)244-273

## TOGO
**Lome (E),** Rue Pelletier Caventou and Rue Vauban; B.P. 852; Tel [228] 21-77-17 and 21-29-91 thru 94; FAX [228]21-79-52

## TRINIDAD AND TOBAGO
**Port-of-Spain (E),** 15 Queen's Park West; P.O. Box 752; Tel (809)622-6372/6, 6176; FAX (809) 628-5462

## TUNISIA
**Tunis (E),** 144 Ave. de la Liberte, 1002 Tunis- Belvedere; Tel [216] (1) 782-566;

## TURKEY
**Ankara (E),** 110 Ataturk Blvd.; APO AE 09823; Tel [90] (4) 126 54 70; FAX

**Istanbul (CG),** 104-108 Mesrutiyet Caddesi, Tepebasi; APO AE 09827-0002; Tel [90] (1) 151 36 02;

**Izmirr (CG),** 92 Ataturk Caddesi (3d Fl.); APO AE 09821; Tel [90] (51) 149426, 131369; FAX 130493

**Adana (C),** Ataturk Caddesi; APO AE 09824; Tel [90] (71) 139106,142145,143774; FAX [90](71)176591

## TURKMENISTAN
**Ashkhabad (E),** Yubilenaya Hotel; Tel [7] (36320 24-49-08

## UGANDA
**Kampala (E),** Parliament Ave.; P.O. Box 7007; Tel [256] (41) 259792/3/5

## UKRAINE
**Kiev (E),**10 Yuria Kotsubinskoh 10; Tel [7] (044) 244-7354; FAX [7] (044) 279-1485

**UNITED ARAB EMIRATES**
**Abu Dhabi (E),** Al-Sudan St.; P.O. Box
4009; Tel [971] (2) 336691; FAX [971] (2)
318441; Chancery 213771; Cons 391786;

**Dubai (CG),** Dubai International Trade
Center; P.O. Box 9343; Tel [971] (4)
371115;

**UNITED KINGDOM**
**London, England (E),** 24/31 Grosvenor Sq.,
W. 1A 1AE; FPO AE 09498-4040; Tel [44]
(71) 499-9000; FAX 409-1637

**Belfast Northern Ireland (CG),** Queen's
House, 14 Queen St., BT1 6EQ; PSC 801,
Box, APO AE 09498;-404 Tel [44] (232)
328239

**Edinburgh, Scotland (CG),** 3 Regent Ter.
EH7 5BW; Tel [44] (31) 556-8315

**URUGUAY**
**Montevideo (E),** Lauro Muller 1776; APO
AA 34035; Tel [598] (2) 23-60-61 and
afterhours 48-77-77; FAX [598](2)48-86-11

**UZBEKISTAN**
**Tashkent (E),** 82 Chelanzar, Tel [7] (3712)
771-081

**VENEZUELA**
**Caracas (E),** Avenida Francisco de Miranda
and Averxida Principal de la Horesta; P.O.
Box 62291, Caracas 1060-A or APO AA
34037; Tel [58] (2) 285 -3111/2222; FAX
[58](2)285

**Maracaibo (C),** Edificio Sofimara, Piso 3,
Calle 77 Con Avenida 13, or APO AA
34037; Tel [58] (61) 84 -253/4, 52-42-55,
84-054/5; FAX [58](61)524255

**WESTERN SAMOA**
**Apia (E),** P.O. Box 3430 Apia; Tel (685)
21-631; FAX (685) 22-030

**REPUBLIC OF YEMEN**
**Sanaa (E),** Dhahr Himyar Zone, Sheraton
Hotel District, P.O. Box 22347 Sanaa,
Republic of Yemen or Sanaa-Dept. of State,
Washington, D.C. 20521-6330;
Tel [967] (2) 238-842/52; FAX
[967] (2) 251-563

**YUGOSLAVIA**
**Belgrade (E),** American Embassy Box 5070;
APO AE 09213-5070; Tel [38] (11) 645-655;
FAX [38](11)645-221

**Zagreb (CG),** Brace Kavurica 2;
AMCONGEN Box 5080; APO AE
09213-5080; Tel [38] (41) 444-800;
FAX [38](41)440-235

**ZAIRE**
**Kinshasa (E),** 310 Avenue des Aviateurs;
APO AE 09828; Tel [243](12)21532, 21628;
FAX [243](12)21232

**Lubumbashi (CG),** 1029 Blvd. Kamanyola;
B.P. 1196; APO AE 09828, Tel
[243](011)222324

**ZAMBIA**
**Lusaka (E),** corner of Independence and
United Na- tions Aves.; P.O. Box 31617; Tel
[260-1] 228-595, 228-601/2/3 FAX [260-1]
251-578

**ZIMBABWE**
**Harare (E),** 172 Herbert Chitapo Aye., P.O.
Box 3340; Tel [263] (4) 794-521; Telex
24591 FAX [263](4)796488

| Note: | E = | Embassy |
|---|---|---|
| | C = | Consulate |
| | CG = | Consulate-General, |
| | | Consul General |
| | BO = | Branch Office (of |
| | | Embassy) |

# APPENDIX  B

## FOREIGN EMBASSIES IN THE UNITED STATES

**AFGHANISTAN**: Emabassy of Afghanistan, 2341 Wyoming Ave. N.W., Washington, DC 20008, (202) 234-3770, FAX (202) 328-3516

**ALBANIA**: Embassy of the Rep. of Albania, 320 East 79th St., New York, NY 10021, (212) 249-2059

**ALGERIA**: Algeria, Democratic and Popular, Rep. of Algeria, 2118 Kalorama Road, Washington, DC 20008, (202 265-2800

**ANGOLA**: Permanent Mission of, Angola to the U.N., 747 - 3rd Avenue, 18th Floor, New York, NY 10017

**ANGUILLA:** Contact Embassy of the United Kingdom, 3100 Massachusetts Ave NW, Washington, DC 20008, (202) 426-1340, FAX (202) 898-4255

**ANTIGUA AND BARBUDA**: Emabassy of Antigua and Barbuda, 2000 N St. NW., Suite 601, Washington, DC 20036, (202) 296-6310

**ARGENTINA**: Embassy of Argentina, 1600 New Hampshire Ave., NW, Washington, DC 20009 , (202) 939-6400 to 6403

**ARMENIA**: Embassy of Armenia, 122 C Street, NW, Suite 360, Washington DC 20001, (202) 393-5983

**AUSTRALIA:** Embassy of Australia, 1601 Massachusetts Ave., NW, Washington, DC 20036, (202) 797-3000, FAX (202) 797-3168

**AUSTRIA**: Embassy of Austria, 2343 Massachusetts Ave., NW, Washington, DC 20008, (202) 483-4474, FAX (202) 483-2743

**AZERBAIJAN:** Contact Consular section, Embassy of Russia, (202) 939-8907

**BAHAMAS**: Embassy of The Commonwealth of The Bahamas , 2220 Massachusetts Ave., NW, Washington, DC 20008, (202) 319-2660, FAX (202) 319-2668

**BAHRAIN:** 3502 International Drive, NW, Washington, DC 20008, (202) 342-0741

**BARBADOS**: Embassy of Barbados, 2144 Wyoming Ave., NW, Washington, DC 20008, (202) 939-9200

**BANGLADESH:** Embassy of Bangladesh, 2201 Wisconsin Ave., NW, Washington, DC 20007, (202) 342-8372

**BELARUS:** Embassy of Belarus, 1511 K Street, NW, Suite 619, Washington DC 20005, (202) 638-2954

**BELGIUM:** Embassy of Belgium, 3330 Garfield St., NW, Washington, DC 20008, (202) 333-6900

**BELIZE**: Embassy of Belize, 3400 International Drive, NW, Suite 2J, Washington, DC 20008, (202) 363-4505, FAX (202) 362-7468

**BENIN:** Embassy of Benin, 2737 Cathedral Ave., NW, Washington, DC 20008, (202) 232-6656, FAX (202) 265-1996

**BHUTAN:** Kingdom of Bhutan, Mission to the United Nations, Two United Nations Plaza, New York, NY 10017, (212) 826-1919

**BOLIVIA:** Embassy of Bolivia, 3014 Massachusetts Ave., NW, Washington, DC 20008, (202) 483-4410, Fax (202) 328-3712

**BOTSWANA:** Embassy of the Rep. of Botswana, 3400 International Dr., NW, Ste. 7M, Washington, DC 20008, (202) 244-4990, FAX (202) 244-4164

**BRITISH VIRGIN ISLANDS:** Contact Embassy of the , United Kingdom, 3100 Massachusetts Ave., NW, Washington, DC 20008, (202) 462-1340, FAX (202) 898-4255

**BRAZIL:** Embassy of Brazil, 3006 Massachusetts Ave., NW, Washington, DC 20008, (202) 745-2700, FAX (202) 745-2827

**BRUNEI:** Embassy of the State , of Brunei Darussalam, 2600 Virginia Ave., NW, Ste. 300, NW Washington, DC 20037, (202) 342-0159, FAX (202) 342-0158

**BULGARIA:** Embassy of the Rep. of Bulgaria, 1621 - 22d St., NW, Washington, DC 20008, (202) 387-7969, FAX (202) 234-7973

**BURKINA FASO:** Embassy of Burkina Faso, 2340 Massachusetts Ave., NW, Washington, DC 20008, (202) 332-5577

**BURMA** (See Myanmar)

**BURUNDI:** Embassy of Burundi, 2233 Wisconsin Ave., NW, Washington, DC 20008, (202) 342-2574

**CAMEROON:** Embassy of Cameroon, 2349 Massachusetts Ave., NW, Washington, DC 20008, (202) 265-8790 to 8794

**CANADA:** Embassy of Canada, 501 Pennsylvania Ave., NW, Washington, DC 20001, (202) 682-1740, FAX (202) 682-7726

**Rep. OF CAPE VERDE:** Embassy of Cape Verde, 3415 Massachusetts Ave., NW, Washington, DC 20007, (202) 965-6820, FAX (202) 965-1207

**CAYMAN ISLANDS:** Contact Embassy of Jamaica, 1850 K St. NW, Suite 355, Washington, DC 20006, (202) 452-0660

**CENTRAL AFRICAN Rep.:** Embassy of Cent. African Rep., 1618 - 22d St., NW, Washington, DC 20008, (202) 483-7800/1

**CHAD:** Embassy of Chad, 2002 R St. NW, Washington, DC 20009, (202) 462-4009, FAX (202) 265-1937

**CHILE:** Embassy of Chile, 1732 Massachusetts Ave., NW, Washington, DC 20036, (202) 785-1746, FAX (202) 887-5475

**CHINA, PEOPLES Rep.:** Embassy of the People's , Rep. of China, 2300 Connectucut Ave., NW, Washington, DC 20008, (202) 328-2500 to 2502

**COLOMBIA:** Embassy of Colombia, 2118 Leroy Place, NW, Washington, DC 20008, (202) 387-8338, FAX (202) 232-8643

**COMOROS:**
Embassy of Comoros, 336 E. 45th St., 2nd Floor, New York, NY 10017, (212) 972-8010, FAX (212) 983-4712

**CONGO, PEOPLE'S Rep.:** Embassy of Congo, 4891 Colorado Ave., NW, Washington, DC 20011, (202) 726-5500/1

**133**

**COSTA RICA:** Embassy of Costa Rica, 1825 Connecticut Ave., NW, Suite 211, Washington, DC 20009, (202) 234-2945, FAX (202) 234-8653

**COTE D'IVOIRE:** Embassy of Cote d'Ivoire, 2424 Massachusetts Ave., NW, Washington, DC 20008, (202) 797-0300

**CROATIA:** Embassy of Croatia, 236 Massachusetts Ave., NE,, Washington DC 20002, (202) 543-5580 or 5608

**CUBA:** Cuban Interest Section, Embassy of Czechoslovak, Socialist Rep., 2639 16th St., NW, Washington, DC 20009, (202) 797-8518

**CYPRUS:** Embassy of the Rep. of Cyprus, 2211 R St., NW, Washington, DC 20008, (202) 462-5772

**CZECH REPUBLIC:** Embassy of the Czech Republic, 3900 Spring of Freedom Street, NW, Washington DC 20008, (202) 363-6315

**DENMARK:** Royal Danish Embassy, 3200 Whitehaven St., NW, Washington, DC 20008, (202) 234-4300, FAX (202) 328-1470

**Rep. OF DJIBOUTI:** Embassy of the Rep. of Djibouti, 1156 - 15th St., NW, Suite 515, Washington, DC 20005, (202) 331-0270, FAX (202) 331-0302

**DOMINICA:** Contact the Embassy of Barbados, 2144 Wyoming Ave., NW, Washington, DC 20008, (202) 939-9200

**DOMINICAN Rep.:** Embassy of the Dominican Rep., 1715 - 22d St., NW, Washington, DC 20008, (202) 332-6280, Fax (202) 265-8057

**ECUADOR:** Embassy of Ecuador, 2535 15th St., NW, Washington, DC 20009, (202) 234-7200

**EGYPT:** Egypt, Arab Rep. of, 2310 Decatur Place, NW, Washington, DC 20008, (202) 232-5400

**EL SALVADOR:** Embassy of El Salvador, 2308 California St., NW, Washington, DC 20008, (202) 265-3480

**EQUATORIAL GUINEA:** Embassy of Equatorial Guinea, 57 Magnolia Ave. (Temporary), Mount Vernon, NY 10553, (914) 667-9664

**ESTONIA:** Embassy of the Republic of Estonia, 9 Rockefeller Plaza, Suite J-1421, New York, NY 10020, (202) 247-1450

**ETHIOPIA:** Embassy of Ethiopia, 2134 Kalorama Rd., NW, Washington, DC 20008, (202) 234-2281

**FIJI:** Embassy of the Rep. of Fiji, 2233 Wisconsin Ave., Suite 240, Washington, DC 20007, (202) 337-8320, FAX (202) 337-1996

**FINLAND:** Embassy of Finland, 3216 New Mexico Ave., NW, Washington, DC 20016, (202) 363-2430, FAX (202) 363-8233

**FRANCE:** Embassy of France, 4101 Reservoir Rd., NW, Washington, DC 20007, (202) 944-6000

**FRENCH GUIANA:** Contact Embassy of France , 4101 Reservoir Rd., NW, Washington, DC 20007, (202) 944-6000

**GABON:** Embassy of Gabon, 2034 - 20th St., NW, Washington, DC 20009, (202) 797-1000

**THE GAMBIA:** Embassy of Gambia, 1030 - 15th St., NW, Suite 720, Washinton, DC 20005, (202) 842-1356/1359,FAX (202) 842-2073

**134**

**GEORGIA:** Contact Embassy of Russia, (202) 939-8907

**Fed. Rep. OF GERMANY:** Embassy of the Fed. , Rep. of Germany, 4645 Reservoir Rd., NW, Washington, DC 20007, (202) 298-4000

**GHANA**: Embassy of Ghana, 3512 International Dr., NW, Washington, DC 20008, (202) 686-4520, FAX (202) 686-4527

**GREECE:** Embassy of Greece, 2221 Massachusetts Ave., NW, Washington, DC 20008, (202) 939-5800, FAX (202) 939-5824

**GRENADA:** Embassy of Grenada, 1701 New Hampshire Ave., NW, Washington, DC 20009, (202) 265-2561,

**GUADELOUPE**: Contact the Embassy of France, 2535 Belmont Rd., NW, Washinton, DC 20008, (202) 328-2600

**GUATEMALA**: Embassy of Guatemala, 2220 R St., NW, Washington, DC 20008, (202) 745-4952, FAX (202) 745-1908

**GUINEA**: Embassy of Guinea, 2112 Leroy Place, NW, Washington, DC 20008, (212) 483-9420

**GUINEA-BISSAU**: Embassy of the Rep. of Guinea-Bissau, 918 - 16th St., NW, Mezzanine Suite, Washington, DC 20006, (202) 872-4222, FAX (202) 872-4226

**GUYANA:** Embassy of Guyana, 2490 Tracy Place NW, Washington, DC 20008, (202) 265-6900

**HAITI:** Embassy of Haiti, 2311 Massachusetts Ave., NW, Washington, DC 20008, (202) 332-4090, FAX (202) 745-7215

**HONDURAS:** Embassy of Honduras, 3007 Tilden St., NW, Washington, DC 20008,

(202) 966-7702/2604/5008/4596,FAX (202) 966-9751

**HUNGARY:** Embassy of the Rep. of Hungary, 3910 Shoemaker St., NW, Washington, DC 20008, (202) 362-6730

**ICELAND**: Embassy of Iceland, 2022 Connecticut Ave., NW, Washington, DC 20008, (202) 265-6653 to 6655, FAX (202) 265-6656

**INDIA:** Embassy of India, 2107 Massachusetts Ave., NW, Washington, DC 20008, (202) 939-7000

**INDONESIA**: Embassy of the Rep. of Indonesia, 2020 Massachusetts Ave., NW, Washington, DC 20036, (202) 775-5200, FAX (202) 775-5365

**IRAN:** Iranian Interests Section, Embassy of Algeria, 2209 Wisconsin Ave., NW, Washington, DC 20007, (202) 965-4990

**IRAQ**: Iraq, Rep. of, 1801 P St., NW, Washington, DC 20036, (202) 483-7500, FAX (202) 462-5066

**IRELAND**: Embassy of Ireland, 2234 Massachusetts Ave., NW, Washington, DC 20008, (202) 462-3939

**ISRAEL**: Embassy of Israel, 3514 International Dr., NW, Washington, DC 20008, (202) 364-5500, FAX (202) 364-5610

**ITALY**: Embassy of Italy, 1601 Fuller St., NW, Washington, DC 20009, (202) 328-5500

**JAMAICA**: Embassy of Jamaica, 1850 K St., NW, Suite 355, Washington, DC 20006, (202) 452-0660, FAX (202) 452-0081

**JAPAN:** Embassy of Japan, 2520 Massachusetts Ave., NW, Washington, DC

**135**

20008, (202) 939-6700, FAX (202) 328-2187

**JORDAN**: Jordan, Hashemite Kingdom of, 3504 International Dr., NW, Washington, DC 20008, (202) 966-2664, FAX (202) 966-3110

**KAZAKHSTAN**: Contact Embassy of Russia, (202) 939-8907

**KENYA:** Embassy of Kenya, 2249 R. St., NW, Washington, DC 20008, (202) 387-6101

**KOREA, SOUTH**: Embassy of Korea, 2370 Massachussets Ave., NW, Washington, DC 20008, (202) 939-5600

**KOREA, DEM. PEOPLE'S REP.**: Contact the licensing Division, Office of Foreign Assets Control, Department of the Treasury, 1331 G St, NW, Washington DC 20220 (202) 622-2480

**KUWAIT:** Embassy of Kuwait, 2940 Tilden St., NW, Washington ,DC 20008, (202) 966-0702, FAX (202) 966-0517

**LAOS**: Embassy of the Lao People's Democratic Republic, , 2222 S St., NW,, Washington DC 20008, (202) 332-6416/7

**LATVIA**: Embassy of Latvia, 4325 - 17th St., NW , Washington, DC 20011, (202) 726-8213/8214

**LEBANON:** Lebanon, 2560 - 28th St., NW, Washington, DC 20008, (202) 939-6300, FAX (202) 939-6324

**LESOTHO**: Embassy of Lesotho, 2511 Massachusetts Ave., NW, Washington, DC 20008, (202) 797-5533, FAX (202) 234-6815

**LIBERIA**: Embassy of Liberia, 5201 - 16th St., NW, Washington, DC 20011, (202) 723-0437 t0 0440

**LIBYA**: Contact the Licensing Division, Office of Foreign Assets Control, Department of the Treasury, 1331 G St., NW Washington 20220, (202) 622-2480

**LITHUANIA**: Embassy of Lithuania, 2622 - 16th St., NW, Washington, DC 20009, (202) 234-5860/2639, FAX (202) 328-0466

**LUXEMBOURG**: Embassy of Luxembourg, 2200 Massachusetts Ave., NW, Washington, DC 20008, (202) 265-4171, FAX (202) 328-8270

**MADAGASCAR:** Embassy of Madagascar, 2374 Massachusetts Ave., NW, Washington, DC 20008, (202) 265-5525/6

**MALAWI**: Embassy of Malawi, 2408 Massachusetts Ave., NW, Washington, DC 20008, (202) 797-1007

**MALAYSIA**: Embassy of Malaysia, 2401 Massachusetts Ave., NW, Washington, DC 20008, Annex: 1900 - 24th St., NW, Washington, DC 20008, (202) 328-2700, FAX (202) 483-7661

**MALDIVES**: Rep. of Maldives, Mission to the United Nations, 820 Second Ave., Suite 800C, New York, NY 10017, (212) 599-6195

**MALI:** Embassy of Mali, 2130 R. St., NW, Washington, DC 20008, (202) 332-2249

**MALTA**: Embassy of Malta, 2017 Connecticut Ave., NW, Washington, DC 20008, (202) 462-3611/2, FAX (202) 387-5470

**MARSHALL ISLANDS:** Embassy of the Rep. of the, Marshall Islands, 2433 Massachusetts Ave., NW 20008, (202) 234-5414, FAX (202) 232-3236

**136**

**MARTINIQUE**: Contact Embassy of France, 4101 Reservoir Rd., NW, Washington, DC 2007, (202) 944-6000

**MAURITANIA:** Embassy of Mauritania, 2129 Leroy Place, NW, Washington, DC 20008, (202) 232-5700/1

**MAURITIUS**: Embassy of Mauritius, 4301 Connecticut Ave., NW, Suite 134, Washington, DC 20008, (202) 244-1491/2, FAX (202) 966-0983

**MEXICO:** Embassy of Mexico, 1911 Pennsylvania Ave., NW, Washington, DC 20006, (202) 728-1600

**MICRONESIA:** Embassy of the Federated States, of Micronesia, 1725 N St., NW, Washington, DC 20036, (202) 223-4383, FAX (202) 223-4391

**MOLDOVA**: Contact Embassy of Russia, (202) 939-8907

**MONGOLIA:** Embassy of the Mongolian, People's Rep., (301) 983-1962, FAX (301) 983-2035

**MONTSERRAT**: Contact the Embassy of, the United Kingdom, 3100 Massachusetts Ave., NW, Washington, DC 20008, (202) 462-1340, FAX (202) 898-4255

**MOROCCO**: Morocco, 1601 - 21st St., NW, Washington, DC 20009, (202) 462-7979, FAX (202) 265-0161

**MOZAMBIQUE:** Embassy of Mozambique, 1990 M St., NW, Suite 570, Washington, DC 20036, (202) 293-7146, FAX (202) 235-0245

**MYANMAR**: Embassy of the Union of Myanmar, 2300 S St., NW, Washington, DC 20008, (202) 332-9044/9045

**NAMIBIA:** Embassy of the Rep. of Namibia, 1605 New Hampshire Ave., NW, Washington, DC 20009, (202) 986-0540, FAX (202) 986-0443

**NEPAL**: Embassy of Nepal, 2131 Leroy Place, NW, Washington, DC 20008, (202) 667-4550

**NETHERLANDS**: Embassy of the Netherlands, 4200 Linnean Ave., NW, Washington, DC 20008, (202) 244-5300 after 6pm 244-5304, FAX (202) 362-3430

**NETHERLAND ANTILLES:** Embassy of the Netherlands, 4200 Linnean Ave., NW, Washington, DC 20008, (202) 244-5300 , FAX (202) 362-3430

**NEW ZEALAND:** Embassy of New Zealand, 37 Observatory Circle, NW, Washington, DC 20008, (202) 328-4800

**NICARAGUA:** Embassy of Nicaragua, 1627 New Hampshire Ave., NW, Washington, DC 20009, (202) 939-6570

**NIGER**: Embassy of Niger, 2204 R St., NW, Washington, DC 20008, (202) 483-4224 to 4227

**NIGERIA**: Embassy of Nigeria, 2201 M St., NW, Washington, DC 20037, (202) 822-1500

**NORWAY**: Royal Norwegian Embassy, 2720 - 34th St., NW, Washington, DC 20008, (202) 333-6000, FAX (202) 337-0870

**OMAN:** Oman, Sultanate of, 2342 Massachusetts Ave., NW, Washington, DC 20008, (202) 387-1980

**PAKISTAN:** Embassy of Pakistan, 2315 Massachusetts Ave., NW, Washington, DC 20008, (202) 939-6200, FAX (202) 387-0484

**137**

**PANAMA:** Embassy of Panama, 2862 McGill Terrace, NW, Washington, DC 20008, (202) 483-1407

**PAPUA NEW GUINEA:** Embassy of Papua New Guinea, 1615 New Hampshire Ave., NW, 3d Floor, Washington, DC 20009, (202) 745-3680, FAX (202) 745-3679

**PARAGUAY:** Embassy of Paraguay, 2400 Massachusetts Ave., NW, Washington, DC 20008, (202) 483-6960, FAX (202) 234-4508

**PERU:** Embassy of Peru, 1700 Massachusetts Ave., NW, Washington, DC 20036, (202)833-9860, FAX (202) 659-8124

**PHILIPPINES:** Embassy of the Philippines, 1617 Massachusetts Ave., NW, Washington, DC 20036, (202) 483-1414, FAX (202) 328-7614

**POLAND:** Embassy of the Rep. of Poland, 2640 - 16th St., NW, Washington, DC 20009, (202) 234-3800 to 3802, FAX (202) 328-6271

**PORTUGAL:** Embassy of Portugal, 2125 Kalorama Rd., NW, Washington, DC 20008, (202) 328-8610

**QATAR:** Qatar, 600 New Hampshire Ave., NW, Suite 1180, Washington, DC 20037, (202) 338-0111 **ROMANIA:** Embassy of Romania, 1607 23rd St., NW, Washington, DC 20008, (202) 232-4747, FAX (202) 232-4748

**RUSSIA:** Embassy of Russia, 1825 Phelps Pl., NW, Washington DC 2008, (202) 939-8907, 8911 or 8913

**RWANDA:** Embassy of Rwanda, 1714 New Hampshire Ave., NW, Washington, DC 20009, (202) 232-2882, FAX (202) 232-4544

**SRI LANKA:** Embassy of Sri Lanka, 2148 Wyoming Ave., NW, Washington, DC 20008, (202) 483-4025

**ST. KITTS and NEVIS:** Embassy of St. Kitts and Nevis, 2100 M St., NW, Suite 608 , Washington, DC 20037, (202) 833-3550, FAX (202) 833-3553

**ST. LUCIA:** Embassy of St. Lucia, 2100 M St., NW, Washington, DC 20037, (202) 463-7378, FAX (202) 887-5746

**ST. MARTIN:**, Contact the Embassy of France, 2535 Belmont Rd., NW, Washington, DC 20008, (202) 328-2600

**ST. VINCENT and the GRENADINES**, Embassy of St. Vincent and, the Grenadines, 1717 Massachusetts Ave., NW, Suite 102, Washington, DC 20036, (202) 462-7806/7846, FAX (202) 462-7807

**SAO TOME AND PRINCIPE,** Embassy of Sao Tome & Principe, 801 Second Ave. Suite 603, New York, NY 10017, (212) 697-4211, FAX (212) 687-8389

**SAUDI ARABIA:** Saudi Arabia, 601 New Hampshire Ave., NW, Washington, DC 20037, (202) 342-3800

**SENEGAL:** Embassy of Senegal, 2112 Wyoming Ave., NW, Washington, DC 20008, (202) 234-0540/1

**SERBIA AND MONTENEGRO:** Contact the Licensing Division, Office of Foreign Assets Control, Department of the Treasury, 1331 G St., NW Washington 20220, (202) 622-2480

**SEYCHELLES:** Permanent Mission of Seychelles to, the United Nations, 820 Second Ave. 900F, New York, NY 10017, (212) 687-9766, FAX (212) 922-9177

**138**

**SIERRA LEONE**: Embassy of Sierra Leone, 1701 - 19th St., NW, Washington, DC 20009, (202) 939-9261

**SINGAPORE**: Embassy of Singapore, 1824 R St. NW, Washington, DC 20009, (202) 667-7555, FAX (202) 265-7915

**SLOVAK REPUBLIC:** Embassy of the Slovak Republic, 3900 Spring of Freedom Street, NW, Washington DC 20008, (202) 363-6315

**SLOVENIA:** Embassy of Slovenia, 1300 19th Street, NW, Washington DC 20036, (202) 828-1650

**SOLOMON ISLANDS:** Embassy of the Solomon Islands, c/o The Permanent Mission, of the Solomon Islands to the UN, 820 Second Ave., Suite 800, New York, NY 10017, (212) 599-6193

**SOMALIA:** Embassy of Somalia, 600 New Hampshire Ave., NW, Suite 710, Washington, DC 20037, (202) 333-5908

**SOUTH AFRICA**: Embassy of South Africa, 3201 New Mexico Ave., NW, Washington, DC 20016, (202) 966-1650

**SPAIN:** Embassy of Spain, 2700 Massachusetts Ave., NW, Washington, DC 20009, (202) 265-0190/1

**SRI LANKA**: Embassy of the Democratic, Socialist Rep. of Sri Lanka, 2148 Wyoming Ave., NW, Washington, DC 20008, (202) 483-4025 to 4028, FAX (202) 232-7181

**SUDAN:** Embassy of Sudan, 2210 Massachusetts Ave., NW, Washington, DC 20008, (202) 338-8565 to 8570, FAX (202) 667-2406

**SURINAME:** Embassy of Suriname, 4301 Connecticut Ave., NW, Suite 108, Washington, DC 20008, (202) 244-7488, FAX (202) 244-5878

**SWAZILAND:** Embassy of the Kingdom, of Swaziland, 3400 International Dr., NW, Washington, DC 20008, (202) 362-6683/6685, FAX (202) 244-8059

**SWEDEN:** Embassy of Sweden, 600 New Hampshire Ave., NW, Suites 1200 and 715, Washington, DC 20037, (202) 944-5600, FAX (202) 342-1319

**SWITZERLAND:** Embassy of Switzerland, 2900 Catherdral Ave., NW, Washington, DC 20008, (202) 745-7900, FAX (202) 387-2564

**SYRIA**: Syrian Arab Rep., 2215 Wyoming Ave., NW, Washington, DC 20008, (202) 232-6313, FAX (202) 234-9548

**TAJIKISTAN**: Contact Russian Embassy, (202) 939-8907

**TANZANIA:** Embassy of Tanzania, 2139 R St., NW , Washington, DC 20008, (202) 939-6125, FAX (202) 797-7408

**THAILAND:** Embassy of Thailand, 2300 Kalorama Rd., NW, Washington, DC 20008, (202) 483-7200

**TOGO**, Embassy of Togo, 2208 Massachusetts Ave., NW, Washington, DC 20008, (202) 234-4212/3

**TRINIDAD AND TOBAGO:** Embassy of Trinidad & Tobago, 1708 Massachusetts Ave., NW, Washington, DC 20036, (202) 467-6490, FAX (202) 785-3130

**TUNISIA:** Tunisia, 1515 Massachusetts Ave., NW, Washington, DC 20005, (202) 862-1850

**TURKEY:** Embassy of the Rep. of Turkey, 1714 Massachusetts Ave., NW, Washington, DC 20036, (202) 659-8200

**TURKMENISTAN:** Contact Russian Embassy, (202) 939-8907

**TURKS AND CAICOS:** Contact the Embassy of the Bahamas, 600 New Hampshire Ave, NW, Washington, DC 20037, (202) 338-3940

**UGANDA:** Embassy of Uganda, 5909 - 16th St., NW, Washington, DC 20011, (202) 726-7100, FAX (202) 726-1727

**UKRAINE:** Embassy of Ukraine, Suite 711, 1828 L street NW,, Washington DC, 20036, (202) 296-6960

**UNITED ARAB EMIRATES:** United Arab Emirates, 600 New Hampshire Ave., NW, Suite 740, Washington, DC 20037, (202) 338-6500

**UNITED KINGDOM:** Embassy of the United Kingdom, 3100 Massachusetts Ave., NW, Washington, DC 20008, (202) 462-1340, FAX (202) 898-4255

**URUGUAY:** Embassy of Uruguay, 1918 F St., NW, Washington, DC 20006, (202) 331-1313

**UZBEKISTAN**: Contact Russian Embassy, (202) 939-8907

**VATICAN CITY:** Apostolic Nunciature, 3339 Massachusetts Ave., NW, Washington, DC 20008, (202) 333-7121

**VENEZUELA**: Embassy of Venezuela, 1099 30th St., NW, Washington, DC 20007, (202) 342-2214

**WESTERN SAMOA:** Embassy of Western Samoa, 1155 - 15th St., NW #510, Washington, DC 20005, (202) 833-1743, FAX (202) 833-1746

**YEMEN, ARAB Rep.:** Yemen Arab Rep., 600 New Hampshire Ave., NW, Washington, DC 20037, (202) 965-4760, FAX (202) 337-2017

**YEMEN, PEOPLE'S DEM. REP.:** Yemen, Peoples' Dem. Rep., 413 East 51st St., New York, NY 10022, (212) 752-3066

**YUGOSLAVIA:** Embassy of the Socialist Fed., Rep. of Yugoslavia, 2410 California St., NW, Washington, DC 20089, (202) 462-6566

**ZAIRE**:Embassy of Zaire, 1800 New Hampshire Ave., NW, Washington, DC 20009, (202) 234-7690/1

**ZAMBIA**: Embassy of Zambia, 2419 Massachusetts Ave., NW, Washington, DC 20008, (202) 265-9717 to 9721

**ZIMBABWE:** Embassy of Zimbabwe, 1608 New Hampshire Ave., NW , Washington, DC 20009, (202) 332-7100

**140**

# *APPENDIX C*

## KEY OFFICERS OF U.S. FOREIGN SERVICE POSTS

**Guide for Business Representatives**

The Key Officers Guide lists key officers at Foreign Service posts with whom American business representatives would most likely have contact. All embassies, missions, consulates general, and consulates are listed.

At the head of each U.S. diplomatic mission are the Chief of Mission (with the title of Ambassador, Minister, or Charge d'Affairs) and the Deputy Chief of Mission. These officers are responsible for all components of the U.S. Mission within a country, including consular posts.

Commercial Officers assist U.S. business through: arranging appointments with local business and government officials, providing counsel on local trade regulations, laws, and customs; identifying importers, buyers, agents, distributors, and joint venture partners for U.S. firms; and other business assistance. At larger posts, trade specialists of the US&FCS perform this function. At smaller posts, commercial interests are represented by economic/commercial officers from the Department of State.

Commercial Officers for Tourism implement marketing programs to expand inbound tourism, to increase the export competitiveness of U.S. travel companies, and to strengthen the international trade position of the United States. These officers are employees of the U.S. Travel and Tourism Administration (USTTA), an agency of the U.S. Department of Commerce with offices in various countries. Additional important markets in Europe, Asia, the Pacific, Latin America are covered by the Foreign Commercial Services and the private sector under USTTA leadership.

Economic Officers analyze and report on macroeconomic trends and trade policies and their implications for U.S. policies and programs.

141

Financial Attaches analyze and report on major financial developments.

Political Officers analyze and report on political developments and their potential impact on U.S. interests.

Labor Officers follow the activities of labor organizations and can supply information on wages, non-wage costs, social security regulations, labor attitudes toward American investments, etc.

Consular Officers extend to U.S. citizens and their property abroad the protection of the U.S. Government. They maintain lists of local attorneys, act as liaison with police and other officials, and have the authority to notarize documents. The Department recommends that business representatives residing overseas register with the consular officer; in troubled areas, even travelers are advised to register.

The Administrative Officer is responsible for the normal business operations of the post, including purchasing for the post and its commissary.

Regional Security Officers are responsible for providing physical, procedural, and personnel security services to U.S. diplomatic facilities and personnel; their responsibilities extend to providing in-country security briefings and threat assessments to business executives.

Security Assistance Officers are responsible for Defense Cooperation in Armaments and foreign military sales to include functioning as primary in-country point of contact for U.S. Defense Industry.

Scientific Attaches follow scientific and technological developments in the country.

Agricultural Officers promote the export of U.S. agricultural products and report on agricultural production and market developments in their area.

The Aid Mission Director is responsible for AID programs, including dollar and local currency loans, grants, and technical assistance.

The Public Affairs Officers is the post's press and cultural affairs specialist and maintains close contact with the local press.

The Legal Attache serves as a representative to the U.S. Department of Justice on criminal matters.

The Communications Program Officer is responsible for the telecommunications, telephone, radio, diplomatic pouches, and records management programs within the diplomatic mission. They maintain close contact with the host government's information/communications authorities on operational matters.

The Information Systems Manager is responsible for the post's unclassified information systems, database management, programming, and operational needs. They liaison with appropriate commercial contacts in the information field to enhance the post's systems integrity.

Business representatives planning a trip overseas should include in their preparations a visit or telephone call to the nearest U.S. Department of Commerce District Office. The District Office can provide extensive information and assistance as well as a current list of legal holidays in the countries to be visited. If desired, the District Officer can also provide advance notice to posts abroad of the representative's visit.

The Department of State, Bureau of Diplomatic Security, can also provide current data on the security situation to interested persons planning trips abroad. American business representatives desiring this information should contact the Diplomatic Security Service, Overseas Support Programs Division (202) 647-3122.

Some of the services jointly provided by the Departments of State and Commerce to U.S. business firms interested in establishing a market for their products or expanding sales abroad include:

-The Trade Opportunities Program (TOP) that provides specific export sales leads of U.S. products and services;

World Traders Data Report (WTDR) that provides detailed financial and commercial information on individual firms abroad upon request from U.S. companies;

-Agent Distributor Service (ADS) that helps U.S. firms find agents or distributors to represent their firms and market their products abroad; and

-Information about foreign markets for U.S. products and services and U.S.-sponsored exhibitions abroad in which American firms can participate and demonstrate their products to key foreign buyers.

**143**

-In all matters pertaining to foreign trade, the nearest U.S. Department of Commerce District Office should be your first point of contact. Foreign trade specialists at these facilities render valuable assistance to U.S. business representatives engaged in international commerce.

For additional information about Foreign Service assistance to American business overseas, or for specialized assistance with unusual commercial problems, you are invited to visit, telephone, or write the Office of Commercial, Legislative, and Public Affairs, Bureau of Economic and Business Affairs, U.S. Department of State, Washington, D.C. 20520-5816. Telephone (202) 647-1942.

# APPENDIX D

## U.S. GOVERNMENT PASSPORT AGENCIES

**APPLY EARLY FOR YOUR PASSPORT!**

**Boston Passport Agency**
Thomas P. O'Neill Fed. Bldg.,
Rm.247
10 Causeway Street
Boston, Massachusetts 02222
*Recording: 617-565-6698
**Public Inquiries: 617-565-6990**

**Chicago Passport Agency**
Suite 380, Kluczynski Federal Bldg.
230 South Dearborn Street
Chicago, Illinois 60604-1564
*Recording: 312-353-5426
**Public Inquiries: 312-353-7155 or 7163**

**Honolulu Passport Agency**
Room C-106, New Federal Bldg.
300 Ala Moana Blvd.
Honolulu, Hawaii 96850
*Recording: 808-541-1918
**Public Inquiries: 808-541-1918**

**Houston Passport Agency**
Concord Towers
1919 Smith Street, Ste. 1100
Houston, Texas 77002
*Recording: 713-653-3159

**Public Inquiries: 713-653-3153**

**Los Angeles Passport Agency**
Room 13100, 11000 Wilshire
Boulevard, Los Angeles, California
90024-3615 *Recording:
213-209-7070
**Public Inquiries: 213-209-7075**

**Miami Passport Agency**
3rd Floor, Federal Office Bldg.
51 Southwest First Avenue
Miami, Florida 33130-1680
*Recording: 305-536-5395 (English)
305-536-4448 (Spanish)
**Public Inquiries: 305-536-4681**

**New Orleans Passport Agency**
Postal Services Building
701 Loyola Avenue, Room T-12005
New Orleans, Louisiana 70113-1931
*Recording: 504-589-6728
**Public Inquiries: 504-589-6161**

**New York Passport Agency**
Room 270, Rockefeller Center
630 Fifth Avenue
New York, New York 10111-0031
*Recording: 212-541-7700
**Public inquiries: 212-541-7710**

145

**Philadelphia Passport Agency**
Room 4426, Federal Bldg.
600 Arch Street
Philadelphia, Pennsylvania
19106-1684, *Recording:
215-597-7482
**Public Inquiries: 215-597-7480**

**San Francisco Passport Agency**
Suite 200, 525 Market Street
San Francisco, California 94105-2773

*Recording: 415-974-7972
**Public Inquiries: 415-974-9941**

**Seattle Passport Agency**
Room 992, Federal Office Bldg.
915 Second Avenue
Seattle, Washington 98174-1091
*Recording: 206-553-7941
**Public Inquiries: 206-553-7945**

**Stamford Passport Agency**
One Landmark Square
Broad and Atlantic Streets
Stamford, Connecticut 06901-2767
*Recording: 203-325-4401
**Public Inquiries: 203-325-3538,
3530**

**Washington Passport Agency**
1425 K Street, N.W.
Washington, D.C. 20524-0002
*Recording: 202-647-0518
**Public Inquiries: 202-647-0518**

-------------
* The 24-hour recording includes general passport information, passport agency location, and hours of operation and information regarding emergency passport services during non-working hours

** For other questions, call Public Inquiries number.

146

# APPENDIX  E

## VISA AND PASSPORT AGENCIES[OG]

### ATLANTA, GA

**International Visa Service, Inc.,** 278 Hilderbrand Dr. NE. Box 720715, Zip, 30328. TEL: 404/843-0005,Continental U.S. (except GA) 800 843-0050. Hours. 9 AM - 5,30 PM (Mon.-Wed., Fri.); 9 AM - 12 Noon (Sat.); 9 AM - 7:30 PM (Thurs.).

### BALTIMORE, MD

**Harbor City Visa Services,** 1635 Eastern Ave., Zip, 21231. TEL: 301/342-8472. Hours, 1 PM - 5 PM (Mon.-Fri.).

**Visa Adventure, Inc.,** 205 Hillendale Ave., Zip: 21227. TEL: 301/242-5602. Hours: 8:30 AM - 4 PM (Mon.-Fri.).

### BOSTON, MA

**Visa Service, Inc.,** 581 Boylston St., Zip: 02116. TEL: 617/266-7646. FAX, 617/262-9829. Hours, 9 AM - 5 PM (Mon.-Fri.).

### CHICAGO, IL

**Adventure Seekers Tours,** 36 W. Randolph, Zip: 60601. TEL: 312/346-9100. Hours, 9:30 AM - 5:30 PM (Mon.-Fri.).

**American Visa Service, Inc.,** 53 W. Jackson, Ste. 803, Zip: 60604. TEL: 312/922-8860. Hours, 9 AM - 5 PM (Mon.-Fri.).

**Chicago Visa Service,** 201 N. Wells, Rm. 430, Zip: 60606. TEL: 312/332-7211. Hours: 9 AM - 5 PM (Mon.-Fri.); 9 AM - 1 PM (Sat.).

**Perry International Inc.,** 100 W. Monroe St., Zip: 60603. TEL: 312/372-2703. Hours: 9 AM - 5 PM (Mon.-Fri.).

### DALLAS, TX

**Dallas Visa Service,** 2755 Valley View Lane, Ste. 103., Zip: 75234. TEL: 214/241-9900. Hours, 8:30 AM - 5 PM (Mon.-Fri.).

**Passport and Visa Express,** 2132 Willowbrook Way, Ste. 100, Zip: 75075. TEL: 214/867-7707.Continental U.S. 800-344-2810; FAX: 214/867-6006. Hours: 7 AM - 7 PM (Mon.-Fri.); 9 AM - 3 PM (sat.).

**Wide World Visas,** Greenville Bank Tower, 7515 Greenville Ave., Ste. 407,

Zip: 75231. TEL: 214/739-5710. Hours: 8:30 AM - 5 PM (Mon.-Fri.).

### DENVER, CO

**International Passport Visas, Inc.,** 1325 S. Colorado Blvd., Ste. 604, Zip: 80222. 24 Hour Answering Service. TEL: 303/753-0424, Continental U.S., AK, HI 800-783-VISA. Hours: 9 AM - 5 PM (Mon.-Sun.).

### FOUNTAIN VALLEY, CA

**South Coast Visa & Passport Service,** 18854 Brookhurst, Zip: 92708. TEL: 714/963-8464. Hours: 9 AM - 5 PM (Mon.-Fri.).

### HOUSTON, TX

**Visas & International Passports,** 507 Dallas St., Ste. 304, Zip: 77002. TEL: 713/759-9119. Continental U.S. 800-876-VISA; FAX: 713/759-9589. Hours, 8 AM - 6 PM (Mon.-Fri.); 10 AM - 3 Pm (Sat.).

**WIde World Visas,** 1200 Smith St., Ste. 875, Zip: 77002. TEL: 713/655-9074, Continental U.S. (except TX), AK, HI 800-527-1861, TX 800-833-5423. Hours: 9 AM - 5 PM (Mon.-Fri.).

### LAKEWOOD, OH

**Adventure International Travel,** 14305 Madison Ave., Zip: 44107. TEL: 216/228-7171. Hours. 9 AM - 6 PM (Mon.-Fri.); 9 AM - 2 PM (Sat.).

### LOS ANGELES, CA

**Consular Visa Assistance,** 4276 Brunswick Ave, Zip: 90039. TEL: 818/241-4202. Hours: 8:30 AM - 5:30 PM (7 Days).

**Intercontinental Visa Services,** Los Angeles World Trade Center, 350 S. Figueroa, Ste. 185. Zip: 90071. TEL: 213/625-7175. Hours, 9 AM - 5 PM (Mon.-Fri.).

**Visas International,** 3169 Barbara Ct., Ste. F, Zip: 90068. TEL: 213/850-1192, Continental U.S. 800-638-1517. Hours. 9 AM - 12 PM 1:30 PM - 5 PM (Mon.-Fri.).

### NEW YORK, NY

**Foreign Visa Service,** 18 E. 93rd St, Zip: 10128. TEL: 212/876-5890. Hours: 9 AM - 5 PM (Mon.-Fri.) & by appointment.

**Mr. Visas Inc.,** 211 E. 43rd St, Zip: 10017. TEL: 212/682-3895. Hours: 9 AM - 7 PM (Mon.-Fri.); 10:30 AM - 2:30 PM (Sat.).

**Passport Plus,** 677 Fifth Ave., Zip: 10022. TEL: 212/759-5540, Continental U.S. (except NY) 800-367-1818. Hours: 9:30 AM - 5:30 PM (Mon.-Fri.).

**Travel Agenda, Inc.** (DBA "VISA PROS"), 119 W. 57th St. Zip: 10019. TEL: 212/265-7887, Continental U.S. 800-683-0119; FAX: 212/581-8144.

Hours. 9:30 AM - 5:30 PM (Mon.-Fri.).

**Visa Center, Inc.,** 507 Fifth Ave., Ste. 904, Zip: 10017. TEL: 212/986-0924. Hours. 9 AM - 4:45 PM (Mon.-Fri.).

**ORANGE, CA**
**Orange County Visa & Passport Service,** 309 N. Rampart, Zip: 92668. TEL: 714/385-2595. Hours. 8:30 AM - 5 PM (Mon.-Fri.).

**Visa Consultants,** 450 E. Chapman Ave., Ste. 102. Zip: 92666. TEL: 714/633 0839, Southern CA 800 441-VISA. Hours: 8:30 AM - 2:30 PM (Mon.-Fri.).

**PHILADELPHIA, PA**

**New York Connection Visa Service,** 1617 JFK Blvd., Ste. 630, Zip: 19103. TEL: 215/564 2300. Continental U.S., AK, HI 800-247-2300; FAX: 215/564-9927. Hours: 9 AM - 6 PM (Mon.-Fri.).

**SALT LAKE CITY, UT**

**The Travel Broker-Express Visa & Passport,** 1061 E. 2100 South, Zip: 84106. TEL: 801/486-7800. Hours: 9 AM - 5 PM (Mon.-Fri.).

**SAN FRANCISCO, CA**

**Trans World Visa Service,** 790 27th Ave., Box 22068, Zip: 94121. TEL: 415/752 6957, Continental U.S. (except CA) 800-848-9980; FAX: 415-752-0804. Hours: 9 AM - 5 PM

(Mon.-Fri.).

**Visa Aides,** 870 Market St., Zip: 94102. TEL: 415/362-7137. Hours: 9 AM - 5 PM (Mon.-Fri.).

**Visas Unlimited,** 582 Market, Ste. 900, Zip: 94104. TEL, 415/421-7351. Hours: 9 AM - 5 PM (Mon.-Fri.).

**Zierer Visa Service,** 703 Market St., Ste. 802, Zip: 94103. TEL: 415/495-5216, Continental U.S. 800-843-9151; FAX: 415/495-4491. Hours: 7 AM - 5 PM (Mon.-Fri.).

**SEATTLE, WA**

**Visa Services Northwest,** Plaza 600 Bldg., Ste. 1900, Zip: 98101. TEL: 206/448 8400. Hours: 9 AM - 4:30 PM (Mon.-Fri.).

**WASHINGTON, DC**

**Atlas Visa Service, Inc.,** 2341 Jefferson Davis Hwy., Ste, 116 (Arlington, VA), Zip: 22202. 24 Hour Answering Service. TEL: 703/418-0800. Hours: 8 AM - 6 PM (Mon.-Fri.).

**Center For International Business & Travel, Inc.,** 2135 Wisconsin Ave. NW, Ste. 400, Zip: 20007. TEL: 202/333-5550, Continental U.S., AK, HI 800-424-2429. Hours: 8:30 AM - 6:30 PM (Mon.-Fri.).

**Diran Visa & Translation Service,** 1511 K St. NW, Ste. 309, Zip: 20005. TEL: 202/638-4328. Hours: 9 AM - 5

**149**

PM (Mon.-Fri.).

**Express Visa**, 150 Wisconsin Ave., Ste. 20, Zip: 20007. 24 Hour Answering Service. TEL: 202/337-2442. Hours: 9 AM - 6 PM (Mon.-Fri.).

**Mercury Visa Service**, 2004 17th St. NW, Zip: 20009. TEL: 202/939-8851, Continental U.S. 800-526-8456; FAX: 202/667-5303. Hours: 8:30 AM - 5 PM (Mon.-Fri.).

**Nader Visa Service, Inc.**, 1325 18th St., NW, Ste. 104, Zip: 20036. TEL: 202/332-7797; 332-7650. Hours: 9 AM - 5 PM (Mon.-Fri.), 10 AM - 12 Noon (Sat.).

**Passport & Visa Services**, 1377 K St. NW, Zip: 20005. TEL: 202/293-6245, Continental U.S. (except DC) 800-237-3270. Hours: 8:30 AM - 5 PM (Mon.-Fri.); 10 AM - 1 PM (Sat.).

**Trav-All Visa Service**, 7311 Rockford Dr., Box 523 (Falls Church, VA), Zip: 22040. TEL: 703/698-1777. Hours: 9 AM - 5 PM (Mon.-Fri.).

**Travel Document Systems**, 734 15th St. NW, Ste. 400, Zip: 20005. TEL: 202/638-3800, Continental U.S. (except DC) 800-424-8472. Hours: 10 AM - 7 PM (Mon.-Fri.).

**Travisa, Inc.**, 2122 P St. NW, Zip: 20037. TEL: 202/436-6166, Continental U.S. (except DC) 800-222-2589. Hours: 8:30 AM - 5:30 PM (Mon.-Fri.).

**Visa Advisors,** 1808 Swann St. NW, Zip: 20009. TEL: 202/797-7976. FAX: 202/667-6708. Hours: 9 AM - 5 PM (Mon.-Fri.).

**Visa Fox International,** 2020 Pennsylvania Ave. NW Ste, 123, Zip: 20006. TEL: 202/785-0787, Continental U.S., AK, HI 800-635-1047. Hours: 9 Am - 5 PM (Mon.-Fri.).

**Visa Passport & Immigration Service,** 815 15th St. NW, Ste. 537, Zip: 20005. TEL: 202/783-6290. Hours: 9 AM - 5:30 PM (Mon.-Fri.).

**Visa Services, Inc.,** 1519 Connecticut Ave. NW, Ste. 300, Zip: 20036. TEL: 202/387-0300, Continental U.S. (except DC) AK, HI 800-222-VISA. Hours: 9 AM - 5:30 PM (Mon.-Fri.).

**Washington Passport & Visa Service, Inc.,** 2318 18th St. NW, Zip: 20009. TEL: 202/234-7667, Continental U.S. (except DC) 800-272-7776; FAX: 202/462-2335. Hours: 9 AM - 5 PM (Mon.-Fri.).

**Zierer Visa Service,** 1521 New Hampshire Ave. NW, Ste. 100, Zip: 20036. TEL: 202/265-3007, Continental U.S. 800-421-6706, FAX: 202/265-3061. Hours: 9 AM - 5:30 PM (Mon.-Fri.).

--------------

**CAUTION:** The listing of these companies (agencies) should not be interpreted as a recommendation from this author or publisher. As always, you must exercise prudence in dealing with any services of this type. Refer to the index for the section entitled passport scam.

**150**

# *APPENDIX F*

## FOREIGN GOVERNMENT TOURIST BOARDS AND OFFICES IN THE U.S.*

**ANGUILLA**
Anguilla Tourist Office; c/o Medhurst & Assoc; 271 Main St. Northport, NY 11768; (516) 261-1234;

**ANTIGUA AND BARBUDA**
Antigua Dept. of Tourism & Trade; 610 5th Ave. Ste 311; New York, NY 10020; (212) 541-4117

**AUSTRALIA**
Australian Natl. Tourist Office; 500 Fifth Ave. Ste 2009; New York, NY 10110; (212) 944-6880

**AUSTRIA**
Austrian Natl. Tourist Office; 500 Fifth Ave. Ste.2009.; New York, NY 10110; (212) 944-6880

**BAHAMAS**
Bahamas Tourist Office; 150 E. 52nd St; 28th Floor, North; New York, NY 10022; (212) 758-2777

**BARBADOS**
Barbados Board of Tourism; 800 2nd Ave. 17th Floor; New York, NY 10017; (212) 986-6516

**BELGIUM**
Belgian Tourist Office; 745 Fifth Avenue; New York, NY 10022; (212) 758-8130

**BERMUDA**
Bermuda Gov't. Travel Info. Center; 310 Madison Avenue; New York, NY 10017; (212) 818-9800

**BONAIRE**
Bonaire Government Tourist Office; 275 7th Ave. 19th floor; New York, NY 10001-6788; (212) 242-7707

**BRITISH VIRGIN ISLANDS**
British Virgin Islands Tourist Board; 370 Lexington Ave., Ste.511; New York, NY 10017; (800) 835-8530

**BRAZIL**
Brazil Tourism Office; 551 5th Ave. Ste. 519; New York, NY 10176; (212) 286-9600

**BULGARIA**
Bulgarian Tourist Office; 161 East 86th Street, 2nd floor; New York, NY 10028; (212) 722-1110

**BURKINA FASO**
Africa Travel Association; 347 Fifth Ave. Suite 610; New York, NY 10036; (212) 447-1926

**151**

**CAMEROON**
Africa Travel Association; 347 Fifth Ave. Suite 610; New York, NY 10036; (212) 447-1926

**CANADA**
Canadian Government - Office of Tourism; 1251 Ave. of the Americas; New York, NY 10020; (212) 581-2280

**CAYMAN ISLANDS**
Cayman Islands Dept of Tourism; 980 N. Michigan Ave., Suite 1260; Chicago, IL. 00611; (312) 944-5602

**CHINA, PEOPLES REPUBLIC**
China Natl. Tourist Office; 50 East 42nd St. Rm. 3126; New York, NY 10165; (212) 867-0271

**CHINA, TAIWAN**
Taiwan Visitors Assoc.; One World Trade Center, Ste. 8855; New York, NY 10048

**COLUMBIA**
Columbian Government Tourist Office; 140 East 57th St. 2nd Floor; New York, NY 10022; (212) 688-0151

**CYPRUS**
Cyprus Tourism Organ.; Cyprus Trade Center; 13 E. 40th St.; New York, NY 10016; (212) 683-5280

**CZECH REPUBLIC**
Cedok Czechoslovakian Travel Office; 10 E. 40th. St.,Suite 1902; New York, NY 10016; (212) 689-9720

**DENMARK**
Danish Tourist Board; 655 Third Ave.; New York, Ny 10017; (212) 949-2333

**DOMINICAN REPUBLIC**
Dominican Rep. Tourist Info. Center; 485 Madison Avenue; New York, NY 10022; (212) 826-0750

**EGYPT**
Egyptian Government Tourist Office; 630 Fifth Avenue; New York, NY 10111; (212) 246-6960

**EL SALVADOR**
El Salvador Tourist Bureau; P.O. Box 818 Dept RB; Radio City, NY 10019

**FINLAND**
Finnish Tourist Board; 655 Third Avenue; New York, NY 10017; (212) 949-2333

**FRANCE**
French Government Tourist Office; 610 Fifth Avenue; New York, NY 10020; (212) 757-1125

**GABON**; Gabon Tourist Information Office; 347 Fifth Ave. Suite 1100; New York, NY 10016; (212) 447-6701

**FEDERAL REPUBLIC OF GERMANY**
German Natl. Tourist Office; 122 E. 42nd St. 52nd Floor; New York, NY 10168; (212) 661-7200

**GHANA**
Ghana Trade & Investment Office; 19 E. 47th St.; New York, NY 10017; (212) 832-1300

**GREAT BRITAIN**
British Tourist Authority; 551 5th Ave, 7th Fkr.; New York, NY. 10176; (212) 986-2200

**GREECE**
Greek Natl. Tourist Organ. ; 645 Fifth Avenue; New York, NY 10022; (212) 421-

**152**

5777

**GRENADA**
Grenada Tourist Office, 820 2nd Ave. Ste.900D, New York, NY 10017; (212) 687-9554

**GUADELOUPE**
French West Indies Tourist Board; 610 Fifth Ave.; New York, NY 10020; (212) 757-1125

**HONG KONG**
Hong Kong Tourist Assoc.; 548 Fifth Ave.; New York, NY 10036; (212) 947-5008

**HUNGARY**
Hungarian Travel Bureau; One Parker Plaza, Suite 1104; Fort Lee, NJ 07024; (201) 592-8585

**ICELAND**
Iceland Tourist Board; 655 Third Ave.; New York, NY 10017; (212) 949-2333

**INDIA**
Government of India Tourist Office; 30 Rockefeller Plaza; New York, NY 10112; (212) 586-4901

**IRELAND**
Irish Tourist Board; 757 3rd Ave.; New York, NY 10017; (212) 418-0800

**ISRAEL**
Isreal Government Tourism Office; 350 Fifth Avenue; New York, NY 10118; (212) 560-0650

**ITALY**
Italian Government Travel Office; 630 Fifth Ave. Suite 1565; New York, NY 10111; (212) 397-5286

**JAMAICA**
Jamaica Tourist Board; 866 Second Avenue.; New York, NY 10017; (212) 688-7650

**JAPAN**
Japan Natl. Tourist Org.; 630 Fifth Ave. Ste. 2101; New York, NY 10111; (212) 757-5640

**JORDAN**
Jordan Torist Office; 545 Fifth Ave. 5th Flr.; New York, NY 10017; (212) 949-0050

**KENYA**
Kenya Tourist Office; 424 Madison Avenue; New York, NY 10017; (212) 486-1300

**KOREA**
Korea Natl. Tourism Corp.; 2 Executive Dr.; Fort Lee, N.J. 07024; (201) 585-0909;

**LESOTHO**
Embassy of Lesotho, Tourist Board; 2511 Massachusettes Ave. NW; Washington, DC 20008; (202) 797-5533

**LIECHTENSTEIN**
Liechtenstein Natl. Tourist Office; 608 Fifth Ave. New York, NY 10020; (212) 757-5944

**LUXEMBURG**
Luxemburg Natl. Tourist Office; 801 Second Ave.; New York, NY 10017; (212) 370-9850

**MALAYSIA**
Malaysian Tourist Center; 420 Lexington Ave. New York, NY 10170 ; (212) 697-8995

**MALDIVES**; (See Sri Lanka)

**MALTA**
Malta Tourism Office; Consulate of Malta;

153

249 E. 35th St. ; New York, NY 10016; (212) 725-2345

**MARTINIQUE**
French West Indies Tourist Board; 610 Fifth Ave.; New York, NY 10020; (212) 757-1125

**MAURITIUS**
Mauritius Government Tourist Office; 40 J. Pask Associates Inc.; 415 Seventh Ave.; New York, NY 10001; (212) 239-8350

**MEXICO**
Mexican Govt. Tourism Office; 405 Park Ave. Suite 1002; New York, NY 10022; (212) 755-7261

**MONACO**
Monaco Govt. Tourist Office; 845 Third Ave.; New York, NY 10022; (212) 759-5227

**MOROCCO**
Moroccan Tourist Board; 20 E. 46th St.; New York, NY 10017; (212) 557-2520

**NETHERLANDS**
Netherlands Board of Tourism Office; 355 Lexington Ave.; New York, NY 10017; (212) 370-7367

**NETHERLAND ANTILLES**
Curacoa Tourist Board; 400 Madison Ave. Suite 311; New York, NY 10017; (212) 751-8266

**NEW ZEALAND**
New Zealand Tourism Office; 10960 Wilshire Blvd.; Los Angeles CA 90024; (213) 477-8241

**NIGERIA**
Nigerian Info. Service Center; 2201 M. St NW; Washington DC 20037; (202) 822-1541

**NORWAY**
Norwegian Tourist Board; 655 Third Ave.; New York, NY 10017; (212) 949-2333

**PANAMA**
Panama Government Tourist Bureau; Airport Exec. Tower 2; 7270 NW 12th St.; Coral Gables, FL 33134

**POLAND**
Polish Natl. Tourist Office; 333 N. Michigan Ave. Suite 228; Chicago, IL 60601; (312) 236-9013

**PORTUGAL**
Portuguese Natl. Tourist Office; 590 Fifth Ave. 4th fl. New York, NY 10036 (212) 354-4403

**ROMANIA**
Romanian Natl. Tourist Office; 573 Third Avenue; New York, NY 10016; (212) 697-6971

**ST. KITTS-NEVIS**
St. Kitts-Nevis Tourist Office; 414 E. 75th St.; New York, NY 10021; (212) 535-1234

**ST. LUCIA**; St. Lucia Tourist Board; 820 2nd Ave. Suite 900, New York, NY 10017 (212) 867-2950

**ST. MAARTEN**
St. Maarten Tourist Office; 275 7th Ave. 19th flr.; New York, NY 10017; (212) 989-0000

**SEYCHELLES**
Seychelles Tourist Office; 820 Second Ave. Suite 900F; New York, NY 10017; (212) 687-9766

**SOUTH AFRICA**
South African Tourist Board; 747 Third

Avenue; New York, NY 10017; (212) 838-8841

## SPAIN
Spanish Government Tourist Office; 665 Fifth Ave.; New York, NY 10022; (212) 759-8822

## SRI LANKA
Sri Lanka Tourist Department; Embassy of Sri Lanka; 2148 Wyoming Ave. NW; Washington, DC 20008; (202) 483-4025

## SWEDEN
Swedish Tourist Board; 655 Third Ave.; New York, NY 10017; (212) 949-2333

## SWITZERLAND
Swiss Natl. Tourist Office; 608 Fifth Ave. ; New York, NY 10020; (212) 757-5944

## TANZANIA
Tanzania Tourist Office; 205 E. 42nd St. ; 13th flr. Rm. 1300; New York, NY 10017; (212) 972-9160

## TOGO
Togo Info. Service; 1706 R St. NW; Washington, DC 20009; (202) 667-8181

## TRINIDAD AND TOBAGO
Trinidad & Tobago ; Tourism Dev. Authority 25 W. 43rd St. Suite 1508 ; New York, NY 10036; (212) 719-0540

## TURKEY
Turkish Government Tourism Office; 821 United Nations Plaza; New York, NY 10017; (212) 687-2194

# *Appendix G*

## HOW TO OBTAIN AN INTERNATIONAL DRIVER'S PERMIT

Although most countries no longer require an International Drivers Permit (IDP), it is advisable to verify in advance if such a permit is required or recommended for the country you plan to visit. Your travel agent, travel advisor, or the country's tourist bureau or Embassy should be able to provide you with that information. You may also contact your local automobile association or the American Automobile Association. One of the important advantages of the IDP is that it is written in nine different, major languages.

Here are the requirements to apply for an International Drivers Permit from the American Automobile Association (AAA).

| Requirements: | (1) | A completed application form; |
|---|---|---|
| | (2) | two recent signed passport size photograph not larger than 2 1/2" by 2 1/2"; |
| | (3) | A $10 permit fee; |
| | (4) | Applicant must be 15 years or older; |
| | *(5) | Applicant must hold a valid U.S. or Territorial Driver's License. |

You may request for an IDP by mail or in person. You are not required to be an AAA member to get and IDP from them. Check your telephone directories for an AAA office in your area you, or you may contact their headquarters at AAA Drive, Heathrow, Florida 32746-5063. Telephone: (407) 444-4000.

---

*Applicants with driving violations may be refused permit.

# *APPENDIX H*

## TO REPORT LOST OR STOLEN CREDIT/CHARGE CARD* OR TO ARRANGE FOR CARD REPLACEMENT

| CARD | IN U.S./CARIBBEAN | OUTSIDE U.S./OVERSEAS |
|---|---|---|
| **VISA** | 800-336-8472 | CALL COLLECT:(314) 275-6690 |
| **VISA GOLD** | 800-847-2911 | CALL COLLECT:(314) 275-6690 |
| **MASTERCARD** | 800-826-2181 | CALL COLLECT:(314) 275-6690 |
| **DINNERS CLUB** | 800-525-9135 | CALL COLLECT:(303) 790-2433 |
| **AMERICAN EXPRESS*** | | |
| Personal Card | 800-528-4800 | CALL COLLECT:(919) 668-6668 |
| Corporate Card | 800-528-2122 | CALL COLLECT:(602) 492-5450 |
| Gold Card | 800-528-2121 | CALL COLLECT:(305) 476-2166 |
| Platinum Card | 800-525-3355 | CALL COLLECT:(602) 492-5450 |
| Optima Card | 800-635-5955 | CALL COLLECT:(602) 492-5450 |
| Travelers Checks | 800-221-7282 | CALL COLLECT:(801) 964-6665 |
| **THOMAS COOK** | | |
| Travelers Checks | 800-223-7373 | CALL COLLECT:(609) 987-7300 |

---

*In the event of a stolen or lost Credit/Charge Card, it is advisable to quickly file a report with the local Police. Request a copy of the report for your file. American Express Cardholders are advised to call or visit the nearest American Express Travel Service Office immediately and/or call collect. Apply the same procedure as with cards, in the event your travelers checks are stolen or lost.

157

# *Appendix I*
## TO SEND
## MONEY/TELEX/TELEGRAM/CABLEGRAM
## (From the U.S.) CALL

### WIRING MONEY

| | |
|---|---|
| **WESTERN UNION** | 800-325-6000 or 800-257-4900 |
| **AMERICAN EXPRESS (MONEYGRAM)** | 800-543-4080.<br>From Abroad CALL COLLECT:<br>(303) 980-3340 |
| **BANK OF AMERICA**<br>**(GLOBAL SELLERS NETWORK)** | 800-227-3460 |
| **CITIBANK** | (212) 657-5161 |
| **BARCLAYS⁺** | (212) 233-4200 |

### TELEX/TELEGRAM/CABLEGRAM

| | |
|---|---|
| **WESTERN UNION** | 800-325-6000 or 800-257-4900 |
| **AT&T (EASYLINK)*** | 800-242-6005 |

---

* May be available only to subscribers.

+ Must have a Barclays account.

158

# APPENDIX J
## INTERNATIONAL AIRLINES

**AER LINGUS**
122 E. 42nd St.
New York, NY 10017
800-223-6537

**AEROFLOT-RUSSIAN AIRLINES**
630 Fifth Ave. Ste. 1709
New York, NY 10111
800-535-9877

**AEROLINEAS ARGENTINAS**
1 Biscayne Tower
Mezzanine Level
Miami, FL 33131
800-333-0276

**AEROMEXICO**
13405 NW Freeway
Houston, TX 77040
800-237-6639

**AEROPERU**
8181 NW 36th St., Ste 5
Miami, FL 33166
800-777-7717

**AIR INDIA**
345 Park Ave.,
New York, NY 10022
800-776-3000

**AIR NEW ZEALAND**
9841 Airport Blvd., Ste.
1020; Los Angeles, CA
90045
800-262-1234

**AIR FRANCE**
888 Seventh Ave
New York, NY 10106
800-237-2747

**AIR JAMAICA**
444 Brickell Ave.
Miami, FL 33131
800-523-5585

**AIR NEW ZEALAND LTD.**
1960 E. Grand Ave.
El Segundo, CA 90245
800-262-1234

**AIR CANADA**
15 W. 50th St.
New York, NY 10020
800-776-3000

**ALITALIA AIRLINES**
666 Fifth Ave.
New York, NY 10019
800-223-5730

**ALL NIPPON AIRWAYS**
Herbalife Building
9800 Lacienega Blvd.
Englewood, CA 90301
800-235-9262

**ALM ANTILLEAN AIRLINES**
1150 NW 72nd Ave.
Miami, FL 33166
800-327-7230

**ALOHA AIRLINES, INC.**
P.O. Box 30028
Honolulu, HI 96820
800-367-5250

**AVIANCA**
6 W. 49th St.
New York, NY 10020
800-284-2622

**AUSTRALIANAIRLINES**
360 Post Street 9th flr.
San Francisco, CA 94108
800-922-5122

**AUSTRIAN AIRLINES**
17-20 Whitestone
Expressway
Whitestone, NY 11357
800-843-0002

**AVIATECA**
6595 NW 36TH St. Ste.
100, Miami, FL 33166
800-327-9832

**BAHAMASAIR**
228 SE 1st St.
Miami, FL 33131
800-222-4262

**BRITISH AIRWAYS**
75-20 Astoria Blvd.
Jackson Heights, NY 11370
800-247-9297

**BWIA INTERNATIONAL**

**159**

330 Biscayne Blvd 3rd Flr.
Miami, FL 33132
800-327-7401

**CANADIAN AIRLINE**
Calgary Administration
Building; 615 18th St. S.E.
Calgary, Alberta T2E6J5
800-426-7000

**CATHEY PACIFIC AIRWAYS**
300 N. Continental Blvd.
Ste 500, El Segando, CA
90245
800-233-2742

**CAYMAN AIRWAYS**
250 Catalonia Ste 506
Coral Gables, FL 33134
800-422-9626

**CHINA AIRLINES, LTD.**
6053 West Century Blvd.
Ste. 800; Los Angeles, CA
90045
800-227-5118

**DELTA AIRLINES, INC.**
Hartfield International
airport
Atlanta, GA 30320
800-221-1212

**DOMINICANA AIRLINES**
1444 Biscayne Blvd.
Miami, FL 33132
800-327-7240

**ECUATORIANA**
Miami Internaional Airport
P.O. Box 522970
Miami, FL 33152
800-328-2367

**EGYPTAIR**
720 Fifth Ave. Ste. 505
New York, NY 10019
800-334-6787

**EL AL ISRAEL AIRLINES**
850 Third Ave.
New York, NY 10022
800-223-6700

**FINNAIR**
10 E. 40th St.
New York, NY 10016
800-950-5000

**GULF AIR**
489 Fifth Ave
New York, NY 10017
800-223-1740

**GUYANA AIRWAYS**
6555 NW 36th, Ste. 207
Miami, FL 33166
800-327-8680

**HAITI TRANS AIR**
7270 N.W. 12th St., Ste.
200; Miami, FL 33126
800-545-9949

**HAWAIIAN AIRLINES**
1164 Bishop St., 8th flr.
Honolulu, HI 96813
800-367-5320

**IBERIA AIRLINES of SPAIN**
1983 Marcus Ave. Ste. 215
Lake Success, NY 11042
800-772-4642

**ICELANDAIR, INC.**
630 Fifth Ave.
New York, NY 10020

800-223-5500

**JAPAN AIR LINES, LTD.**
655 Fifth Ave.
New York, NY 10022
800-525-3663

**K.L.M.-ROYAL DUTCH AIRLINES**
437 Madison Ave.
New York, NY 10022
800-556-7777

**KOREAN AIRLINES**
1813 Wilshire, Blvd.
Los Angeles, CA 90057
800-421-8200

**KUWAIT AIR LINES**
30 Rockefeller Plaza
New York, NY 10020
800-458-9284

**LAN-CHILE AIRLINES**
PENTHOUSE
9700 South Dixie Highway
Miami, FL 33156
800-735-5526

**LASCA**
1600 NW Le-jeune Rd. Ste.
200; Miami, FL 33126
800-225-2272

**LOT-POLISH AIRLINES**
21 E. 51st St.
New York, NY 10022
800-223-0593

**LTU INTERNATIONAL AIRWAYS**
(800) 888-0200

**160**

**LUFTHANSA**
750 Lexington Ave.
New York, NY 10022
800-645-3880

**MEXICANA AIRLINES**
9841 Airport Blvd. Ste. 220
Los Angeles, CA 90045-
9990
800-531-7923

**NIGERIA AIRWAYS**
15 E. 51st St.
New York, NY 10022
212-935-2700

**NORTHWESTERN
AIRLINES**
(800) 447-4747

**NORTHWEST ORIENT
EXPRESS**
5101 North West Dr.
St. Paul, MN 55111
612-726-2111

**OLYMPIC AIRWAYS**
647 Fifth Ave.
New York, NY 10022
800-223-1226

**PHILIPPINE AIRLINES**
447 Sutter St.
San Francisco, CA 94081
800-435-9725

**QANTAS AIRWAYS**
360 Post St.
San Francisco, CA 94108
800-227-4500

**ROYAL AIR MAROC**
55 East 59th St. Ste. 17b
New York, NY 10022

800-344-6726

**ROYAL JORDANIAN
AIRLINES**
535 Fifth Ave
New York, NY 10017
800-223-0470

**SABENA-BELGIAN
WORLD AIRLINES**
125 Community Dr.
Great Neck, NY 11021
800-955-2000

**SAUDI ARABIAN
AIRLINES**
747 Third Ave.
New York, NY 10017
800-472-8342

**SCANDINAVIAN
AIRLINES SYSTEM**
138-02 Queens Blvd.
Jamaica, NY 11435
800-221-2350

**SINGAPORE AIRLINES**
510 W. Sixth St. Ste. 506
Los Angeles, CA 90014
800-742-3333

**SURINAME AIRWAYS**
5775 Blue Lagoon Dr. #320
Miami, FL 33126
800-327-6864

**SWISSAIR**
608 Fifth Ave.
New York, NY 10020
800-221-4750

**TACA INTERNATIONAL
AIRLINES**
New Orleans International
Airport

800 Airlines Highway
P.O. Box 20047
New Orleans, LA 70141
800-535-8780

**TAP AIR PORTUGAL**
399 Market St.
Newark, NJ 07105
800-221-7370

**THAI AIRWAYS**
720 Olive Way, Ste 1400
Seattle, WA 98101
800-426-5204

**TRANS WORLD
AIRWAYS, INC.**
100 Soth Bedford Rd.
Mount Kisco, New York
10549
800-892-4141

**TRINIDAD & TOBAGO
AIRLINES**
(See BIWA)

**UNITED AIRLINES**
11555 West Touhy
Chicago, IL 60666
800-241-6522

**UTA FRENCH AIRLINES**
9841 Airport Blvd., Ste.
1000; Los Angeles, CA
90045
800-282-4484

**VARIG BRAZILIAN
AIRLINES**
622 Third Ave
New York, NY 10017
800-468-2744

**VIASA-VENEZUELAN**
INTERNATIONAL
AIRWAYS
1101 Brickell Ave., 6th flr.
Miami, FL 33131
800-327-5454


**VIRGIN AIR**
C/O Cyril King Airport
U.S. Virgin Islands 00803
800-522-3084

**WORLD AIRWAYS, INC.**
P.O. Box 2332
Oakland, CA 94614
415-577-2500

**YUGOSLAV AIRLINES**
630 Fifth Ave., Ste 3155
New York, NY 10111
800-334-5890

**AIRLINES OPERATING
WITHIN THE
CARIBBEAN ZONE**

**AMERICAN EAGLE** (A
subsidiary of American
Airlines)
(800) 433-7300

**AIR BVI**
(809) 774-6500

**AIR ANGUILLA**
(809) 497-2643

**TYDEN AIR**
(809) 497-2719

**WINDWARD ISLANDS
AIRWAYS**
(809) 775-0183

162

# *APPENDIX K*

## INTERNATIONAL AIRLINES TWO-LETTER CODES

| | | | |
|---|---|---|---|
| Aer Lingus (Irish) | EI | CSA-ceslovenske Airline | OK |
| Aermexico | AM | Delta Airlines | DL |
| Aeroflot-Russian Airlines | SU | Dominicana Airlines | DO |
| Aerolineas Argentinas | AR | Eastern Airlines | EA |
| Aeroperu | PL | Ecuatoriana | EU |
| Air Canada | AC | Egyptair | MS |
| Air New Zealand | NZ | El Al Israel Airlines | LY |
| Air Jamaica | JM | Empresa Ecuatoriana | EU |
| Air Pacific | FJ | Finnair | AY |
| Air China | CA | Garuda Indonesian Airways | GA |
| Air Lanka | UL | Ghana Airways | GH |
| Air Algerie | AH | Gulf Air | GF |
| Air Afrique | RH | Guyana Airways | GY |
| Air France | AF | Hawaiian Airlines | HA |
| Air New Zealand-International | TE | Hugfelag-Icelandair | FI |
| Air India | AI | Iberia | IB |
| ALIA-Royal Jordanian Airlines | RJ | Iraqi Airways | IA |
| Alitalia | AZ | Japan Airlines | JL |
| All Nippon Airways | NH | Kenya Airways | KQ |
| Aloha airlines, Inc. | AQ | KLM-Royal Dutch Airlines | KL |
| American Airlines | AA | Korean Airlines | KE |
| Ansett Airlines of Australia | AN | Kuwait Airways | KU |
| Ansett Airlines of S. Australia | GJ | LACSA-Lineas | LR |
| Austrian Airlines | OS | Lan-chile Airlines | LA |
| Avianca | AV | LAP-Lineas Aereas Paraguayas | PZ |
| Aviateca | GU | Lloyd Aero Boliviano | LB |
| Bahamasair | UP | Lufthansa German Airlines | LH |
| British Airways | BA | Luxair-Luxembourg Airlines | LG |
| Caribbean Airways | IQ | Malaysian Airline System | MH |
| Cathay Pacific Airways | CX | Nigerian Airways | WT |
| China Airlines | CI | Olympic Airways | OA |
| Continental Airlines, Inc. | CO | Pakistan International Airlines | PK |

**163**

| | |
|---|---|
| Phillippine Airlines | PR |
| Quantas Airways | QF |
| Royal Nepal Airlines | RA |
| Royal Air Maroc | AT |
| Sabena-Belgian World Airlines | SN |
| SAS-Scandinavian Airlines | SK |
| Saudi Arabian Airline | SV |
| Singapore Airlines | SQ |
| South African Airways | SA |
| Suriname Airways | PY |
| Swissair | SR |
| TACA International Airlines | TA |
| TAP Air Portugal | TP |
| Thai Airways International | TG |
| Trinidad and Tobago Airways(BWI) | BW |
| TWA-Trans World Airlines, Inc. | TW |
| United Airlines | UA |
| UTA | UT |
| Varig, SA | RG |
| VIASA-Venezuelan | VA |
| Virgin Air | ZP |
| Yugoslav Airlines | JU |

# *APPENDIX L*

## COMPARATIVE CLOTHING SIZES

### Suits and Overcoats (men)

| American | 32 | 34 | 36 | 38 | 40 | 42 | 44 | 46 |
|---|---|---|---|---|---|---|---|---|
| Continental | 42 | 44 | 46 | 48 | 50 | 52 | 54 | 56 |
| British | 32 | 34 | 36 | 38 | 40 | 42 | 44 | 46 |

#### Dresses and Suits (women)

| American | 6 | 8 | 10 | 12 | 14 | 16 | 18 |
|---|---|---|---|---|---|---|---|
| Continental | 36 | 38 | 40 | 42 | 44 | 46 | 48 |
| British | 8 | 10 | 12 | 14 | 16 | 18 | 20 |

### Shirts (men)

| American | 14 | 14.5 | 15 | 15.5 | 16 | 16.5 | 17 | 17.5 |
|---|---|---|---|---|---|---|---|---|
| Continental | 36 | 37 | 38 | 39 | 41 | 42 | 43 | 44 |
| British | 14 | 14.5 | 15 | 15.5 | 16 | 16.5 | 17 | 17.5 |

### Women's Hosiery

| American | 8 | 8.5 | 9 | 9.5 | 10 | 10.5 |
|---|---|---|---|---|---|---|
| Continental | 0 | 1 | 2 | 3 | 4 | 5 |
| British | 8 | 8.5 | 9 | 9.5 | 10 | 10.5 |

### Socks

| American | 8.5 | 9 | 9.5 | 10 | 10.5 | 11 | 11.5 |
|---|---|---|---|---|---|---|---|
| Continental | 36/37 | 37/38 | 38/39 | 39/40 | 40/41 | 41/42 | 42/43 |
| British | 8.5 | 9 | 9.5 | 10 | 10.5 | 11 | 11.5 |

### Shoes(Men)

| American | 7 | 8 | 8.5 | 9.5 | 10.5 | 11 | 11.5 | 12 | 13 |
|---|---|---|---|---|---|---|---|---|---|
| Continental | 39.5 | 41 | 42 | 43 | 44 | 44.5 | 45 | 46 | 47 |
| British | 6 | 7 | 7.5 | 8.5 | 9.5 | 10 | 10.5 | 11 | 12 |

### Shoes (women)

| American | 6 | 6.5 | 7 | 7.5 | 8 | 8.5 | 9 |
| Continental | 38 | 38 | 39 | 30 | 40 | 41 | 42 |
| British | 4.5 | 5 | 5.5 | 6 | 6.5 | 7 | 7.5 |

## Children's Clothes

| American | 2 | 4 | 6 | 8 | 10 | 12 | 14 |

**Continental**

| Height (cm) | 115 | 125 | 135 | 150 | 155 | 160 | 165 |
| Age | 5 | 7 | 9 | 12 | 13 | 14 | 15 |

**British**

| Height (in) | 38 | 43 | 48 | 55 | 58 | 60 | 62 |
| Age | 2-3 | 4-5 | 6-7 | 9-10 | 11 | 12 | 13 |

## Shoes (children)

| American | 1 | 2 | 3 | 4.5 | 5.5 | 6.5 | 8 | 9 | 10 | 11 | 12 | 13 |
| Continental | 32 | 33 | 34 | 36 | 37 | 38.5 | 24 | 25 | 27 | 28 | 29 | 30 |
| British | 13 | 1 | 2 | 3 | 4 | 5.5 | 7 | 8 | 9 | 10 | 11 | 12 |

166

# APPENDIX *M*

## INTERNATIONAL WEIGHTS AND MEASURES

## CONVERSION TABLES

### DISTANCE

1 mile (Mi) = 1.609 Kilometers (Km)
1 kilometer (Km) = .6214 miles (Mi)
1 inch = 2.54 centimeter (cm)
1 centimeter = .3937 inches (in)
1 foot = .3048 meters (m)
1 meter = 3.281 feet (ft)

### VOLUME (capacity)

### IMPERIAL WEIGHT MEASURE

1 Imperial gallon = 4.5 liters (L)
1 liter (L) = .222 Imperial gallon (IGal)
Imperial gallons are larger than U.S. gallons
1mperial gallon = 1.2 U.S. gallons

### TEMPERATURE

Degrees Fahrenheit (F⁰) = 9/5 x Degrees Centigrade + 32
Degrees Centigrade/Celsuis (C⁰) = (5/9 Degrees Fahrenheit - 32)

### SPEED

1 Mile per hour (MPH) = 1.6 (KMH)
1 kilometer per hour (KMH) = .625 (MPH)

### WEIGHTS

1 ounce (oz) = 28.349 grams (gm)
1 gram (gm) = .0353 ounces (oz)
1 pound (lb) = .4536 Kilograms (Kg)
1 Kilogram (Kg) = 2.205 pounds (lb)

**167**

## QUICK CONVERSION CHART

| In = Cm | Kg = Lb | Gal = L |
|---|---|---|
| 1 = 2.54 | 1 = 2.21 | 1 = 3.79 |
| 2 = 5.08 | 2 = 4.41 | 2 = 7.57 |
| 3 = 7.63 | 3 = 6.61 | 3 = 11.35 |
| 4 = 10.16 | 4 = 8.82 | 4 = 15.14 |
| 5 = 12.70 | 5 = 11.02 | 5 = 18.93 |
| 6 = 15.24 | 6 = 13.23 | 6 = 22.71 |
| 7 = 17.78 | 7 = 15.43 | 7 = 26.50 |
| 8 = 20.32 | 8 = 17.64 | 8 = 30.28 |
| 9 = 22.86 | 9 = 19.84 | 9 = 34.16 |
| 10 = 25.40 | 10 = 22.05 | 10 = 37.94 |
| 11 = 27.94 | 50 = 110.23 | 50 = 189.70 |
| 12 = 30.48 | 100 = 220.46 | 100 = 379.40 |

| Cm = In | Mi = Km | L = Gal |
|---|---|---|
| 1 = 0.40 | 1 = 1.61 | 1 = 0.26 |
| 2 = 0.80 | 2 = 3.22 | 2 = 0.53 |
| 3 = 1.20 | 3 = 4.83 | 3 = 0.79 |
| 4 = 1.60 | 4 = 6.44 | 4 = 1.06 |
| 5 = 2.00 | 5 = 8.05 | 5 = 1.32 |
| 6 = 2.40 | 6 = 9.66 | 6 = 1.58 |
| 7 = 2.80 | 7 = 11.27 | 7 = 1.85 |
| 8 = 3.20 | 8 = 12.88 | 8 = 2.11 |
| 9 = 3.50 | 9 = 14.48 | 9 = 2.38 |
| 10 = 3.90 | 10 = 16.09 | 10 = 2.64 |
| 11 = 4.30 | 50 = 80.47 | 50 = 13.20 |
| 12 = 4.70 | 100 = 160.90 | 100 = 26.40 |

| Lb = Kg | Km = Mi | TEMPERATURE |
|---|---|---|
| | | F = C |
| 1 = 0.45 | 1 = 0.62 | 32 = 0 |
| 2 = 0.91 | 2 = 1.24 | 40 = 5 |
| 3 = 1.36 | 3 = 1.86 | 50 = 10 |
| 4 = 1.81 | 4 = 2.49 | 60 = 15 |
| 5 = 2.27 | 5 = 3.11 | 70 = 20 |
| 6 = 2.72 | 6 = 3.73 | 75 = 25 |
| 7 = 3.18 | 7 = 4.35 | 85 = 30 |
| 8 = 3.63 | 8 = 4.97 | 105 = 40 |
| 9 = 4.08 | 9 = 5.59 | 140 = 60 |
| 10 = 4.54 | 10 = 6.21 | 175 = 80 |
| 50 = 22.68 | 50 = 31.07 | |
| 100 = 45.36 | 100 = 62.14 | |

**SPEED**
**MPH = KMH**
 20 = 32
 30 = 48
 40 = 64
 50 = 80
 60 = 96
 70 = 112
 80 = 128
 90 = 144
100 = 160

# APPENDIX N

## INTERNATIONAL SYSTEMS
## OF WEIGHTS & MEASURES

| | |
|---|---|
| AFGHANISTAN | M |
| ALBANIA | M |
| ANGOLA | M |
| ANGUILLA | M,I |
| ANTIGUA & BARBUDA | I* |
| ARGENTINA | M |
| ARMENIA | M |
| AUSTRALIA | M |
| AUSTRIA | M |
| AZERBAIJAN | M |
| BAHAMAS | I |
| BAHRAIN | M |
| BANGLADESH | I* |
| BARBADOS | M |
| BELGIUM | M |
| BELIZE | I |
| BERMUDA | M,I |
| BHUTAN | M |
| BOLIVIA | M |
| BOTSWANA | M |
| BRAZIL | M |
| BRITISH VIRGIN IS | I |
| BRUNEI | I** |
| BULGARIA | M |
| BURKINA FASO | M |
| BURUNDI | M |
| BYELARUS | M |
| CAMBODIA | M |
| CAMEROON | M |
| CANADA | M |
| CAYMAN IS | I |
| CENTRAL AFRICAN REP. | M |
| CHAD | M |
| CHILE | M |
| CHINA, PEOPLES REP. | M* |
| CHINA, TAIWAN | M |
| COLOMBIA | M |
| COMOROS | M |
| CONGO, PEOPLE'S REP. | M |
| COSTA RICA | M |
| COTE D'IVOIRE | M |
| CUBA | M |
| CYPRUS | M*,I* |
| CZECHOSLOVAKIA | M |
| DENMARK | M |
| DOMINICA | I* |
| DOMINICAN REP. | I* |
| ECUADOR | M |
| EGYPT | M* |
| EL SALVADOR | M* |
| EQUATORIAL GUINEA | M |
| ESTONIA | M |
| ETHIOPIA | M* |
| FIJI | M |
| FINLAND | M |
| FRANCE | M |
| FRENCH GUIANA | M |
| FRENCH ANTILLES | M |
| FRENCH POLYNESIA | M |
| GABON | M |
| GEORGIA | M |
| GERMANY | M |
| GHANA | M |
| GREECE | M |

170

| | | | |
|---|---|---|---|
| GRENADA | M | MAURITANIA | M |
| GUADELOUPE | M | MAURITIUS | M |
| GUATEMALA | M | MEXICO | M |
| GUINEA | M | MOLDOVA | M |
| GUINEA-BISSAU | M | MONACO | M |
| GUYANA | M | MONGOLIA | M |
| HAITI | M | MONTSERRAT | I* |
| HONDURAS | M* | MOROCCO | M |
| HONG KONG | M | MOZAMBIQUE | M |
| HUNGARY | M | NAMIBIA | M |
| ICELAND | M | NAURU | M |
| INDIA | M,I* | NETHERLANDS | M |
| INDONESIA | M | NETHERLANDS ANTILLES | M |
| IRAN | M* | NEW ZEALAND | M |
| IRAQ | M* | NICARAGUA | M* |
| IRELAND | I* | NIGER | M |
| ISRAEL | M | NIGERIA | M |
| ITALY | M | NORWAY | M |
| JAMAICA | M,I | OMAN | M,I* |
| JAPAN | M | PAKISTAN | M,I* |
| JORDAN | M | PANAMA | M,I |
| KAZAKHSTAN | M | PAPUA NEW GUINEA | M |
| KENYA | M | PARAGUAY | M |
| KOREA, NORTH | M | PERU | M |
| KOREA, SOUTH | M* | PHILIPPINES | M |
| KUWAIT | M | PORTUGAL | M |
| KYRGYZSTAN | M | QATAR | M* |
| LAOS | M | REP. OF CAPE VERDE | M |
| LATVIA | M | ROMANIA | M |
| LEBANON | M | RUSSIA | M |
| LESOTHO | M | RWANDA | M |
| LIBERIA | I | SAN MARINO | M |
| LIBYA | M | SAO TOME & PRINCIPE | M |
| LIECHTENSTEIN | M | SAUDI ARABIA | M |
| LITUANIA | M | SENEGAL | M |
| LUXEMBOURG | M | SEYCHELLES | I* |
| MADAGASCAR | M | SIERRA LEONE | M |
| MALAWI | M | SINGAPORE | M* |
| MALAYSIA | M* | SOMALIA | M,I |
| MALI | M | SOUTH AFRICA | M |
| MALTA | M | SPAIN | M |
| MARTINIQUE | M | SRI LANKA | M* |

| | |
|---|---|
| ST. VINCENT | I |
| ST. KITTS | I |
| ST. LUCIA | I |
| ST.PIERRE & MIQUELON | M |
| SUDAN | I* |
| SURINAME | M |
| SWEDEN | M |
| SWITZERLAND | M |
| SYRIA | M |
| TAJIKISTAN | M |
| TANZANIA | M |
| THAILAND | M* |
| THE GAMBIA | I* |
| TOGO | M |
| TONGA | M |
| TRINIDAD & TOBAGO | I* |
| TUNISIA | M |
| TURKEY | M |
| TURKMENISTAN | M |
| TURKS & CAICOS | I |
| UGANDA | M |
| UKRAINE | M |
| UNITED ARAB EMIRATES | |
| | I,M |
| UNITED KINGDOM | I* |
| URUGUAY | M |
| UZBEKISTAN | M |
| VENEZUELA | M |
| VIETNAM | M |
| YEMEN, P.D.M. | I* |
| YUGOSLAVIA | M |
| ZAIRE | M |
| ZAMBIA | M |
| ZIMBABWE | M |

metrication program is being introduced.

**I\*\*** = Imperial and /or local systems of Weights and Measures are being used.

**M** = Metric system of Weights and Measures is in use.

**M\*** = Traditional systems of Weights and Measures is still in use.

**M,I** = Metric and Imperial systems of Weights and Measures are in use.

----------------------

**I** = Imperial system of Weights and Measures is in use.

**I\*** = Imperial system of Weights and Measures is in use, however

# APPENDIX O

## INTERNATIONAL GUIDE TO TIPPING*

|  | HOTELS | TAXIS | OTHERS |
|---|---|---|---|
| ANDORRA | 10-20% | 10% | YES |
| ANGUILLA | D | D | YES |
| ANTIGUA & BARBUDA | 10% | D | YES |
| ARGENTINA | 10-22% | 10% | YES |
| ARMENIA | YES | OD | OD |
| AUSTRALIA | 10% | D | YES |
| AUSTRIA | 10-15% | 10% | YES |
| AZERBAIJAN | YES | OD | OD |
| BAHAMAS | 15% | 15% | YES |
| BANGLADESH | 5-10% | 5-10% | YES |
| BARBADOS | 10% | 10% | YES |
| BELARUS | YES | OD | OD |
| BELGIUM | 15% | D | YES |
| BELIZE | D 10% | D | YES |
| BENIN | D | D | D |
| BOLIVIA | 10-23% | D | YES |
| BRAZIL | D | YES | |
| BURMA | 10% | 10% | YES |
| CAMEROON | 10% | D | YES |
| CANADA | 15-20% | 15-20% | YES |
| CAYMAN IS | NC 10-15% | NC | YES |
| CHILE | 10% | NC | YES |
| CHINA, PEOPLES REP. | F | F | F |
| CHINA, TAIWAN | D 10% | D 10% | YES |
| COLUMBIA | 10% | NC | YES |
| COSTA RICA | 10% | NC | YES |
| COTE D'IVOIRE | 5-10% | 5-10% | YES |
| CYPRUS | 10% | NT | YES |
| CZECHOSLOVAKIA | OD 5-10% | 5-10% | YES |

173

| | | | |
|---|---|---|---|
| DENMARK | 15% | upto 15% | YES |
| DOMINICA | 10% | D | YES |
| DOMINICAN REP. | 10% | | |
| ECUADOR | 10% | NC | YES |
| EGYPT | 10-12% | 10% | YES |
| ETHIOPIA | 5-10% | NC | YES |
| FIJI | D | D | YES |
| FINLAND | 14-15% | NT | YES |
| FRANCE | upto 25% | 15% | YES |
| FRENCH GUIANA | 12 1/2% | NC | YES |
| GEORGIA | | | |
| GERMANY | 10% | 5% | YES |
| GHANA | YES | YES | YES |
| GIBRALTAR | 10-12% | 10% | YES |
| GREECE | 10-15% | 10% | YES |
| GRENADA | D | D | YES |
| GUADELOUPE | 10-15% | YES | |
| GUATEMALA | 10% | 10% | YES |
| GUINEA | D | D | YES |
| GUYANA | 10% | 10% | YES |
| HAITI | NC 10% | D | YES |
| HONDURAS | 10% | 10% | YES |
| HONG KONG | 10-15% | 10% | YES |
| HUNGARY | OD 10-15% | YES | YES |
| ICELAND | NC | NC | NC |
| INDIA | 10% | NC | YES |
| INDONESIA | NC 10% | NC 10% | YES |
| IRELAND | 10-15% | YES | YES |
| ISRAEL | 10% | NC | YES |
| ITALY | 12-15% | 15% | YES |
| JAMAICA | 15% | 10-20% | YES |
| JAPAN | NC 10-20% | NC | YES |
| JORDAN | 10% | 10% | YES |
| KAZAKHSTAN | OD | OD | OD |
| KENYA | 10-15% | 10% | YES |
| KOREA, SOUTH | NC 10% | NC 10-15% | YES |
| KUWAIT | 10% | D | YES |
| KYRGYZSTAN | OD | OD | OD |
| LATVIA | NT | 10-20% | YES |
| LIBERIA | 10-15% | NC | YES |
| LIECHTENSTEIN | 10-15% | | |
| LITHUANIA | NC | NC | NC |

**174**

| | | | |
|---|---|---|---|
| LUXEMBOURG | NC 10-20% | 15-20% | YES |
| MALAYSIA | NC 10% | NC 10% | YES |
| MALTA | 10% | 10% | YES |
| MARTINIQUE | 10-15% | D | YES |
| MEXICO | 7-15% | D | YES |
| MOLDOVA | OD | OD | OD |
| MONTSERRAT | 10% | 10% | YES |
| MOROCCO | 10-15% | 10-15% | YES |
| NEPAL | | | YES |
| NETHERLANDS | 15% | 10-15% | YES |
| NEW CALEDONIA | | F | F |
| NEW ZEALAND | NC 10% | NC | |
| NICARAGUA | 10% | NC | YES |
| NIGERIA | 10% | D | YES |
| NORWAY | 15% | D | YES |
| PAKISTAN | 5-10% | D | YES |
| PANAMA | 10-15% | NC | YES |
| PAPUA NEW GUINEA | NC | NC | NC |
| PARAGUAY | 10% | 5-12% | YES |
| PERU | 5-10% | NC | YES |
| PHILIPPINES | 10% | D 10% | YES |
| POLAND | 10% | 10% | YES |
| PORTUGAL | 10-15% | 15% | YES |
| ROMANIA | NC | NC | |
| RUSSIA | 10-15% | 10-15% | YES |
| SAUDI ARABIA | 10-15% | NC | YES |
| SENEGAL | 10% | D | YES |
| SEYCHELLES | 10% | D | YES |
| SINGAPORE | OD | 10% | OD |
| SOUTH AFRICA | 10% | 10% | YES |
| SPAIN | 5-10% | 10-15% | YES |
| SRI LANKA | 10% | D | YES |
| ST. KITTS | D | D | YES |
| ST. LUCIA | 10% | 10% | YES |
| ST. VINCENT | 10-15% | 10-15% | YES |
| ST. MAARTEN | 10% | 10% | YES |
| SURINAME | 10% | NC | YES |
| SWEDEN | 12-15% | 10-15% | YES |
| SWITZERLAND | 12-15% | 12-15% | YES |
| TAJIKISTAN | OD | OD | OD |
| TANZANIA | 5% | (OD) D | YES |
| THAILAND | D 10% | NC | YES |

**175**

| | | | |
|---|---|---|---|
| **TOGO** | OD | OD | |
| **TRINIDAD & TOBAGO** | 10% | 10-15% | YES |
| **TUNISIA** | 10% | 10% | YES |
| **TURKEY** | 10-15% | D | YES |
| **TURKMENISTAN** | OD | OD | OD |
| **UKRAINE** | OD | OD | OD |
| **UNITED KINGDOM** | 12-15% | 10-15% | YES |
| **URUGUAY** | 10% | 10% | YES |
| **UZBEKISTAN** | OD | OD | OD |
| **VENEZUELA** | 10% | NC | YES |
| **YUGOSLAVIA** | 10% | 10% | YES |
| **ZAIRE** | 10% | D | YES |
| **ZAMBIA** | 10% | OD | YES |

**xxx**    YES, persons who perform other services such as porters, luggage handlers, door persons, etc. may be tipped or may expect to be tipped. Tipping and amount of tip is at your discretion.

**D**   =   Tipping is expected. Amount of tip is at your discretion.

**OF**   =   Tipping is Officially Discouraged although privately welcome.

**NC**   =   Tipping is not customary, nevertheless welcome.

**NT**   =   Not usually tipped

**F**   =   Tipping is prohibited

# APPENDIX  P

## INTERNATIONAL TIME ZONES

(TIME DIFFERENCE, IN HOURS, BETWEEN U.S.EASTERN STANDARD TIME AND FOREIGN CAPITAL CITIES)

| COUNTRIES | HOURS |
|---|---|
| AFGHANISTAN | 9.5 |
| ALBANIA | 6 |
| ALGERIA** | 6 |
| AMERICAN SAMOA | -6 |
| ANDORRA | 6 |
| ANGUILLA | 1 |
| ANTIGUA & BARBUDA | 1 |
| ARGENTINA | 2 |
| ARMENIA | 8 |
| AUSTRALIA* | 15 |
| AUSTRIA | 6 |
| AZERBAIJAN | 8 |
| BAHAMAS | 0 |
| BAHRAIN | 8 |
| BANGLADESH | 11 |
| BARBADOS | 1 |
| BELGIUM | 6 |
| BELIZE | -1 |
| BENIN | 6 |
| BERMUDA | 1 |
| BHUTAN | 11 |
| BOLIVIA | 1 |
| BOTSWANA | 7 |
| BRAZIL* | 2 |
| BRITISH VIRGIN IS | 1 |
| BRUNEI | 13 |
| BULGARIA | 7 |
| BURKINA FASO | 5 |
| BURMA | 11.5 |
| BURUNDI | 7 |
| BYELARUS | 8 |
| CAMBODIA | 12 |
| CAMEROON | 6 |
| CANADA* | 0 |
| CAYMAN IS | 0 |
| CENTRAL AFRICAN REP. | 6 |
| CHAD | 6 |
| CHILE** | 1 |
| CHINA, PEOPLES REP. | 13 |
| CHINA, TAIWAN | 13 |
| COLUMBIA | 0 |
| COMOROS | 8 |
| CONGO, PEOPLE'S REP | 6 |
| COSTA RICA | -1 |
| COTE D'IVOIRE | 5 |
| CUBA** | 0 |
| CYPRUS | 7 |
| CZECH REP. | 6 |
| DENMARK | 6 |
| DOMINICA | 1 |
| DOMINICAN REP. | 0 |
| ECUADOR | 0 |
| EGYPT | 7 |
| EL SALVADOR | -1 |
| ESTONIA | 8 |

| | | | |
|---|---|---|---|
| **EQUATORIAL GUINEA** | 6 | **KOREA, NORTH** | 14 |
| **ETHIOPIA** | 8 | **KUWAIT** | 8 |
| **FAEROW IS** | 5 | **KYRGYZSTAN** | 11 |
| **FIJI** | 17 | **LAOS** | 12 |
| **FINLAND** | 7 | **LATVIA** | 8 |
| **FRANCE** | 6 | **LEBANON** | 7 |
| **FRENCH POLYNESIA** | -5 | **LESOTHO** | 7 |
| **FRENCH ANTILLES** | 1 | **LIBERIA** | 5 |
| **FRENCH GUIANA** | 2 | **LIBYA** | 6 |
| **GABON** | 6 | **LIECHTENSTEIN** | 6 |
| **GEORGIA** | 6 | **LITUANIA** | 8 |
| **GHANA** | 5 | **LUXEMBOURG** | 6 |
| **GIBRALTAR** | 6 | **MADAGASCAR** | 8 |
| **GREECE** | 7 | **MALAWI** | 7 |
| **GREENLAND** | 2 | **MALAYSIA\*** | 13 |
| **GRENADA** | 1 | **MALDIVES** | 10 |
| **GUADELOUPE** | 1 | **MALI** | 5 |
| **GUAM** | 15 | **MALTA** | 6 |
| **GUANTANAMO BAY** | 0 | **MARSHALL IS** | 17 |
| **GUATEMALA** | -1 | **MAURITANIA** | 5 |
| **GUINEA** | 5 | **MAURITIUS** | 9 |
| **GUINEA-BISSAU** | 5 | **MAYOTTE IS** | 8 |
| **GUYANA** | 2 | **MEXICO\*** | 1 |
| **HAITI** | 0 | **MICRONESIA\*** | 16 |
| **HONDURAS** | -1 | **MOLDOVA** | 8 |
| **HONG KONG** | 13 | **MONACO** | 6 |
| **HUNGARY** | 6 | **MONGOLIA** | 13 |
| **ICELAND** | 5 | **MONTSERRAT** | 1 |
| **INDIA** | 10.5 | **MOROCCO** | 5 |
| **INDONESIA\*** | 12 | **MOZAMBIQUE** | 7 |
| **IRAN** | 8.5 | **MUSTIQUE** | 1 |
| **IRAQ** | 8 | **NAMIBIA** | 7 |
| **IRELAND** | 5 | **NAURU** | 17 |
| **ISRAEL** | 7 | **NEPAL** | 10.5 |
| **ITALY** | 6 | **NETHERLANDS** | 6 |
| **JAMAICA\*\*** | 0 | **NETHERLANDS ANTILLES** | 1 |
| **JAPAN** | 14 | **NEW CALEDONIA** | 16 |
| **JORDAN** | 7 | **NEW ZEALAND\*\*** | 17 |
| **KAZAKHSTAN** | 11 | **NICARAGUA** | -1 |
| **KENYA** | 8 | **NIGER** | 6 |
| **KIRIBATI** | -5 | **NIGERIA** | 6 |
| **KOREA, SOUTH** | 14 | **NORWAY** | 6 |

178

| | | | | |
|---|---|---|---|---|
| OMAN | 9 | TANZANIA | 8 |
| PAKISTAN | 10 | THAILAND | 12 |
| PANAMA | 0 | THE GAMBIA | 5 |
| PAPUA NEW GUINEA | 15 | TOGO | 5 |
| PARAGUAY | 2 | TONGA | 18 |
| PERU | 0 | TRANSKEI | 7 |
| PHILIPPINES | 13 | TRINIDAD & TOBAGO | 1 |
| POLAND | 6 | TUNISIA | 6 |
| PORTUGAL | 5 | TURKEY | 7 |
| PUERTO RICO | 1 | TURKMENISTAN | 10 |
| QATAR | 8 | TURKS & CAICOS** | 0 |
| REP. OF DJIBOUTI | 8 | U.S.A. | 0 |
| REP. OF CAPE VERDE | 4 | UGANDA | 8 |
| REUNION IS | 9 | UKRAINE | 8 |
| ROMANIA | 7 | UNION IS | 1 |
| RUSSIA | 8 | UNITED KINGDOM** | 5 |
| RWANDA | 7 | UNITED ARAB EMIRATES | 9 |
| SAIPAN | 15 | URUGUAY | 2 |
| SAN MARINO | 6 | UZBEKISTAN | 11 |
| SAO TOME & PRINCIPE | 5 | VATICAN CITY | 6 |
| SAUDI ARABIA | 8 | VENEZUELA | 1 |
| SENEGAL | 5 | WESTERN SAMOA | -6 |
| SEYCHELLES | 9 | YEMEN, .P.D.R. | 8 |
| SIERRA LEONE | 5 | YEMEN, ARAB REP. | 8 |
| SINGAPORE | 13 | YUGOSLAVIA | 6 |
| SOLOMON IS | 16 | ZAIRE* | 6 |
| SOMALIA | 8 | ZAMBIA | 7 |
| SOUTH AFRICA | 7 | ZIMBABWE | 7 |
| SPAIN | 6 | | |
| SRI LANKA | 10.5 | | |
| ST. MARTIN | 1 | | |
| ST. LUCIA | 1 | | |
| ST. KITTS-NEVIS | 1 | | |
| ST. PIERRE & MIQUELON | 2 | | |
| ST. VINCENT | 1 | | |
| SUDAN | 7 | | |
| SURINAME | 2 | | |
| SWAZILAND | 7 | | |
| SWEDEN | 6 | | |
| SWITZERLAND | 6 | | |
| SYRIA | 7 | | |
| TAJIKISTAN | 11 | | |

\*       Countries with multiple Time Zones. Hours indicated may be different depending on your location in these countries.

\*\*       Countries with varying time, depending on the month.

**179**

# APPENDIX  Q

## INTERNATIONAL ELECTRICITY
## REQUIREMENTS

| COUNTRIES: | (Volts/AC) |
|---|---|
| AFGHANISTAN | 20/50 AC |
| ALGERIA | 110-115/50, 220/50 AC* |
| ANDORRA | 125/50 AC |
| ANGUILLA | 220 |
| ANTIGUA | 110/60 AC |
| ARGENTINA | 220/60 AC |
| ARMENIA | 220/50 |
| AUSTRALIA | 240 AC |
| AUSTRIA | 220/50 |
| AZERBAIJAN | 220/50 |
| BAHAMAS | 120/60 AC |
| BAHRAIN | 220/50 AC |
| BANGLADESH | 220 AC |
| BARBADOS | 110/50 AC |
| BELGIUM | 220/50 AC |
| BELIZE | 110/220/60 AC |
| BENIN | 220/50 |
| BERMUDA | 110/60 AC |
| BHUTAN | 110-220/50 AC* |
| BOTSWANA | 220 |
| BRAZIL+ | 110/60; 220/60, 127/60 AC* |
| BRITISH VIRGIN IS | 115-210/60 AC |
| BULGARIA | 220/50 AC |
| BURKINA FASO | 220/50 |
| BURMA | 220/50 AC |
| BURUNDI | 220/50 |
| BYELARUS | 220/50 |

| COUNTRIES: | (Volts/AC) |
|---|---|
| CAMEROON | 110-220 |
| CANADA | 110/60 AC |
| CAYMAN ISLANDS | 110/60 AC |
| CENTRAL AF. REP. | 220 |
| CHAD | 220 |
| CHILE+ | 220/50 AC |
| CHINA | 110/50 |
| CHINA, TAIWAN | 110/60 AC |
| COLOMBIA | 150/60 AC, 110/60** |
| COMOROS | 220/50 |
| CONGO, REP. | 220/50 |
| COSTA RICA | 110/60 AC |
| COTE D'IVOIRE | 220/50 AC |
| CUBA | 110/60 |
| CYPRUS++ | 240/50 AC |
| CZECH REP. | 220/50 AC |
| DENMARK | 220/50 |
| DOMINICA | 220-240/50 AC |
| DOMINICAN REP. | 110/60 AC |
| ECUADOR | 110/60 AC |
| EGYPT | 220/50, 110-120/50* |
| EL SALVADOR | 110/60 |
| ESTONIA | 220/50 |
| EQUAT. GUINEA | 220/50 |
| ETHIOPIA | 220/60 AC |
| FIJI | 240/50 AC |
| FINLAND | 220/60 AC |
| FRANCE | 220/50 |
| FRENCH GUIANA | 220 & 110/50 AC |

180

| | | | |
|---|---|---|---|
| GABON | 220/240/50 | MALAYSIA | 220/50 AC |
| GEORGIA | 220/50 | MALI | 220 |
| GERMANY | 220/50 AC | MALTA | 240/50 AC |
| GHANA | 220-240/50 AC | MARTINIQUE | 220/50 AC |
| GIBRALTAR | 240-250/50 AC | MAURITANIA | 220/50 |
| GREECE+ | 220/50 AC | MAURITIUS | 220/230 |
| GRENADA | 220-240/50 Ac | MEXICO | 110/60 AC |
| GUADELOUPE | 220/50 AC | MICRONESIA | 110/60 AC |
| GUAM | 120/60 AC | MOLDOVA | 220/50 |
| GUATEMALA | 110/60 AC | MONTSERRAT | 230/60 AC |
| GUINEA | 220/50 | MOROCCO | 110-120/50 AC |
| GUYANA | 110-120/60 AC | MOZAMBIQUE | 220/50 |
| HAITI | 110/60 AC | NAMIBIA | 220/240/60 |
| HONDURAS | 110 or 220/60 AC* | NEPAL | 220/50 AC |
| HONG KONG++ | 200-220/60 AC | NETHERLANDS ANT. | 110-130/50,120/60AC* |
| HUNGARY | 220/50 AC | NETHERLANDS | 220/50 AC |
| ICELAND | 220/50 AC | NEW CALEDONIA | 220/50 AC |
| INDIA+ | 220/50 AC | NICARAGUA | 110/60 AC |
| INDONESIA | 220/50 AC | NIGER | 220-240/50 |
| IRAN | 220/50 | NIGERIA++ | 220/50 AC |
| IRAQ | 220 DC | NORWAY | 220/50 AC |
| IRELAND | 220/50 AC | OMAN | 220/240/50 |
| ISRAEL | 220/50 AC | PAKISTAN | 220/240/50 AC |
| ITALY | 220/50, 110-127/50 AC* | PANAMA | 110/60 AC |
| JAMAICA | 110/50 AC | PAPUA NEW GUINEA | 240 AC |
| JAPAN | 110/50, 100/60 AC* | PARAGUAY+ | 220/50 AC |
| JORDAN | 220/50 AC | PERU | 220/60 AC |
| KAZAKHSTAN | 220/50 | PHILIPPINES | 220/60 AC |
| KENYA | 220/50 AC | POLAND | 220/50 AC |
| KOREA, SOUTH | 110/60 AC | PORTUGAL | 210-220/50 AC |
| KUWAIT | 240/50 AC | PUERTO RICO | 110-115/60 AC |
| KYRGYZSTAN | 220/50 | QATAR | 220/50 |
| LATVIA | 220/50 | REP. OF DJIBOUTI | 220/50 |
| LEBANON | 110-220/50 | CAPE VERDE | 220/50 |
| LESOTHO | 220 AC | ROMANIA | 220/50 |
| LIBERIA | 120/60 AC | RUSSIA | 220/50 |
| LIBYA | 220/50 | RWANDA | 220/50 |
| LIECHTENSTEIN | 220/50 AC | SAUDI ARABIA | 110 & 120/60 AC |
| LITHUANIA | 220/50 | SENEGAL | 110 & 220/50 AC |
| LUXEMBOURG | 220/110 | SEYCHELLES | 240/50 AC |
| MADAGASCAR | 220/50 | SIERRA LEONE | 220/50 |
| MALAWI | 220 | | |

| | |
|---|---|
| SINGAPORE++ | 230-250 AC |
| SAO TOME & PRIN. | 220/50 |
| SOMALIA | 220/50 |
| SOUTH AFRICA | 220-230/50 AC |
| SPAIN | 110-220/50 AC |
| SRI LANKA | 230-240/50 AC |
| ST. KITTS | 230/60 AC |
| ST. LUCIA | 220/50 AC |
| ST. MARTIN | 220/60 AC |
| ST. VINCENT | 220-230/50 AC |
| SUDAN | 240 AC |
| SURINAME | 110-115/60 AC |
| SWAZILAND | 240/50 |
| SWEDEN+ | 220/50 AC |
| SWITZERLAND | 220/50 AC |
| TAJIKISTAN | 220/50 |
| TANZANIA | 240/50/60 AC |
| THAILAND | 220/50 AC |
| TOGO | 220/50 AC |
| TONGA | 220 AC |
| TRINIDAD & TOB. | 110/60 AC |
| TUNISIA 110-115/50, 220/50 AC* | |
| TURKEY | 220/50 |
| TURKMENISTAN | 220/50 |
| TURKS & CAICOS | 110/60 |
| U.S.A | 110-115/60 AC |
| UKRAINE | 220/50 |
| UNITED ARAB EM.240/415 AC | |
| UNITED KINGDOM | 220/50 AC |
| URUGUAY | 220/50 AC |
| UZBEKISTAN | 220/50 |
| VENEZUELA | 110/60 AC |
| YEMEN, ARAB REP. | 220/50 AC |
| YEMEN, P.D.R | 220/240/50 |
| YUGOSLAVIA | 220/50 AC |
| ZAIRE | 220/50 |
| ZAMBIA | 220/50 AC |
| ZIMBABWE++ | 220/240/50 |

------------------

\*              Electricity requirements vary
in some parts of the country.

+  Some parts of the country still use DC.

++ In some or most parts of the country,
you may need three square pin plugs.

**182**

# *APPENDIX R*

## INTERNATIONAL TELEPHONE DIALING CODES

**COUNTRY/COUNTRY**
**City & Codes          CODE**


**Algeria          213**

City code not required.

**American Samoa    684**

City code not required.

**Andorra          33**

Use 628 for all cities.

**Anguilla         809**

Dial 1 + 809 + Local Number.

**Antigua          809**
Dial 1 + 809 + Local Number.

**Argentina        54**

Bahia Blanca 91. Buenos Aires 1, Cordoba
51, Corrientes 783, La Plata 21,
Mar Del Plata 23, Mendoza 61, Merlo 220,
Posadas 752, Resistencia 772,
Rio Cuarto 586, Rosario 41, San Juan 64,
San Rafael 627, Santa Fe 42, Tandil 293

**Aruba            297**
Use 8 for all cities.
**Ascension Island    247**
City code not required.

**Australia        61**
Adelaide 8, Ballarat 53, Brisbane 7,
Canberra 62, Darwin 89, Geelong 52,
Gold Coast 75, Hobart 02, Launceston 03,
Melbourne 3, Newcastle 49, Perth 9,
Sydne 2, Toowoomba 76, Townsville 77,
Wollongong 42

**Austria          43**

Bludenz 5552, Graz 316, Innsbruck 5222,
Kitzbuhel 5356, Klagenfut 4222,
Krems An Der Donau 2732, Linz Donau
732, Neunkirchen Niederosterreich 2635,
Salzburg 662, St. Polten 2742, Vienna 1,
Villach 4242, Wels 7242,
Wiener Neustadt 2622

**Bahamas          809**

Dial 1 + 809 + Local Number.

**Bahrain**          973
City code not required.

**Bangladesh**          880
Barisal 431, Bogra 51, Chittagong 31,


Comilla 81, Dhaka 2, Khulna 41,
Maulabi Bazar 861, Mymensingh 91,
Rajshaki 721, Sylhet 821

**Barbados**          809


Dial 1 + 809 + Local Number.

**Belgium**          32
Antwerp 3, Bruges 50, Brussels 2, Charleroi
71, Courtrai 56, Ghent 91, Hasselt 11,
La Louviere 64, Leuven 16, Libramont 61,
Liege 41, Malines 15, Mons 65,
Namur 81, Ostend 59, Verviers 87

**Belize**          501
Belize City (City code not required),
Belmopan 08, Benque Viejo Del Carmen
093, Corozal Town 04, Dangviga 05,
Independence 06, Orange Walk 03,
Punta Gorda 07, San Ignacio 092

**Benin**          229
City code not required.

**Bermuda**          809
Dial 1 + 809 + Local Number.
**Bolivia**          591
Cochabamba 42, Cotoga 388, Guayafamerin
47, La Belgica 923, La Paz 2, Mineros 984,
Montero 92, Oruro 52, Portachuelo 924,
Saavedra 924, Santa Cruz 33, Trinidad 46,
Warnes 923

**Botswana**          267
Francistown 21, Gaborone 31, Jwaneng 38,
Kanye 34, Lobatse 33, Mahalapye 41,
Maun 26, Mochudi 37, Molepoloe 32,
Orapa 27, Palapye 42, Ramotswana 39,
Selibe (Phikwe) 8, Serowe 43

**Brazil**          55
Belem 91, Belo Horizonte 31, Brasilia 61,
Curitiba 41, Fortaleza 85, Goiania 62,
Niteroi 21, Pelotas 532, Porto Alegre 512,
Recife 81, Rio de Janeiro 21, Salvador 71,
Santo Andre 11, Santos 132, Sao Paulo 11,
Vitoria 27

**British Virgin Islands**          809
Dial 1 + 809 + Local Number in the
following cities: Anegada, Camanoe Island,
Guana Island, Josh Vah Dyke, Little Thatch,
Marina Cay, Mosquito Island, North Sound,
Peter Island, Salt Island, Tortola, Virgin
Gorda.

**Brunei**          673
Bandar Seri Begawan 2, Kuala Belait 3,
Mumong 3, Tutong 4

**Bulgaria**          359
Kardjali 361, Pazardjik 34, Plovdiv 32,
Sofia 2, Varna 52

**Burkina Faso**          226
Bobo Dioulasso 9, Fada N'Gorma 7,
Koudougou 4, Ouagadougou 3

**Burma**          95
Akyab 43, Bassein 42, Magwe 63,
Mandalay 2, Meikila 64, Moulmein 32,
Pegu 52, Prom 53, Rangoon 1

**Cameroon**          237
City code not required.

**184**

**Canada**      **NPA's**

Dial 1 + Area Code + Local Number.

**Cape Verde Islands  238**

City code not required.

**Caymen Islands      809**
Dial 1 + 809 + Local Number.

**Chile      56**
Chiquayante 41, Concepcion 41, Penco 41, Recreo 31, San Bernardo 2, Santiago 2, Talcahuano 41, Valparaiso 32, Vina del Mar 32

**China      86**
Beijing (Peking) 1, Fuzhou 591, Ghuangzhou (Canton) 20, Shanghai 21

**Colombia      57**
Armenia 60, Barranquilla 5, Bogota 1, Bucaramanga 73, Cali 3, Cartagena 59, Cartago 66, Cucuta 70, Giradot 832, Ibague 82, Manizales 69, Merdellin 42, Neiva 80, Palmira 31, Pereira 61, Santa Marta 56

**Costa Rica      506**
City code not required.

**Cyprus      357**
Kythrea 2313, Lapithos 8218, Lamaca 41, Lefkonico 3313, Limassol 51, Moni 5615, Morphou 71, Nicosia 2, Paphos 61, Platres 54, Polis 63, Rizokarpaso 3613, Yialousa 3513. The following cities are handled by the Turkish Telephone Network.
Use country code 90 for Turkey: Famagusta 536, Kyrenia 581, and Lefka 57817.

**Czechoslovakia      42**
Banska Bystrica 88, Bratislava 7, Brno 5, Ceske Budejovice 38, Decin 412, Havirov 6994, Hradec Kralove 49, Kablonec Nad Nisou 428, Karvina 6993, Kosice 95, Most 35, Ostrava 69, Pizen 19, Prague (Praha) 2, Usti Nad Labem 47, Zilina 89

**Denmark      45**
City code not required.

**Djibouti      253**
City code not required.

**Dominica      809**
Dial 1 + 809 + Local Number.

**Dominican Republic   809**
Dial 1 + 809 + Local Number.

**Ecuador      593**
Ambato 2, Cayambe 2, Cuenca 7, Esmeraldas 2, Guayaquil 4, Ibarra 2; Loja 4, Machachi 2, Machala 4, Manta 4, Portoviejo 4, Quevedo 4, Quito 2, Salinas 4, Santa Domingo 2, Tulcan 2

**Egypt      20**
Alexandria 3, Answan 97, Asyut 88, Benha 13, Cairo 2, Damanhour 45, El Mahallah (El Kubra) 43, El Mansoura 50, Luxor 95, Port Said 66, Shebin El Kom 48, Sohag 93, Tanta 40

**El Salvador      503**
City code not required.

**Estonia      7**
Tallinn 0142

**Ethiopia      251**
Addis Ababa 1, Akaki 1, Asmara 4, Assab

185

3, Awassa 6, Debre Zeit 1, Dessie 3,
Dire Dawa 5, Harrar 5, Jimma 7, Makale 4,
Massawa 4, Nazareth 2, Shashemene 6

**Faeroe Islands      298**
City code not required.

**Fiji Islands      679**
City code not required.

**Finland      358**
Epoo-Ebbo 15, Helsinki 0, Joensuu 73,
Jyvaskyla 41, Kuopio 71, Lahti 18,
Lappeenranta 53, Oulu 81, Port 39,
Tammefors-Tampere 31, Turku 21,
Uleaborg 81, Vaasa 61, Vanda-Vantaa 0

**France      33**
Aix-en-Provence 42, Bordeaux 56, Cannes
93, Chauvigny 49, Cherbourge 33,
Grenoble 76, Le Havre 35, Lourdes 62,
Lyon 7, Marseille 91, Nancy 8, Nice 93,
Paris 1, Rouen 35, Toulouse 61, Tours 47

**French Antilles      596**
City code not required.

**French Guiana      594**
City code not required.

**French Polynesia   689**
City code not required.

**Gabon Republic    241**
City code not required.

**Gambia      220**
City code not required.

**Georgia      7**
Sukhumi 88122, Tblisi 8832

**Germany East      7**
Berlin 2, Cottbus 59, Dresden 51, Erfurt 61,
Frankfurt 30, Gera 70, Halle/Saale 46,
Karl-Marx-Stadt 71, Leipzig 41, Magdeburg
91, Neubrandenburg 90, Postdam 33,
Rostock 81, Schwerin (Meckl) 84, Suhl 66,
Zittau 522

**Germany West      49**
Bad Homburg 6172, Berlin 30, Bonn 228,
Bremen 421, Cologne (Koln) 221,
Dusseldorf 211, Essen 201, Frankfurt 69,
Hamburg 40, Heidellberg 6221, Koblenz
261, Mannheim 621, Munich 89, Numberg
911, Stuttgart 711, Wiesbaden 6121

**Ghana      233**
City code not required.

**Gibraltar      350**
City code not required.

**Greece      30**
Argos 751, Athens (Athinai) 1, Corinth 741,
Iraklion (Kristis) 81, Kavala 51,
Larissa 41, Patrai 61, Piraeus Pireefs 1,
Rodos 241, Salonica (Thessaloniki) 31,
Sparti 731, Thessaloniki 31, Tripolis 71,
Volos 421, Zagora 426

**Greenland      299**
Goatham 2, Sondre Stromfjord 11, Thule 50

**Grenada      809**
Dial 1 + 809 + Local Number.

**Guadeloupe      590**
City code not required.

**Guam      671**
City code not required.

**186**

**Guantanemo Bay    5399**
City code not required.

**Guatemala    502**
Guatemala City 2. All other cities 9.

**Guinea    224**
City code not required.

**Guyana    592**
Anna Regina 71, Bartica 5, Beteryerwaging 20, Cove & John 29, Georgetown 2, Ituni 41, Linden 4, Mabaruma 77, Mahaica 28, Mahalcony 21, New Amsterdam 3, New Hope 66, Rosignol 30, Timehri 61, Vreed-En-Hoop 64, Whim 37

**Haiti    509**
Cap-Haitien 3, Cayes 5, Gonalve 2, Port au Prince 1

**Honduras    504**
City code not required.

**Hong Kong    852**
Castle Peak 0, Cheung Chau 5, Fan Ling 0, Hong Kong 5, Kowloon 3, Kwai Chung 0, Lamma 5, Lantau 5, Ma Wan 5, Peng Chau 5, Sek Kong 0, Sha Tin 0, Tai Po 0, Ting Kau 0, Tsun Wan 0

**Hungary    36**
Abasar 37, Balatonaliga 84, Budapest 1, Dorgicse 80, Fertoboz 99, Gyongyos 37, Kaposvar 82, Kazincbarcika 48, Komlo 72, Miskolc 46, Nagykaniza 93, Szekesfehervar 22, Szolnok 56, Varpalota 80, Veszprem 80, Zalaegerzeg 92

**Iceland    354**

Akureyi 6, Hafnafijorour 1, Husavik 6,

Keflavik Naval Base 2, Rein 6, Reykjavik 1, Reyorarjorour 7, Sandgerol 2, Selfoss 9. Siglufijorour 6, Stokkseyri 9, Suoavik 4, Talknafijorour 4, Varma 1, Vik 9

**India    91**

Ahmedabad 272, Amritsar 183, Bangalore 812, Baroda 265, Bhopal 755, Bombay 22 Calcutta 33, Chandigarh 172, Hyderabad 842, Jaipur 141, Jullundur 181, Kanpur 512, Madras 44, New Dehli 11, Poona 212, Surat 261

**Indonesia    62**
Bandung 22, Cirebon 231, Denpasar (Bali) 361, Jakarta 21, Madiun 351, Malang 341, Medan 61, Padang 751, Palembang 711, Sekurang 778, Semarang 24, Solo 271, Surabaya 31, Tanjungkarang 721, Yogykarta 274

**Iran    98**

Abadan 631, Ahwaz 61, Arak 2621, Esfahan 31, Ghazvin 281, Ghome 251, Hamadan 261, Karadj 2221, Kerman 341, Mashad 51, Rasht 231, Rezaiyeh 441, Shiraz 71, Tabriz 41, Tehran 21

**Iraq    964**
Baghdad 1, Basiah 40, Diwanyia 36, Karbala 32, Kirkuk 50, Mosul 60, Nasryia 42

**Ireland    353**
Arklow 402, Cork 21, Dingle 66, Donegal 73, Drogheda 41, Dublin 1, Dundalk 42, Ennis 65, Galway 91, Kildare 45, Killamey 64, Sligo 71, Tipperary 62, Tralee 66, Tullamore 506, Waterford 51, Wexford 53

**Israel          972**
Afula 65, Ako 4, Ashkelon 51, Bat Iam 3,
Beer Sheva 57, Dimona 57, Hadera 63,
Haifa 4, Holon 3, Jerusalem 2, Nazareth 65,
Netania 53, Rehovot 8, Tel Aviv 3,
Tiberias 67, Tsefat 67

**Italy          39**
Bari 80, Bologna 51, Brindisi 831, Capri
81, Como 31, Florence 55, Genoa 10,
Milan 2, Naples 81, Padova 49, Palermo
91, Pisa 50, Rome 6, Torino 11, Trieste 40,
Venice 41, Verona 45

**Ivory Coast          225**
City code not required.

**Jamaica          809**
Dial 1 + 809 + Local Number.

**Japan          81**
Chiba 472, Fuchu (Tokyo) 423, Hiroshima
82, Kawasaki (Kanagawa) 44, Kobe 78,
Kyoto 75, Nagasaki 958, Nagoya 52, Nahat
(Okinawa) 988, Osaka 6, Sapporo 11,
Sasebo 956, Tachikawa (Tokyo) 425, Tokyo
3, Yokohama 45, Yokosuka (Kanagawa) 468

**Jordan          962**
Amman 6, Aqaba 3, Irbid 2, Jerash 4,
Karak 3, Maam 3, Mafruq 4, Ramtha 2,
Sueeleh 6, Sult 5, Zerqa 9

**Kazakhstan          7**
Alma-Ata 3272, Chimkent 3252, Guryev
31222

**Kenya          254**
Anmer 154, Bamburi 11, Embakasi 2,
Girgiri 2, Kabete 2, Karen 2882, Kiambu
154, Kikuyu 283, Kisumu 35, Langata 2,
Mombasa 11, Nairobi 2, Nakuru 37, Shanzu

11, Thika 151, Uthiru 2

**Kiribati          686**
City code not required.

**Korea          82**
Chung Ju 431, Chuncheon 361, Icheon 336,
Incheon 32, Kwangju (Gwangju) 62,
Masan 551, Osan 339, Osan Military
(333+414), Pohang 562, Pusan (Busan) 51,
Seoul 2, Suwon (Suweon) 331, Taegu
(Daegu) 53, Ulsan 552, Wonju (Weonju)
371

**Kuwait          965**
City code not required.

Kyrgyzstan          7
Osh 33222, Pishpek 3312

**Latvia          7**
Riga 0132

**Lebanon          961**
Beirut 1, Juniyah 9, Tripoli 6, Zahlah 8

**Lesotho          266**
City code not required.

**Liberia          231**

City code not required.

**Libya          218**

Agelat 282, Benghazi 61, Benina 63, Derma
81, Misuratha 51, Sabratha 24, Sebha
71, Taigura 26, Tripoli 21, Tripoli
International Airport 22, Zawai 23, Zuara
25

**Liechtenstein      41**

Use 75 for all cities.

**Lithuania      7**
Vilnius 0122

**Luxembourg      352**
City code not required.

**Macao      853**
City code not required.

**Malawi      265**
Domasi 531, Likuni 766, Luchenza 477, Makwasa 474, Mulanje 465, Namadzi 534, Njuli 664, Thondwe 533, Thornwood 486, Thyolo 467, Zomba 50, City code not required for other cities.

**Malaysia      60**
Alor Star 4, Baranang 3, Broga 3, Cheras 3, Dengil 3, Ipoh 5, Johor Bahru 7, Kajang 3, Kepala Batas 4, Kuala Lampur 3, Machang 97, Maran 95, Port Dickson 6, Semenyih 3, Seremban 6, Sungei Besi 3, Sungei Renggam 3

**Maldives      960**
City code not required.

**Mali      223**
City code not required.

**Malta      356**
City code not required.

**Marshall Islands      692**
Ebeye 871, Majuro 9

**Mauritius      230**
City code not required.

**Mayotte Islands      269**
City code not required.

**Mexico      52**
Acapulco 748, Cancun 988, Celaya 461, Chihuahua 14, Ciudad Juarez 16, Conzumel 987, Culiacan 671, Ensenda 667, Guadalajara 36, Hermosillo 621, La Paz 682, Mazatlan 678, Merida 99, Mexicali 65, Mexico City 5, Monterrey 83, Puebla 22, Puerto Vallarta 322, Rasarito 661, San Luis Potosi 481, Tampico 121, Tecate 665, Tijuana 66, Torreon 17, Veracruz 29

**Micronesia      691**
Kosrae 851, Ponape 9, Truk 8319, Yap 841

**Moldova      7**
Kishinev 0422

**Monaco      33**
Use 93 for all cities.

**Mongolian People's Rep.      976**
Ulan Bator 1

**Montserrat      809**
Dial 1 + 809 + Local Number.

**Morocco      212**
Agardir 8, Beni-Mellal 48, Berrechid 33, Casablanca (City code not required). El Jadida 34, Fes 6, Kenitra 16, Marrakech 4, Meknes 5, Mohammedia 32, Nador 60, Oujda 68, Rabat 7, Tanger (Tangiers) 9, Tetouan 96

**Mustique**          **809**
Dial 1 + 809 + Local Number.

**Namibia**          **264**
Gobabis 681, Grootfontein 673, Industria
61, Keetmanshoop 631, Luderitz 6331,
Mariental 661, Okahandja 622, Olympia 61,
Otjiwarongo 651, Pioneerspark 61,
Swakopmund 641, Tsumeb 671, Windhoek
61, Windhoek Airport 626

**Nauru Island**          **674**
City code not required.

**Nepal**          **977**
City code not required.

**Netherlands**          **31**
Amsterdam 20, Arnhem 85, Eindhoven 40,
Groningen 50, Haarlem 23, Heemstede
23, Hillegersberg 10, Hoensbraoek 45,
Hoogkerk 50, Hoogvliet 10, Loosduinen 70,
Nijmegen 80, Oud Zuilen 30, Rotterdam 10,
The Hague 70, Utrecht 30

**Netherlands Antilles**   **599**
Bonaire 7, Curacao 9, Saba 4, Eustatius 3,
St. Maarten 5

**Nevis**          **809**
Dial 1 + 809 + Local Number.

**New Caledonia**          **687**
City code not required.

**New Zeland**          **64**
Auckland 9, Christchurch 3, Dunedin 24,
Hamilton 71, Hastings 70, Invercargill 21,
Napier 70, Nelson 54, New Plymouth 67,
Palmerston North 63, Rotorua 73,
Tauranga 75, Timaru 56, Wanganui 64,
Wellington 4, Whangarei 89

**Nicaragua**          **505**
Boaco 54, Chinandega 341, Diriamba 42,
Esteli 71, Granada 55, Jinotepe 41,
Leon 311, Managua 2, Masatepe 44,
Masaya 52, Nandaime 45, Rivas 461,
San Juan Del Sur 466, San Marcos 43,
Tipitapa 53

**Niger Republic**          **227**
City code not required.

**Nigeria**          **234**
Lagos 1 (Only city direct dial)

**Niue**          **683**

**Norfolk Island**          **672**

**Norway**          **47**
Arendal 41, Bergen 5, Drammen 3,
Fredrikstad 32, Haugesund 47,
Kongsvinger 66, Kristiansund N. 73, Larvik
34, Moss 32, Narvik 82, Oslo 2,
Sarpsborg 31, Skien 35, Stavanger 4,
Svalbard 80, Tonsberg 33, Trondheim 7

**Oman**          **968**
City code not required.

**Pakistan**          **92**
Abbotabad   5921,   Bahawalpur   621,
Faisalabad 411, Gujtanwala 431,
Hyderabad 221, Islamabad 51, Karachi 21,
Lahore 42, Multan 61, Okara 442,
Peshawar 521, Quetta 81, Sahiwal 441,
Sargodha 451, Sialkot 432, Sukkur 71

**Palm Island**          **809**
Dial 1 + 809 + Local Number.

**Panama          507**
City code not required.

**Papau New Guinea  675**
City code not required.

**Paragua          595**
Asuncion 21, Ayolas 72, Capiata 28,
Concepcion 31, Coronel Bogado 74,
Coronel Oviedo 521, Encarnacion 71,
Hermandarias 63, Ita 24, Pedro J. Caballero
36, Pilar 86, San Antonio 27, San Ignacio
82, Stroessner: Ciudad Pte. 61, Villarica
541, Villeta 25

**Peru              51**
Arequipa 54, Ayacucho 6491, Callao 14,
Chiclayo 74, Chimbote 44, Cuzco 84,
Huancavelica 6495, Huancayo 64, Ica 34,
Iquitos 94, Lima 14, Piura 74, Tacna 54,
Trujillo 44

**Phillippines      63**
Angeles 55, Bacolod 34, Baguio City 442,
Cebu City 32, Clark Field (military) 52,
Dagupan 48, Davao 35, Lloilo City 33,
Lucena 42, Manila 2, San Fernando:
La Union 46, San Fernando: Pampanga 45,
San Pablo 43, Subic Bay Military Base 89,
Subic Bay Residential Housing 89, Tarlac
City 47

**Poland            48**
Bialystok 85, Bydgoszcz 52, Crakow
(Krakow) 12, Gdansk 58, Gdynia 58,
Katowice 32, Lodz 42, Lubin 81, Olsztyn
89, Poznan 48, Radom 48, Sopot 58,
Torun 56, Warsaw 22

**Portugal          351**
Alamada 1, Angra Do Heroismo 95,
Barreiro 1, Beja 84, Braga 53,

Caldas Da Rainha 62, Coimbra 39, Estoril
1, Evora 66, Faro 89, Horta 92,
Lajes AFB 95, Lisbon 1, Madalena 92,
Madeira Islands 91, Montijo 1,
Ponta Del Gada 96, Porto 2, Santa Cruz
(Flores) 92, Santarem 43, Setubal 65,
Velas 95, Vila Do Porto 96, Viseu 32

**Qatar             974**
City code not required.

**Reunion Island    262**
City code not required.

**Romania           40**
Arad 66, Bacau 31, Brasov 21, Bucharest 0,
Cluj-Napoca 51, Constanta 16, Crajova 41,
Galati 34, Lasi 81, Oradea 91, Pitesti 76,
Ploiesti 71, Satu-Mare 97, Sibiu 24,
Timisoara 61, Tirgu Mures 54

**Russia            7**
Magadan   41300,   Moscow   095,   St.
Petersburg 812

**Rwanda            250**
City code not required.

**St. Kitts         809**
Dial 1 + 809 + Local Number.

**St. Lucia         809**
Dial 1 + 809 + Local Number.

**St. Pierre & Miquelon  508**
City code not required.

**St. Vincent       809**
Dial 1 + 809 + Local Number.

**Saipan            670**
Capitol Hill 322, Rota Island 532, Susupe

City 234, Tinian Island 433

**San Marino        39**
Use 541 for all cities.

**Saudi Arabia        966**
Abha 7, Abqaiq 3, Al Khobar 3, Al Markazi
2, Al Ulaya 1, Damman 3, Dhahran
(Aramco) 3, Jeddah 2, Khamis Mushait 7,
Makkah (Mecca) 2, Medina 4, Najran 7,
Qatif 3, Riyadh 1, Taif 2, Yenbu 4

**Senegal        221**
City code not required.

**Seychelles Islands    248**
City code not required.

**Sierra Leone        232**
Freetown 22, Juba 24, Lungi 25, Wellington
23

**Singapore        65**
City code not required.

**Solomon Island        677**
City code not required.

**South Africa        27**
Bloemfontein 51, Cape Town 21, De Aar
571, Durban 31, East London 431, Gordons
Bay 24, Johannesburg 11, La Lucia 31,
Pietermaritzburg 331, Port Elizabeth 41,
Pretoria 12, Sasolburg 16, Somerset West
24, Uitenhage 422, Welkom 171

**Spain        34**
Barcelona 3, Bibao 4, Cadiz 56, Ceuta 56,
Granada 58, Igualada 3, Las Palmas de Gran
Canaria 28, Leon 87, Madrid 1, Malaga 52,
Melilla 52, Palma De Mallorca 71,
Pamplona 48, Santa Cruz de Tenerife 22,

Santander 42, Seville 54, Torremolinos 52,
Valencia 6

**Sri Lanka        94**
Ambalangoda 97, Colombo Central 1, Galle
9, Havelock Town 1, Kandy 8, Katugastota
8, Kotte 1, Maradana 1, Matara 41,
Negomgo 31, Panadura 46, Trincomalee 26

**Suriname        597**
City code not required.

**Swaziland        268**
City code not required.

**Sweden        46**
Alingsas 322, Boras 33, Eskilstuna 16,
Gamleby 493, Goteborg 31, Helsinborg 42,
Karlstad 54, Linkoping 13, Lund 46, Malmo
40, Norrkoping 11, Stockholm 8, Sundsvall
60, Trelleborg 410, Uppsala 18, Vasteras 21

**Switzerland        41**
Baden 56, Basel 61, Berne 31, Davos 83,
Fribourg 37, Geneva 22, Interlaken 36,
Lausanne 21, Lucerne 41, Lugano 91,
Montreux 21, Neuchatel 38, St. Gallen 71,
St. Moritz 82, Winterthur 52, Zurich 1

**Taiwan        886**
Changhua 47, Chunan 36,
Chunghsing-Hsintsun 49, Chungli 34,
Fengyuan 4, Hsiaying 6, Hualien 38,
Kaohsiung 7, Keelung 2, Lotung 39,
Pingtung 8, Taichung 4, Tainan 6, Taipei 2,
Taitung 89, Taoyuan 33

**Tajikistan        7**
Dushanbe 3772

**Tanzania        255**
Dar Es Salaam 51, Dodoma 61, Mwanza

68, Tanga 53

**Thailand          66**
Bangkok 2, Burirum 44, Chanthaburi 39, Chien Mai 53, Cheingrai 54, Kamphaengphet 55, Lampang 54, Nakhon Sawan 56, Nong Khai 42, Pattani 73, Pattaya 38, Ratchaburi 32, Saraburi 36, Tak 55, Ubon Ratchathani 45

**Togo          228**
City code not required.

**Tonga Islands          676**
City code not required.

**Trinidad & Tabago 809**
Dial 1 + 809 + Local Number.

**Tunisia          216**
Agareb 4, Beja 8, Bizerte 2, Carthage 1, Chebba 4, Gabes 5, Gafsa 6, Haffouz 7, Hamman-Souse 3, Kairouan 7, Kef 8, Khenis 3, Medenine 5, Tabarka 8, Tozeur 6, Tunis 1

**Turkey          90**
Adana 711, Ankara 41, Antalya 311, Bursa 241, Eskisehir 221, Gazianter 851, Istanbul 1, Izmir 51, Izmit 211, Kayseri 351, Konya 331, Malatya 821, Mersin 741, Samsun 361

**Turka & Caicos          809**
Dial 1 + 809 + Local Number.

**Turkmenistan          7**
Ashkkhabad 3632, Chardzhou 37822

**Tuvalu          688**

**Ukraine          7**
Kharkiv 0572, Kyiv 044, Lviv 0322

**Uganda          256**
Entebbe 42, Jinja 43, Kampala 41, Kyambogo 41

**Union Island          809**
Dial 1 + 809 + Local Number.

**United Arab Emirates   971**
Abu Dhabi 2, Ajman 6, Al Ain 3, Aweer 58, Dhayd 6, Dibba 70, Dubai 4, Falaj-al-Moalla 6, Fujairah 70, Jebel Ali 84, Jebel Dhana 52, Khawanij 58, Ras-al-Khaimah 77, Sharjan 6, Tarif 53, Umm-al-Quwain 6

**United Kingdom          44**
Belfast 232, Birmingham 21, Bournemouth 202, Cardiff 222, Durham 385, Edinburgh 31, Glasgow 41, Gloucester 452, Ipswich 473, Liverpool 51, London (Inner) 71, London (Outer) 81, Manchester 61, Nottingham 602, Prestwick 292, Sheffield 742, Southampton 703

**Uruguay          598**
Atlantida 372, Colonia 522, Florida 352, La Paz 322, Las Piedras 322, Los Toscas 372, Maldonado 42, Mercedes 532, Minas 442, Montevideo 2, Parque De Plata 372, Paysandu 722, Punta Del Este 42, Salinas 372, San Jose 342, San Jose De Carrasco 382

**Uzbekistan          7**
Karish 37522, Samarkand 3662, Tashkent 3712

**Vanuatu, Rep. of          678**

**Vatican City          39**
Use 6 for all cities.

**Venezuela          58**
Barcelona 81, Barquisimeto 51, Cabimas 64,
Caracas 2, Ciudad Bolivar 85, Coro 68,
Cumana 93, Los Teques 32, Maiquetia 31,
Maracaibo 61, Maracay 43, Maturin 91,
Merida 74, Puerto Cabello 42, San Cristobal
76, Valencia 41

**Vietnam          84**
Hanoi 4, Ho Chi Minh City 8

**Wallis & Futuna Islands  681**

**Western Samoa          685**
City code not required.

**Yeman (North)          967**
Al Marawyah 3, Al Qaidah 4, Amran 2,
Bayt Al Faquih 3, Dhamar 2, Hodeidah 3,
Ibb 4, Mabar 2, Rada 2, Rawda 2, Sanaa 2,
Taiz 4, Yarim 4, Zabid 3

**Yugoslavia          38**
Belgrade (Beograd) 11, Dubrovnik 50,
Leskovac 16, Ljubjana 61, Maribor 62,
Mostar 88, Novi Sad 21, Pirot 10, Rijeka
51, Sarajevo 71, Skopje 91, Split 58,
Titograd 81, Titovo-Uzice 31, Zagreb 41

**Zaire          243**
Kinshasa 12, Lubumbashi 222

**Zambia          260**
Chingola 2, Kitwe 2, Luanshya 2, Lusaka 1,
Ndola 26

**Zimbabwe          263**
Bulawayo 9, Harare 0, Mutare 20

# *APPENDIX S*

## CURRENCIES OF THE WORLD

COUNTRY  UNIT      1 Unit = 100 Unless stated otherwise

| | | |
|---|---|---|
| **AFGHANISTAN** | Afghani | Puls |
| **ALBANIA** | Lek | Quintar |
| **ALGERIA** | Dinar | Centimes |
| **ANGOLA** | Kwanza | Lweis |
| **ANGUILLA** | E.C. Dollar | Cents |
| **ARGENTINA** | Peso | Centavos |
| **ARMENIA**˙ | Rubles | Kopeks |
| **AUSTRALIA** | Australian Dollar | Cents |
| **AUSTRIA** | Schilling | Groschen |
| **AZERBAIJAN**⁺ | Rubles | Kopek |
| **BAHAMAS** | Bahamian Dollar | Cents |
| **BAHRAIN** | Bahrain Dinar | 1000 Fils |
| **BANGLADESH** | Taka | Poisha |
| **BARBADOS** | Dollar | Cents |
| **BELGIUM** | Belgian Franc | Centimes |
| **BELIZE** | Dollar | Cents |
| **BENIN** | Franc (CFA) | --- |
| **BERMUDA** | Dollar | Cents |
| **BHUTAN** | Ngultrum | |
| **BOLIVIA** | Boliviano | Centavos |
| **BOTSWANA** | Pula | Thebe |
| **BRAZIL** | Cruzeiro | Centavos |
| **BRITISH VIRGIN IS** | Dollar USC | Cents |
| **BRUNEI** | Brunei Dollar | Cents |
| **BULGARIA** | Lev | Stotinki |
| **BURKINA FASO** | Franc (CFA) | --- |

**195**

| | | |
|---|---|---|
| **BURMA** | Kyat | Pyas |
| **BURUNDI** | Burundi Franc | Centimes |
| **BYELARUS'** | Rubles | Kopeks |
| **CAMBODIA** | Riel | |
| **CAMEROON** | Franc (CFA) | --- |
| **CANADA** | Canadian Dollar | Cents |
| **CAYMAN IS** | Cayman Is. Dollar | Cents |
| **CENTRAL AFRICAN REP.** | Franc (CFA) | Centimes |
| **CHAD** | Franc (CFA) | Cents |
| **CHILE** | Chilean Peso | Centesimos |
| **CHINA, PEOPLES REP.** | Ren Min Bi | Fen |
| **CHINA, TAIWAN** | New Taiwan Dollar | |
| **COLOMBIA** | Colombian Peso | Centavos |
| **COMOROS** | Franc (CFA) | --- |
| **CONGO, PEOPLE'S REP.** | Franc (CFA) | --- |
| **COSTA RICA** | Colon | Cenavos |
| **COTE D'IVOIRE** | Franc (CFA) | --- |
| **CUBA** | Peso | Centavos |
| **CYPRUS** | Cyprus Pound | 1000 Mills |
| **CZECH REPUBLIC** | Koruna | Halers |
| **DENMARK** | Krone | Ore |
| **DOMINICA** | E.C. Dollar | Cents |
| **DOMINICAN REP.** | Peso | Centavos |
| **ECUADOR** | Sucre | Centavos |
| **EGYPT** | Egyptian Pound | Piastres |
| **EL SALVADOR** | Colon | Centavos |
| **EQUATORIAL GUINEA** | Ekuele | Centimos |
| **ETHIOPIA** | Birr | Cents |
| **FAEROE IS** | Faeroese | Krona |
| **FIJI** | Fiji Dollar | Cents |
| **FINLAND** | Markka | Penni |
| **FRANCE** | French Franc | Centimes |
| **FRENCH POLYNESIA** | Franc | Centimes |
| **FRENCH GUIANA** | Franc | Centimes |
| **GABON** | Franc (CFA) | --- |
| **GEORGIA'** | Rubles | Kopek |
| **GERMANY** | Mark | Pfennig |
| **GHANA** | Cedi | Pesawas |
| **GIBRALTAR** | Pound | Pence |
| **GREECE** | Drachma | Lepta |
| **GRENADA** | E.C. Dollar | Cents |
| **GUATEMALA** | Quetzal | Centavos |

**196**

| | | |
|---|---|---|
| **GUINEA** | Franc | Couris |
| **GUINEA-BISSAU** | Peso | Centavos |
| **GUYANA** | Guyana Dollar | Cents |
| **HAITI** | Gourde | Centimes |
| **HONDURAS** | Lempira | Centavos |
| **HONG KONG** | Hong Kong Dollar | Cents |
| **HUNGARY** | Forint | Fillers |
| **ICELAND** | Icelandic Krona | Aur |
| **INDIA** | Indian Rupee | Naya Paise |
| **INDONESIA** | Rupiah | Sen |
| **IRAN** | Iranian Rial | Dinars |
| **IRAQ** | Iraqi Dinar | 1000 Fils |
| **IRELAND** | Irish Pound | Pence |
| **ISRAEL** | New Shekel | 10 Agorot |
| **ITALY** | Lira          --- | |
| **JAMAICA** | Jamaican Dollar | Cents |
| **JAPAN** | Yen          --- | |
| **JORDAN** | Jordanian Dinar | 1000 Fils |
| **KAMPUCHEA** | Riel | Centimes |
| **KAZAKHSTAN** | Ruble | |
| **KENYA** | Kenya Shilling | Cents |
| **KIRIBATI** | Australian Dollar | Cents |
| **KOREA, NORTH** | Won | Jun |
| **KOREA, SOUTH** | Won | Chon |
| **KUWAIT** | Kuwaiti Dinar | 1000 Fils |
| **KYRGYZSTAN'** | Rubles | Kopeks |
| **LAOS** | Kip Pot Po | Centimes |
| **LATVIA'** | Rubles | Kopeks |
| **LEBANON** | Lebanese Pound | Piastres |
| **LESOTHO** | Loti | Licente |
| **LIBERIA** | Liberian Dollar | Cents |
| **LIBYA** | Libyan Dinar | 1000 Dirham |
| **LIECHTENSTEIN** | Franc | |
| **LUXEMBOURG** | Luxembourg Franc | Centimes |
| **MADAGASCAR** | Franc | Centimes |
| **MALAWI** | Kwacha | Tambala |
| **MALAYSIA** | Ringgit | Sen |
| **MALDIVES** | Rufiyaas | Laree |
| **MALI** | Mali Franc | Centimes |
| **MALTA** | Maltese Lira | Cents |
| **MAURITANIA** | Ouguiya | 5 Khoums |
| **MAURITIUS** | Mauritian Rupee | Cents |

**197**

| | | |
|---|---|---|
| **MEXICO** | Mexican Peso | Centavos |
| **MICRONESIA** | U.S. Dollar | Cents |
| **MOLDOVA** | Rubles | Kopeks |
| **MONACO** | Franc | |
| **MONGOLIA** | Tugrik | |
| **MONTSERRAT** | E. Caribbean Dollar | Cents |
| **MOROCCO** | Dirham | Centimes |
| **MOZAMBIQUE** | Metical | Centavos |
| **NAMIBIA** | Rand | |
| **NAURU** | Australian Dollar | |
| **NEPAL** | Nepalese Rupee | Pice |
| **NETHERLANDS ANTILLES** | Guilder | Cents |
| **NETHERLANDS** | Guilder | Cents |
| **NEW ZEALAND** | New Zealand Dollar | Cents |
| **NEW CALEDONIA** | Franc | Centimes |
| **NICARAGUA** | Cordoba | Centavos |
| **NIGER** | Franc (CFA) | --- |
| **NIGERIA** | Naira | Kobos |
| **NORWAY** | Norwegian Krone | Ore |
| **OMAN** | Rial | 1000 Baizas |
| **PAKISTAN** | Pakistani Rupee | Paisa |
| **PANAMA** | Balboa | Cents |
| **PAPUA NEW GUINEA** | Kina | Toea |
| **PARAGUAY** | Guaranie | Centimos |
| **PERU** | Sol | Centavos |
| **PHILIPPINES** | Philippine Peso | Centavos |
| **POLAND** | Zloty | Groszy |
| **PORTUGAL** | Potuguese Escudo | Centavos |
| **PUERTO RICO** | U.S. Dollar | Cents |
| **QATAR** | Qatar Riyal | Dirhams |
| **REP. OF CAPE VERDE** | Escudo | Centavos |
| **REP. OF DJIBOUTI** | Franc | Centimes |
| **REUNION ISLAND** | Franc | Centimes |
| **ROMANIA** | Lei | Bani |
| **RUSSIA** | Ruble | Kopeks |
| **RWANDA** | Rwandese Franc | Centimes |
| **SAN MARINO** | Lira | |
| **SAO TOME** | Dobra | --- |
| **SAUDI ARABIA** | Saudi Riyal | Hallalah |
| **SENEGAL** | Franc (CFA) | --- |
| **SEYCHELLES** | Seychelles Rupee | Cents |
| **SIERRA LEONE** | Leone | Cents |

**198**

| | | |
|---|---|---|
| **SINGAPORE** | Singapore Dollar | Cents |
| **SOLOMON IS** | Dollar | Cents |
| **SOMALIA** | Somali Schilling | Cents |
| **SOUTH AFRICA** | Rand | Cents |
| **SPAIN** | Spanish Peseta | Centimos |
| **SRI LANKA** | Sri Lanka Rupee | Cents |
| **ST. KITTS-NEVIS** | E.C. Dollar | Cents |
| **ST. VINCENT** | E.C. Dollar | Cents |
| **ST. LUCIA** | E.C. Dollar | Cents |
| **SUDAN** | Sudanese Pound | Piastres |
| **SURINAME** | Surinam Guilder | Cents |
| **SWAZILAND** | Lilangeni | Cents |
| **SWEDEN** | Swedish Kronor | Ore |
| **SWITZERLAND** | Franc | Centimes |
| **SYRIA** | Syrian Pound | Piastre |
| **TAJIKISTAN** | Rubles | Kopeks |
| **TANZANIA** | Tanzanian Shilling | Cents |
| **THAILAND** | Baht | Satang |
| **THE GAMBIA** | Dalasi | Batut |
| **TOGO** | Franc (CFA) | --- |
| **TONGA** | Pa'anga | Seniti |
| **TRINIDAD & TOBAGO** | Dollar | Cents |
| **TUNISIA** | Tunisian Dinar | 1000 Millimes |
| **TURKEY** | Turkish Lira | Kurus |
| **TURKMENISTAN** | Rubles | Kopeks |
| **TURKS & CAICOS** | U.S. Dollar | Cents |
| **U.S.A** | Dollar | Cents |
| **UGANDA** | Uganda Shilling | Cents |
| **UKRAINE** | Rubles | Kopeks |
| **UNITED ARAB EMIRATES** | UAE Dirham | Fils |
| **UNITED KINGDOM** | Pound Sterling | Pence |
| **URUGUAY** | New Uruguayan Peso | Centimos |
| **UZBEKISTAN** | Rubles | Kopeks |
| **VANUATU REP.** | Vatu | Centimes |
| **VENEZUELA** | Bolivar | Centimos |
| **VIETNAM** | Dong | 10 Hao |
| **YEMEN, ARAB REP.** | Yemeni Rial | Fils |
| **YEMEN, P.D.R.** | Yemeni Dinar | 1000 Fils |
| **YUGOSLAVIA** | Yugoslav Dinar | Paras |
| **ZAIRE** | Zaire | Makutas |
| **ZAMBIA** | Zambian Kwacha | Ngwee |
| **ZIMBABWE** | Zimbabwe Dollar | Cents |

**199**

**CFA** = Communaute Financiere Africaine

**E.C.** = East Caribbean

\* = Several of the countries of the former Soviet Union are in the process of introducing their own currency. For now most are still using and accepting the Soviet Ruble.

# APPENDIX T

## COUNTRIES: BANKING, BUSINESS AND SHOPPING HOURS

**AFGHANISTAN**
Business/Shopping Hours: 8:AM - 6:AM (Sun-Thur) Businesses are closed Thursday and Friday afternoons

**ALGERIA**
Banking Hours: 9:AM - 4:PM (Sun-Thur)
Business Hours: 8:AM - 12:Noon, 1:PM - 5:PM (Sat-Wed)
Businesses are closed Thursday and Friday

**AMERICAN SAMOA**
Banking Hours: 9:AM - 2:PM (Mon-Thur) 9:AM - 5:PM (Fri)

**ANDORRA**
Banking Hours: 9:AM - 1:PM; 3:PM - 7:PM;
Business Hours: 9:AM - 1:PM; 3:PM - 7:PM,
Shopping Hours: 10:AM - 1:PM; 3:PM - 8:PM

**ANGUILLA**
Banking Hours: 8:AM - 12:00 Noon (Mon-Fri);
3:PM (Fri), Business Hours: 8:AM - 4:PM, Shopping Hours: 8:AM - 5:PM (Mon-Sat)

**ANTIGUA AND BARBUDA**
Banking Hours: 8:AM - 1:PM (Mon,Tue,Wed,Thur) 8:AM - 1:PM & 3:PM - 5:PM (Fri),Business Hours: 8:AM - 12:Noon & 1:PM - 4:PM (Mon-Fri), Shopping Hours: 8:AM - 12:Noon & 1:PM - 5:PM (Mon-Sat)

**ARMENIA**
Banking Hours: 9:AM - 6:PM, Business Hours:

9:AM - 6:PM, Shopping Hours: 8:AM - 9:PM

**ARGENTINA**
Banking Hours: 10:AM - 4:PM, (Mon-Fri),
Business Hours: 9:AM - 6:PM (Mon-Fri),
Shopping Hours: 9:AM - 8:PM (Mon-Sat)

**AUSTRALIA**
Banking Hours: 10:AM - 3:PM, (Mon-Thur);
10:AM - 5:PM (Fri)
Banks are closed on Saturdays
Business/Shopping Hours: 9:AM - 5:30PM (Mon-Thur); 8:30AM - 12:Noon (Sat)

**AUSTRIA**
Banking Hours: 8:AM - 12:30 PM, 1:30 - 3:30, PM (Mon, Tue, Wed, Fri); 1:30 - 5:30PM(Thur),
Business Hours: 8:30 AM - 4:30 PM, Shopping Hours: 8:AM - 6:PM (Mon - Fri); 8:AM - 12:Noon (Sat)

**AZERBAIJAN**
Banking Hours: 9:AM - 6:PM
Business Hours: 9:AM - 6:PM
Shopping Hours: 8:AM - 9:PM

**BAHAMAS**
Banking Hours: 9:30AM - 3:PM (Mon-Thur);
9:30AM - 5:PM (Fri)

**BAHRAIN**
Banking Hours: 7:30AM - 12:Noon (Sat-Wed);
7:30AM - 11:AM Thur)

**201**

**BARBADOS**
Banking Hours: 8:AM - 3:PM (Mon-Thur); 8:AM - 1:PM & 3:PM - 5:PM (Fri), Business Hours: 8:30AM - 4:PM (Mon-Fri), Shopping Hours: 8:AM - 4:PM (Mon-Fri); 8:AM - 12:Noon (Sat)

**BANGLADESH**
Banking Hours: 9:30AM - 1:30PM, (Mon-Thur); 9:AM - 11:AM (Fri- Sat)Business/ShoppingHours: 9:AM - 9:PM (Mon-Fri); 9:AM - 2:PM (Sat)

**BELARUS**
Banking Hours: 9:AM - 6:PM
Business Hours: 9:AM - 6:PM
Shopping Hours: 9:AM - 9:PM

**BELGIUM**
Banking Hours: 9:AM - 3:PM (Mon-Fri), Business Hours: 9:AM - 12:Noon & 2:PM - 5:30PM, Shopping Hours: 9:AM - 6:PM (Mon-Sat)

**BELIZE**
Banking Hours: 8:AM - 1:PM (Mon-Fri); 3:PM - 6:PM (Fri) ;Business Hours: 8:AM - 12:Noon; 1:PM - 5:PM (Mon-Fri); Shopping Hours: 8:AM - 4:PM (Mon-Sat)

**BENIN**
Banking Hours: 8:AM - 11:AM; 3:PM - 4:PM (Mon-Fri); Business Hours: 8:AM - 12:30PM; 3:PM - 6:30PM (Mon-Fri); Shopping Hours: 9:AM - 1:PM, 4:PM - 7:PM (Mon-Sun)

**BERMUDA**
Business/Shopping: 9:AM - 5:PM (Mon-Sat)

**BOLIVIA**
Banking Hours: 9:AM - 12:Noon & 2:PM - 4:PM (Mon-Fri); Business Houre: 9:AM - 12:Noon & 2:30PM   6:PM (Mon-Fri); Shopping Hours: 9:AM - 6:PM; 9:AM - 12:Noon (Sat)

**BOSNIA HERZEGOVINA**
Banking Hours: 7:AM - Noon or &:AM - 7:PM;

Business Hours: 8:AM - 3:30 PM; Shopping Hours: 8:AM - 8:PM (Mon-Fri)

**BOTSWANA**
Banking Hours: 8:15 - 12:45PM (Mon-Fri), 8:15AM - 10:45 AM (Sat); Shopping Hours: 8:AM - 6:PM (Mon-Sat)

**BRITISH VIRGIN ISLANDS**
Banking Hours: 9:AM - 2:PM (Mon-Fri); Business Hours: 8:30AM - 2:00PM & 4:PM - 5:PM (Mon-Fri); Shopping Hours: 8:AM - 5:PM (Mon-Sat)

**BRAZIL**
Banking Hours 10:AM - 4:30PM (Mon-Fri); Shopping Hours: 9:AM - 6:30PM (Mon-Fri) & 9:AM - 1:PM (Sat)

**BURKINA FASO**
Business Hours: 7:AM - 12:Noon, 3:PM - 5:PM (Mon-Fri); Shopping Hours: 7:AM - 12:Noon, 2:PM - 7:PM (Mon-Sat)

**BURMA**
Banking Hours: 10:AM - 2:PM (Mon-Fri); 10:AM - 12:Noon (Sat); Bussiness/Shopping Hours: 9:30Am - 4:PM (Mon-Sat)

**BURUNDI**
Business Hours: 8:AM - 12:Noon (Mon-Fri); Shopping Hours: 8:AM - 6:PM (Mon-Sat)

**CAMEROON**
Banking Hours: French Speaking Part: 8:AM - 11:AM, 2:30PM - 4:PM (Mon-Fri)English Speaking Part: 8:AM - 2:PM (Mon-Fri); Business Hours: French Speaking Part: 7:30AM - 12: Noon, 2:30PM - 6:PM (Mon-Fri); English Speaking Part: 7:30AM - 2:30PM - (Mon-Fri), 7:30AM - 1:PM; Shopping Hours: 8:AM - 12:30PM, 4:PM - 7:PM (Mon-Sat)

**REPUBLIC OF CAPE VERDE**
Banking Hours: 8:AM - 12: Noon (Mon-Fri); Business Hours: 8:AM - 12: Noon (Mon-Fri)

**CAYMAN ISLANDS**
Banking Hours: 9:AM - 2:30PM (Mon-Thur) & 9:AM -PM, :30PM -4:30PM (Fri); Business Hours: 8:30AM - 5:PM; Shopping Hours: 8:30AM - 5:PM

**CENTRAL AFRICAN REPUBLIC**
Banking Hours: 8:AM - 11:30AM (Mon-Fri); Shopping Hours: 7:30AM - 9:PM (Mon-Sun)

**CHAD**
Banking Hours: 7:AM - 11:AM (Mon-Thur, Sat), 7:AM - 10:AM (Fri); Business Hours: 7:AM - 2:PM (Mon-Thur, Sat), 7:AM -12: Noon (Fri);Shopping Hours: 8:AM - 1:PM, 4:PM - 6:PM (Mon-Sat)

**CHILE**
Banking Hours: 9:AM - 1:PM & 2:30PM - 6:PM (Mon-Fri); 9:AM -2:PM (Sat); Shopping Hours: 9:AM - 1:PM & 2:30PM - 6:PM (Mon-Fri)

**CHINA, PEOPLES REPUBLIC**
Banking Hours: varies (Mon-Sat)

**CHINA, TAIWAN**
Banking Hours: 9:AM - 3:30PM (Mon-Fri); 9:AM - 12:Noon (Sat)

**COLUMBIA**
Banking Hours: 9:AM - 3:PM (Mon-Thur); 9:AM - 3:30 (Fri); Business Hours: 8:30AM - 5:PM (Mon-Fri);ShoppingHours: 10:AM - 7:PM (Mon-Sat)

**COMOROS ISLAND**
Banking Hours: 9:AM - 12:30PM, 3:PM - 5:PM (Mon-Fri), 9:AM - 12:30PM (Sat); Shopping Hours: 8:AM - 8:PM (Mon-Sat)

**CONGO, PEOPLE'S REPUBLIC**
Banking Hours: 7:AM - 2:PM (Mon-Fri); Shopping Hours: 7:AM - 7:PM (Mon-Sat)

**COSTA RICA**
Banking Hours: 9:AM - 3:PM (Mon-Fri);

Shopping Hours: 8:30AM - 11:30AM & 2:PM - 6:PM (Mon-Fri) 8:30AM - 11:30AM (Sat)

**COTE D'IVOIRE**
Banking Hours: 8:AM - 11:30AM, 2:30PM - 4:PM (Mon-Fri); Business Hours: 8:AM - 12:Noon, 2:30PM - 5:30PM (Mon-Fri); Shopping Hours: 8:30AM - 12:Noon, 2:30PM - 7:PM (Mon-Sat)

**CUBA**
Banking Hours: 9:AM - 3:PM (Mon-Fri); Business Hours: 8:30AM - 12:30PM & 1:30PM - 5:30PM (Mon - Fri); Shopping Hours: 9:AM - 5:PM (Mon-Fri); 9:AM - 12:Noon (Sat)

**CYPRUS**
Banking Hours: 8:30AM - 12: Noon (Mon-Sat); Business Hours: 8:AM - 1:PM, 2:30PM - 6:PM (Mon-Fri) 8:AM -i:PM (Sat); Shopping Hours: 8:AM - 1:PM; 4:PM - 7:PM (Mon-Fri) Closed Wednesday and Saturday afternoons.

**CZECH REPUBLIC**
Banking Hours: 8:AM - 4:PM (Mon-Fri); Business Hours: 8:30AM - 5:PM; Shopping Hours: 9:AM - 6:PM (Mon-Fri), 9:AM - 1:PM (Sat)

**DENMARK**
Banking Hours: 9:30AM - 4:PM (Mon,Tue,Wed, & Fri), 9:30AM -6:PM (Thur); Business Hours: 8:AM - 4:PM (Mon-Fri); Shopping Hours: 9/10:AM - 5:30/7:PM (Mon-Thur) 9/10:AM - 7/8:PM (Fri) 9/10:AM - 1/2:PM (Sat)

**REPUBLIC OF DJIBOUTI**
Banking Hours: 7:15AM - 11:45AM (Sun-Thur); Shopping Hours: 7:30AM - 12:Noon, 3:30PM - 7:30PM (Sat-Thur)

**DOMINICA**
Banking Hours: 8:AM - 1:PM (Mon-Fri); 3:PM - 5:PM (Fri); Business Hours: 8:AM - 1:PM & 2:PM - 4:PM (Mon-Fri); 8:AM - 1:PM (Sat); Shopping Hours: 8:AM - 1:PM & 2:PM - 4:PM

**203**

(Mon-Fri); 8:AM- 1:PM (Sat)

## DOMINICAN REPUBLIC
Banking Hours: 8:AM - 12:Noon (Mon-Fri); Business Hours: 9:AM - 6:PM (Mon-Fri) & 9:AM -12:Noon(Sat); Shopping Hours: 8:30AM - 12:Noon & 2:30PM - 6:PM (Mon-Fri); 8:30AM - 1:PM (Sat)

## ECUADOR
Banking Hours: 9:AM - 1:30PM (Mon-Fri) Shopping Hours: 8:30AM - 12:30PM (Mon-Sat) & 3:30PM - 7:PM (Mon-Sat)

## EGYPT
Banking Hours: 8:30AM - 1:PM (Mon-Thur, Sat), 10:AM - 12:Noon (Sat); Shopping Hours: 10:AM - 7:PM (Tue-Sat), 10:AM - 8:PM (Mon - Thur)

## EL SALVADOR
Banking Hours: 8:AM - 12:Noon & 2:PM - 4:PM (Mon-Fri); Shopping Hours: 8:AM - 12:Noon & 2:30PM - 6:PM (Mon-Sat)

## EQUATORIAL GUINEA
Banking Hours: 8:AM - 3:PM (Mon-Fri), 8:AM - 1:PM(Sat); Business Hours; 8:AM - 3:PM (Mon-Fri), 8:AM - 1:PM (Sat); Shopping Hours: 8:AM -3:PM, 5:PM - 7:PM (Mon-Sat)

## ESTONIA
Banking Hours: 9:AM - 3:PM; Business Hours: 9:AM - 6PM; Shopping Hours: 9:am - 9:PM (Mon-Sat)

## ETHIOPIA
Banking Hours: 9:AM - 5:PM (Mon-Fri); Business Hour: 8:AM - 12:Noon, 1:PM - 4:PM (Mon-Fri); Banks close for 3 hours for lunch

## FIJI
Banking Hours: 10:AM - 3:PM (Mon-Thur); 10:AM - 4:PM (Fri)usiness/Shopping Hours: 8:AM - 5:PM

## FINLAND
Banking Hours: 9:15AM - 4:15PM (Mon-Fri); Business Hours: 8:30AM - 4:PM (Mon-Fri);Shopping Hours: 9:AM - 5/6:PM (Mon-Fri), 9:AM - 2/3:PM (Sat)

## FRANCE
Banking Hours: 9:AM - 4:30PM (Mon-Fri); Business Hours: 9:AM - 12:Noon; 2:PM - 6:PM (Mon-Fri), 9:AM - 12:Noon (Sat); Shopping Hours: 9:AM - 6:30PM (Tue-Sat)

## FRENCH GUIANA
Banking Hours: 7:15AM - 11:45AM (Mon,Tue,Thur, Fri); 7:AM -12:Noon (Wed)

## GABON
Banking Hours: 7:AM - 12:Noon (Mon-Fri); Business Hours: 8:AM - 12:Noon, 3:PM - 6:PM (Mon-Fri); Shopping Hours: 8:AM - 12:Noon, 4:PM - 7:PM (Mon-Sat)

## GEORGIA
Shopping Hours: 9:AM - 7:PM

## THE GAMBIA
Banking Hours: 8:AM - 1:PM (Mon-Fri); 8:AM - 11:AM (Sat); Business/Shopping Hours: 8:AM - 5:PM (Mon-Fri); 8:AM -12:Noon (Sat)

## FEDERAL REPUBLIC OF GERMANY
Banking Hours: 8:30AM - 12:30PM; 1:45PM - 3:45PM (Mon-Fri), Thur- 5:45PM; Business Hours: 8:AM - 5:PM; Shopping Hours: 8:AM - 6:30PM (Mon-Fri), 8:AM - 2:PM (Sat)

## GHANA
Banking Hours: 8:30AM - 2:PM (Mon-Fri); Business Hours: 8:30AM - 5:PM (Mon-Fri); Shopping Hours: 8:30AM - 5:PM (Mon-Sat)

## GIBRALTAR
Banking Hours: 9:AM - 3:30PM (Mon-Fri), 4:30PM - 6:PM (Fri); Business Hours: 9:AM - 6:PM; Shopping Hours: 9:AM - 1:PM & 3:30PM - 7:PM (Mon-Fri), 9:-1:PM (Sat)

## GREECE
Banking Hours: 8:AM - 2:PM (Mon-Fri); Business Hours: 8:30AM - 1:30PM, 4:PM - 7:30PM; Shopping Hours: 8:AM - 2:30PM (Mon, Wed, Sat), 8:AM - 1:30PM, 5:PM- 8:PM (Tue, Thur, Fri)

## GRENADA
Banking Hours: 8:AM - 12:Noon (Mon-Fri) & 2:30 PM - 5:PM (Fri); Business Hours: 8:AM - 4:PM (Mon-Fri) 8:AM - 11:45 AM (Sat)Shopping Hours: 8:AM - 4:PM (Mon Fri); 8:AM - 11:45 AM (Sat)

## GUADELOUPE
Banking Hours: 8:AM - 12:Noon & 2:PM - 4:PM; Shopping Hours: 9:AM - 1:PM & 3:PM - 6:PM (Mon-Fri); Sat mornings

## GUATEMALA
Banking Hours: 9:AM - 3:PM (Mon-Fri); Shopping Hours: 9:AM - 7:PM (Mon-Sat)

## GUINEA,REPUBLIC
Banking Hours: 7:30AM - 3:PM (Mon-Sat); Business Hours: 7:30 - 3:PM (Mon-Sat);Shopping Hours: 8:AM - 6:PM (Mon-Sun)

## GUYANA
Banking Hours: 8:AM - 12:30PM; (Mon-Fri); Business Hours: 8:AM - 4:PM (Mon-Fri); Shopping Hours: 8:AM - 12:Noon; 2:PM - 4:PM

## HAITI
Banking Hours: 9:AM - 1:PM (Mon-Fri); Business Hours: 8:AM - 5:PM (Mon-Fri); 8:AM - 12:Noon (Sat); Shopping Hours: 8:AM - 5:PM (Mon-Fri); 8:AM - 12:Noon (Sat)

## HONDURAS
Banking Hours: 9:AM - 3:30PM (Mon-Fri); Shopping Hours: 8:AM - 6:30PM (Mon-Sat)

## HONG KONG
Banking Hours: 10:AM - 3:PM (Mon-Fri); 9:AM - 12:Noon (Sat)

Business/Shopping Hours: 9:AM - 5:PM; 9:AM - 1:Pm (Sat)

## HUNGARY
Banking Hours: 8:30AM - 3:PM (Mon-Sat); Business Hours: 8:30AM - 5:PM; Shopping Hours: 10:AM - 6:PM (Mon-Fri); 10:AM - 2:PM (Sat)

## ICELAND
Banking Hours: 9:15AM - 4:PM (Mon-Fri); Business Hours: 9:AM - 5:PM (Mon-Fri); Shopping Hours: 9:AM - 6:PM (Mon-Fri); 9:AM - 12:Noon (Sat)

## INDIA
Banking Hours: 10:30AM - 2:30PM (Mon-Fri); 10:30AM - 12:30PM (Sat) Business/Shopping Hours:Government Offices: 10:AM - 1:PM; 2:PM - 5:PM (Mon-Sat); Non-Gov't Offices: 9:30AM - 1:PM; 2:PM - 5:PM (Mon-Sat)

## INDONESIA
Banking Hours: 10:AM - 3:PM (Mon-Fri); 9:AM - 12:Noon (Sat)

## IRAN
Banking Hours: 8:AM - 1:PM; 4:PM - 6:PM (Sat-Thur);Business/ShoppingHours:Gov'tOffice: 8:AM - 4:30PM (Sat-Wed) Non-Gov't. Offices: 8:AM - 4:30PM (Sat-Thur) Offices closed on Friday

## IRELAND
Banking Hours: 10:AM - 12:30PM; 1:30PM - 3:PM (Mon-Fri); Business Hours: 9:AM - 1:PM, 2:PM - 5:PM;Shopping Hours: 9:AM - 5:30PM (Mon-Sat)

## ISRAEL
Banking Hours: 8:30AM - 12:30PM; 4:PM - 5:30PM (Sun-Tue,Thur) 8:30AM -12:30PM (Wed); 8:30AM -12:Noon (Fri); Business Hours: Non-Gov't Office: 8:AM - 4:PM (Mon-Fri) Offices close early on Friday

## ITALY
Banking Hours: 8:35AM - 1:35PM; 3:PM - 4:PM (Mon-Fri); Business Hours: 8:30AM - 12:30PM, 3:30PM-7:30PM; Shopping Hours: 9:AM - 1:PM, 3:30/4:PM - 7:30/8:PM

## JAMAICA
Banking Hours: 9:AM - 2:PM (Mon - Thur); 9:AM - 12:Noon & 2:PM- 5:PM (Fri); Business Hours: 8:AM - 4:PM; Shopping Hours: 8:30AM - 4:30PM

## JAPAN
Banking Hours: 9:AM - 3:PM (Mon-Fri); 9:AM 12:Noon(Sat); Business/Shopping: 9:AM - 5:PM (Mon-Fri); 9:AM - 12:Noon (Sat)

## JORDAN
Banking Hours: 8:AM - 12:30PM (Sat-Thur) Business/Shopping Hours: 8:AM - 6:PM (Sat-Thur)

## KENYA
Banking Hours: 9:AM - 2:PM (Mon - Fri); 9:AM - 11;AM (1st & last saturday of month); Business Hours: 8:30AM - 4:30PM (Mon -Fri), 8:30 - 12:Noon (Sat); Shopping Hours: 8:30AM - 12:30PM, 2:PM - 5:PM (Mon - Sat)

## KOREA, SOUTH
Banking Hours: 9:30AM - 4:30PM (Mon-Fri); 9:30AM - 11:PM (Sat) Business/Shopping Hours: 9:AM - 5:PM (Mon-Fri): 9:AM - 1:PM (Sat)

## KUWAIT
Banking Hours: Mostly in the morning; Business/Shopping Hours: Gov't Offices: 7:30AM - 1:30PM Non-Gov't Offices: 7:30AM - 2:30PM (Sat-Wed);7:AM - 1:PM; 5:PM - 8:PM

## KYRGYZSTAN
Banking Hours: 9:AM - 6:PM Business Hours: 9:AM - 6:PM Shopping Hours: 8:AM - 9:PM

## LATVIA
Banking Hours: 9:AM - 12:Noon Business Hours: 9:AM - 6:PM Shopping Hours: 8:Am - 10:PM

## LEBANON
Banking Hours: 8:30AM - 12:30PM (Mon-Fri); 8:30AM - 12:Noon (Sat)

## LESOTHO
Banking Hours: 8:30AM - 1:PM (Mon-Fri); 9:AM - 11:AM (Sat); Business Hours: 8:AM - 4:30PM (Mon-Fri); Shopping Hours: 8:AM - 4:30PM (Mon-Fri); 8:AM - 1:PM (Sat)

## LIBERIA
Banking Hours: 9:AM - 5:PM (Mon-Sat); Business Hours: 9:AM - 6:PM (Mon-Sat)

## LIBYA
Banking Hours: 8:AM - 4:PM (Sat-Thur); Business Hours: 8:AM - 4:PM (Sat-Thur)

## LIECHTENSTEIN
Banking Hours: 8:30AM - 12:Noon, 1:30 - 4:30PM (Mon-Fri); Business Hours: 8:AM - 12:Noon, 2:30PM - 6:PM ; Shopping Hours: 8:AM - 12:15PM, 2:PM - 6:30PM (Mon-Fri), 8:AM - 4:PM (Sat)

## LITHUANIA
Banking Hours: 9:AM - 12:Noon; Business Hours: 9:AM - 1:PM, 2:PM - 6:PM (Mon-Sat)

## LUXEMBOURG
Banking Hours: 9:AM - 12:Noon; 2:PM - 5:PM (Mon-Sat); Business Hours: 9:AM - 12:Noon, 2:PM - 5:30PM; Shopping Hours: 8:AM - 12:Noon, 2:PM - 6:PM (Mon-Sat)

## MADAGASCAR
Banking Hours: 8:AM - 11:AM, 2:PM - 4:PM (Mon-Fri); Shopping Hours: 9:AM - 6:PM (Mon-Sat); Business Hours: 8:AM - 12:Noon, 2:PM - 6:PM (Mon-Fri)

**MALAWI**
Banking Hours: 8:AM - 1:PM (Mon-Fri); Business Hours: 7:30AM - 5:PM (Mon-Fri);Shopping Hours: 8:AM - 6:PM

**MALAYSIA**
Business/Shopping Hours: 8:30/9:AM - 1:PM, 2:30PM - 4:30PM (Mon-Fri); 9:AM - 1:PM (Sat) Gov't Offices: 9:AM - 4:30Pm (Mon-Fri); 9:AM -1:PM (Sat)

**MALI**
Banking Hours: 8:AM - 12:Noon, 2:PM - 4:PM (Mon-Fri); Business Hours: 7:30AM - 2:30PM (Mon-Sat), 7:30AM - 12:30PM (Fri); Shopping Hours: 9:AM - 8:PM (Mon-Sat)

**MALTA**
Banking Hours: 8:30AM - 12:30PM (Mon-Fri), 8:30AM - 11:30AM (Sat); Business Hours: 8:30AM - 5:30PM (Mon-Fri), 8:30AM - 1:PM (Sat); Shopping Hours: 9:AM - 1:PM, 4:PM - 7:PM (Mon-Fri), 9:AM -1:PM, 4:PM - 8:PM (Sat)

**MARTINIQUE**
Banking Hours: 7:30AM - 4:PM (Mon-Fri); Shopping Hours: 8:30AM - 6:PM (Mon-Fri); 8:30AM - 1:PM (Sat)

**MAURITANIA**
Banking Hours: 8:AM - 3:PM (Sun-Thur); Business Hours: 8:AM - 3:PM (SunThur); Shopping Hours: 8:AM - 1:PM, 3:PM - 6:PM (Sun-Thur)

**MAURITIUS**
Banking Hours: 10:AM - 2:PM (Mon - Fri), 9:30AM - 11:30AM (Sat); Shopping Hours: (Varies) 9:AM - 5:PM (Mon-Fri), 9:AM -12:Noon (Sat, Sun)

**MEXICO**
Banking Hours: 9:AM - 1:30PM (Mon-Fri); Business Hours: 9:AM - 6:PM (Mon-Fri); Shopping Hours: 10:AM - 5:PM (Mon-Fri);

10:AM - 8:/9:PM

**MICRONESIA**
Banking Hours: 9:30Am - 2:30PM (Mon-Fri)

**MONACO**
Banking Hours: 9:AM - 12:Noon, 2:PM - 4:PM (Mon-Fri); Business Hours: 8:30AM - 6:PM; Shopping Hours: 9:AM - 12:Noon, 2:PM - 7:PM (Mon-Sat)

**MONTSERRAT**
Banking Hours: 8:AM - 1:PM (Mon-Thur); Business Hours: 8:AM - 4:PM; Shopping Hours: 8:AM - 4:PM

**MOROCCO**
Banking Hours: 8:30AM - 11:30AM, 3:PM - 5:30PM (Mon-Fri); Business Hours: 8:30AM - 12:Noon,2:30PM - 6:30PM (Mon-Fri), 8:30AM - 12:Noon (Sat); Shopping Hours: 8:30AM - 12:Noon, 2:PM - 6:30PM (Mon-Sat)

**MOZAMBIQUE**
Banking Hours: 7:30 -12:Noon, 2:PM - 5:PM (Mon-Fri), 7:30AM - 12:Noon (Sat); Business Hours: 7:30AM - 12:Noon, 2:PM - 5:PM (Mon-Fri), 7:30AM - 12:Noon (Sat)

**NAMIBIA**
Banking Hours: 9:AM - 3:30PM (Mon-Fri), 8:30AM - 11:AM (Sat)Business Hours: 8:30AM - 5:PM (Mon-Fri); Shopping Hours: 8:30AM - 5:30PM (Mon-Fri) 9:AM - 1:PM (Sat)

**NEPAL**
Banking Hours: 10:AM - 3:PM (Sat-Thur);10:AM - 12:Noon (Sat)

**NETHERLANDS**
Banking Hours: 9:AM - 4/5:PM (Mon-Fri); Business Hours: 8:30 - 5:30PM; Shopping Hours: 8:30/9:AM - 5:30/6:PM (Mon-Fri)

**NETHERLANDS ANTILLES**
Banking Hours: 8:30AM - 11:AM; 2:PM - 4:PM

(Mon-Fri); Business/Shopping Hours:8:AM - 12:Noon; 2:PM - 6:PM (Mon-Sat)

### NEW CALEDONIA
Banking Hours: 7:AM - 10:30AM; 1:30PM - 3:30PM (Mon-Fri); 7:30 - 11:AM (Sat)

### NEW ZEALAND
Banking Hours: 10:AM - 4:PM (Mon-Fri); Business/Shopping Hours: 9:AM - 5:PM (Mon-Fri)

### NIGARAGUA
Banking Hours: 8:30AM - 12:Noon; 2:PM - 4:PM (Mon-Fri); 8:30AM - 11:30AM (Sat); Business/Shopping Hours: 8:AM - 5:30PM (Mon-Sat)

### NIGER
Banking Hours: 7:30AM - 12:30PM, 3:30PM - 5:PM; Business Hours: 7:30AM - 12:30:PM, 3:30PM - 6:30PM; Shopping Hours: 7:30AM - 12:30PM, 3:30PM - 6:30PM

### NIGERIA
Banking Hours: 8:AM - 3:PM (Mon), 8:AM - 1:30PM (Tues-Fri):; Business Hours: Gov't Offices: 7:30AM - 3:30PM (Mon-Fri) Private Firms: 8:AM - 5:PM (Mon-Fri)

### NORWAY
Banking Hours: 8:15AM - 3:30PM (Mon, Tue, Wed, Fri); 8:15AM - 5:PM (Thur); Business Hours: 9:AM - 4:PM; Shopping Hours: 9:AM - 5:PM (Mon-Fri); 9:AM - 6/7:PM (Thur); 9:AM-1/2:PM (Sat)

### PAKISTAN
Banking Hours: 9:AM - 1:PM (Mon-Thur); 9:AM - 11:30AM (Sat)   Business/Shopping Hours: 9:30AM - 1:PM (Mon-Thur); 9:AM -10:30AM (Sat)

### PANAMA
Banking Hours: 8:30AM - 1:PM (Mon-Fri); Business Hours: 8:30AM - 12:30PM & 1:30PM -

4:PM (Mon-Fri)); Shopping Hours: 8:30AM - 6:PM (Mon-Sat)

### PARAGUAY
Banking Hours: 7:AM - 12:Noon (Mon-Fri); Shopping Hours: 7:AM - 12:Noon & 3:PM - 7:PM

### PERU
Banking Hours: 9:AM - 1:PM (Mon-Fri); Business Hours: 9:AM - 5:PM (Mon-Fri); Shopping Hours: 9:AM - 7:PM (Mon-Sat)

### PHILIPPINES
Banking Hours: 9:AM - 6:PM (Mon-Fri); 9:AM 12:30 (Sat);

### POLAND
Banking Hours: 8:AM - 1:PM; Business Hours: 8:30AM - 3:30PM; Shopping Hours: 9:AM - 8:PM

### PORTUGAL
Banking Hours: 8:AM - 3:PM (Mon-Fri); Business Hours: 10:AM - 6:PM; Shopping Hours: 9:AM - 1:PM, 3:PM - 7:PM (Mon-Fri), 9:AM -12:Noon (Some Shops)

### PUERTO RICO
Banking Hours: 9:AM - 5:PM (Mon-Fri); Business Hours: 8:AM - 5:PM (Mon-Fri); Shopping Hours: 9:AM - 6:PM (Mon-Sat)

### QATAR
Banking Hours: 7:30AM - 11:30AM (Sat-Thur)

### REUNION ISLAND
Business/Shopping Hours: 8:AM - 12:Noon; 2:PM - 6:PM

### ROMANIA
Banking Hours: 8:30 - 11:30AM; Business Hours: 8:AM - 4:PM (Mon-Fri), 8:AM - 12:30PM (Sat); Shopping Hours: 9:AM - 1:PM, 4:PM-6/8:PM

### RUSSIA
Banking Hours: 9:AM - 6:PM; Business Hours: 9:AM - 6:PM; Shopping Hours: 9:AM - 9:PM (Mon-Sat)

### RWANDA
Banking Hours: 8:AM - 11:AM, 2:PM - 5:PM (Mon-Fri), 8:AM -1:PM (Sat); Business Hours: 7:AM - 12:Noon, 2:PM - 6:PM (Mon-Fri); Shopping Hours: 8:AM - 6:PM (Mon-Fri), 11:AM - 6:PM (Sat)

### SRI LANKA
Banking Hours: 9:AM - 1:PM (Mon-Fri); 9:am - 11:AM (Sat)

### ST. KITTS & NEVIS
Banking Hours: 8:AM - 1:PM (Mon-Fri); 8:AM - 1:PM; 3:PM -5:PM (Fri); Business Hours: 8:AM - 12:Noon, 1:PM - 4:30PM (Mon, Tues); 8:AM - 12:Noon; 1:PM - 4:PM (Wed Thur, Fri); Shopping Hours: 8:AM - 12:Noon, 1:PM -4:PM Shops closed on Thursday afterNoons

### ST. LUCIA
Banking Hours: 8:AM - 12:30PM (Mon-Thur); 8:AM - 12:Noon & 3:PM - 5:PM (Fri); Shopping Hours: 8:AM - 4:30PM (Mon-Fri); 8:AM - 1:PM (Sat)

### SAN MARINO
Banking Hours: 8:30AM - 12:Noon, 2:30PM - 3:15PM; Business Hours: 8:AM - 12:Noon, 2:PM - 6:PM; Shopping Hours: 8:AM - 12:Noon 3:PM - 7:PM

### ST. MAARTEN
Banking Hours: 8:30AM - 1:PM (Mon-Thur); 8:30AM - 1:PM & 4:PM - 5:PM (Fri); Business Hours: 8:AM -12:Noon & 2:PM - 6:PM; Shopping Hours: 8:AM - 12:Noon & 2:PM - 6:PM

### ST. MARTIN
Banking Hours: 9:AM - 12:Noon & 2:PM - 3:PM (Mon-Fri); Shopping Hours: 9:AM - 12/12:30 &

2:PM - 6:PM (Mon-Sat)

### SAO TOME AND PRINCIPE
Banking Hours: 7:30AM - 12:30PM, 2:30PM - 4:30PM (Mon-Fri); Businss Hours: 7:30AM - 12:30PM, 2:30PM - 4:30PM (Mon-Fri); Shopping Hours: 9:AM - 12:30PM, 2:30PM - 6:PM (Mon-Sat)

### ST. VINCENT & THE GRENADINES
Banking Hours: 8:AM - 12/1:PM (Mon - Thur); 8:AM - 12:/1:PM & 2:/3:PM -5:PM (Fri) ;Business Hours: 8:AM - 12:Noon & 1:PM - 4:PM (Mon - Fri); 8:AM- 12:Noon (Sat)

### SAUDI ARABIA
Banking Hours: 7/8:AM - 2:30PM (Sat-Thur); Business Hours: Gov't Offices: In Winter 8:AM - 4:PM (Sat- Wed); In Summer 7:AM - 3:PM; During Ramadan 8:AM - 2:PM Others: 8:30AM-1:30PM; 4:30AM -8PM (Sat-Thur) closed Friday

### SENEGAL
Banking Hours: 8:AM - 11:AM, 2:30PM - 4:30PM (Mon-Fri);Business Hours: 8:AM - 12:Noon , 3:PM - 6:PM (Mon-Fri), 8:AM - 12:Noon (Sat); Shopping Hours: 8:AM - 7:PM (Mon-Sat)

### SEYCHELLES
Banking Hours: 8:30AM - 1:30PM (Mon-Sat); Business Hours: 8:AM - 12:Noon, 1:PM - 4:PM (Mon-Fri); Shopping Hours: 8:AM - 5:PM (Mon-Fri), 8:AM - 1:PM (Sat)

### SIERRA LEONE
Banking Hours: 9:AM - 2:PM (Mon-Fri); Business Hours: 9:AM - 2:PM (Mon-Fri); Shopping Hours: 9:AM - 6:PM (Mon-Sat)

### SINGAPORE
Banking Hours: 10:AM - 3:PM (Mon-Fri); 9:30AM - 11:30AM (Sat); Business Hours: Gov't: 9:AM - 4:30PM (Mon-Fri); 9:AM - 1:PM (Sat);Shopping Hours: 9:AM - 6:PM (Mon-Sat)

**209**

## SOUTH AFRICA
Banking Hours: 9:AM - 3:PM (Mon,Tue,Thur,Fri); 9:AM - 1:PM (Wed); 9:AM -11:AM (Sat); Business/Shopping Hours: 8:30AM - 5:PM (Mon-Fri); 8:30AM - 12:Noon(Sat) Some stores

## SPAIN
Banking Hours: 9:AM - 2:PM (Mon-Fri), 9:AM - 1: PM (Sat); Business Hours: 9:AM - 2:PM, 4:PM - 7:PM; Shopping Hours: 9:AM - 1:PM, 4:PM - 8:PM

## SUDAN
Banking Hours: 8:30AM - 12:Noon (Sat-Thur); Business/Shopping Hours: 8:AM - 1:PM; 5:PM - 8:PM (Sat-Thur)

## SURINAME
Banking Hours: 8:AM - 3:PM (Mon-Fri); Business Hours: 7:AM - 3:PM (Mon-Fri); Shopping Hours: 7:30AM - 4:PM (Mon-Fri)

## SWEDEN
Banking Hours: 9:30AM - 3:PM (Mon,Tue,Wed,Fri), 9:30AM -3:PM, 4:PM - 5:30PM (Thur); Business Hours: 8:AM - 5:PM; Shopping Hours: 9:30AM - 6:PM (Mon-Fri), 9:30AM - 1:PM (Sat), Noon - 4:PM (Sun)

## SWITZERLAND
Banking Hours: 8:30AM - 4:30PM (Mon-Fri); Business Hours: 8:AM - 12:Noon; 2:PM - 6:PM; Shopping Hours: 8:AM - 12:15PM, 1:30PM - 6:30AM (Mon-Fri); 8:AM - 4:PM (Sat)

## SYRIA
Banking Hours: 8:AM - 12:30PM (Sat-Thur) Business Hours: 8:AM - 1:30PM; 4:30PM - 9:PM (Sat-Thur)

## TANZANIA
Business/Shopping Hours: 8:AM - 5/6:PM (Mon-Sat)

## TAJIKISTAN

## [untitled]
Bankng Hours: 9:AM - 6:PM
Business Hours: 9:AM - 6:PM
Shopping Hours: 8:AM - 9:PM

## THAILAND
Business/Shopping Hours: 8:30AM - 7/8:PM

## TOGO
Banking Hours: 7:30AM - 11:30AM; 1:30 - 3:30PM (Mon-Fri); Business/Shopping Hours: 8:AM - 6:PM (Mon-Fri); Sat morning

## TONGA
Banking Hours: 9:30AM - 4:30PM (Mon-Fri)

## TRINIDAD AND TOBAGO
Banking Hours: 9:AM - 2:PM (Mon-Thur) & 9:AM - 12:Noon; 3:PM -5:PM (Fri); Shopping Hours: 8:AM - 4:PM (Mon-Fri); 8:AM - 12:Noon (Sat)

## TUNISIA
Banking Hours: 8:AM - 11:AM; 2:PM - 4:PM (Mon-Fri)

## TURKEY
Banking Hours: 8:30AM - 12:Noon, 1:30 - 5:PM (Mon-Fri); Business Hours: 8:30AM - 12:30PM, 1:30PM - 5:30PM; Shopping Hours: 9:AM - 1:PM, 2:PM - 7:PM (Mon-Sat)

## TURKMENISTAN
Banking Hours: 9:AM - 6:PM
Business Hours: 9:AM - 6:PM
Shopping Hours: 8:AM - 9:PM

## TURKS AND CAICOS
Banking Hours: 8:30AM - 3:30PM
Business Hours: 8:30AM - 5:PM
Shopping Hours: 9:AM - 7:PM

## UKRAINE
Banking Hours: 9:AM - 6:PM
Business Hours: 9:AM - 6:PM
Shopping Hours: 8:AM - 9:PM

**UNITED KINGDOM**
Banking Hours: (Varies) England & Wales: 9:AM - 3:PM (Mon-Fri) Scotland: 9:30 - 12:30PM, 1:30 - 3:30PM (Mon - Wed), 9:30AM -12:30PM, 1:30 - 3:30PM, 3:30PM -4:30PM-6PM (Thur) 9:30AM - 3:30PM (Fri), North Ireland: 10:AM - 3:30PM (Mon - Fri); Business Hours: 9:AM - 5:PM; Shopping Hours: 9:AM - 5:30PM

**UZBEKISTAN**
Banking Hours: 9:AM - 6:PM
Business Hours: 9:AM - 6:PM
Shopping Hours: 8:AM - 9:PM

**URUGUAY**
Banking Hours: 1:PM - 5:PM (Mon-Fri); Business Hours: 7:AM - 1:30PM (Mon-Fri) Summer & 12:30 - 7:PM (Mon-Fri) Winter; Shopping Hours: 10:AM - 7:PM (Mon-Sat)

**VENEZUELA**
Banking Hours: 9:AM - 12:Noon & 3:PM - 5:PM (Mon-Fri); Business Hours: 8:AM - 12:Noon & 2:PM - 5:PM (Mon-Fri); Shopping Hours: 9:AM - 12:Noon & 2:PM - 5:PM (Mon-Sat)

**VIETNAM**
Banking Hours: 8:AM - 11:30AM; 2:PM - 4:PM (Mon-Fri); 8:AM - 11:AM (Sat)

**WESTERN SAMOA**
Banking Hours: 9:30AM - 3:PM (Mon-Fri); 9:30AM - 11:30AM (Sat)

**YUGOSLAVIA**
Banking Hours: 7:AM - 12:Noon or 7:AM - 7:PM; Business Hours: 8:AM - 12:30PM; Shopping Hours: 8:AM - 12:Noon, 4:PM - 8:PM or 8:AM - 8:PM (Mon-Fri) 8:AM - 3:PM (Sat)

**ZAIRE**
Banking Hours: 8:AM - 11:30 (Mon-Fri); Business/Shopping Hours: 8:AM - 12:Noon; 3:PM - 6:PM (Mon- Sat)

**ZAMBIA**
Banking Hours: 8:AM - 1:PM (Mon-Fri); 8:AM - 11:AM (Sat); Business/Shopping Hours: 8:AM - 5:PM (Mon-Fri); 8:AM - 3:PM (Sat)

**ZIMBABWE**
Banking Hours: 8:30AM - 2:PM (Mon,Tue, Thur, Fri); 8:30AM -12:Noon (Wed); 8:30AM - 11:AM (Sat); Business/Shopping Hours: 8:AM - 5:PM

**211**

# APPENDIX U

## COUNTRIES AND OFFICIAL LANGUAGES

| COUNTRY | OFFICIAL LANGUAGE | OTHER LANGUAGES |
|---|---|---|
| AFGHANISTAN | Dari, pashto | Uzbek, Turkmen |
| ALBANIA | Albanian | Greek |
| ALGERIA | Arabic | Berber, French |
| ANDORRA | Catalan | Spanish, French |
| ANGOLA | Portuguese | |
| ANTIGUA & BARBUDA | English | |
| ARGENTINA | Spanish | English, Italian, German |
| ARMENIA | Armenian | Azerbaijani, Russian |
| AUSTRALIA | English | |
| AUSTRIA | German | |
| AZERBAIJAN | Azeerbaijani | Russian, Armenian |
| BAHAMAS | English | Creole |
| BAHRAIN | Arabic | English, Farsi, Urdu |
| BANGLADESH | Bangla (Bengali) | English |
| BARBADOS | English | |
| BELARUS | Byelorussian | Russian |
| BELGIUM | Dutch (Flemish) | French, German |
| BELIZE | English | Spanish, Garifuna, Mayart |
| BENIN | French | Fon, Adja, |
| BERMUDA | English | |
| BHUTAN | Dzongkha | Tibeatan & Nepalese |
| BOLIVIA | Spanish | Quechua, Aymara |
| BOSNIA-HERCEGORVINA | Serb, Croat, Albanian | |
| BOTSWANA | English | Tswana |
| BRAZIL | Portuguese | Spanish, English |
| BRITISH VIRGIN IS. | English | |
| BRUNEI | Malay | English, Chinese |
| BULGARIA | Bulgarian | |
| BURKINA FASO | French | |
| BURMA | Burmese | |
| BURUNDI | French, Kirundi | Swahili |

212

| | | |
|---|---|---|
| CAMBODIA | Cambodian (Khmer) | French |
| CAMEROON | English, French | |
| CANADA | English, French | |
| CENTRAL AFRICAN REP. | French | Sango, Arabic, |
| CHAD | French | Arabic |
| CHILE | Spanish | |
| CHINA, PEOPLES REP. | Chinese | |
| CHINA, TAIWAN | Chinese | |
| COLUMBIA | Spanish | |
| COMOROS | French | Abrabic, Shaafi Islam |
| CONGO, PEOPLE'S REP. | French | |
| COSTA RICA | Spanish | |
| COTE D'IVOIRE | French | |
| CROATIA | Croat | Serb |
| CUBA | Spanish | |
| CYPRUS | Greek, Turkish, English | |
| CZECH REP. | Czech & Slovak | Hungarian |
| DENMARK | Danish | |
| DOMINICA | English | |
| DOMINICAN REP. | Spanish | |
| ECUADOR | Spanish | Quechua |
| EGYPT | Arabic | |
| EL SALVADOR | Spanish | Nahua |
| ESTONIA | Estonian | Russian |
| ETHIOPIA | Amharic | tigrinya, Orominga, Arabic |
| FAEROW ISLANDS | Danish, Faroese | |
| FIJI | English | Fiji |
| FINLAND | Finnish | Swedish |
| FRANCE | French | |
| FRENCH POLYNESIA | French | Tahitian, Chinese |
| FRENCH GUIANA | French | |
| FRENCH ANTILLES | French | |
| GABON | French | Fang |
| GEORGIA | Georgian | Russian, Armenian |
| GERMANY | German | |
| GHANA | English | Akan |
| GIBRALTAR | English | Spanish |
| GREECE | Greek | |
| GREENLAND | Danish | Greenlandic, Inuit |
| GRENADA | English | |
| GUADELOUPE | French | Creole |
| GUAM | English | Chamorro, Tagalog |

| | | |
|---|---|---|
| **GUATEMALA** | Spanish | |
| **GUINEA** | French | |
| **GUINEA-BISSAU** | Portuguese | Crioulo |
| **GUYANA** | English | |
| **HAITI** | French | Creole |
| **HONDURAS** | Spanish | |
| **HONG KONG** | Chinese (Cantonese) | English |
| **HUNGARY** | Magyar | |
| **ICELAND** | Icelandic | |
| **INDIA** | Hindi | English |
| **INDONESIA** | Indonesian | Javanese, Sundanese |
| **IRAN** | Farsi | Turkish, Kurdish, Arabic |
| **IRAQ** | Arabic | Kurdish, Assyrian, Armenian |
| **IRELAND** | English, Gaelic | Irish |
| **ISRAEL** | Hebrew, Arabic | Yiddish, English |
| **ITALY** | Italian | |
| **JAMAICA** | English | Creole |
| **JAPAN** | Japanese | |
| **JORDAN** | Arabic | |
| **KAZAKHSTAN** | Kazakh | Russian, German, Ukraine |
| **KENYA** | English | Swahili |
| **KIRIBATI** | English | Gilbertese |
| **KOREA, SOUTH** | Korean | |
| **KOREA, NORTH** | Korean | |
| **KUWAIT** | Arabic | English |
| **KYRGYZSTAN** | Kirghiz | Russian, Uzbek |
| **LAOS** | Lao | French, Tai |
| **LATVIA** | Latvian | Russian |
| **LEBANON** | Arabic | French, Armenian, English |
| **LESOTHO** | English | Sesotho, Zulu, Xhosa |
| **LIBERIA** | English | |
| **LIBYA** | Arabic | |
| **LIECHTENSTEIN** | German | |
| **LITHUANIA** | Lithuanian | Russian, Polish |
| **LUXEMBOURG** | French, German | Luxembourgish |
| **MADAGASCAR** | Malagasy, French | |
| **MALAWI** | Chichewa, English | Tombuka |
| **MALAYSIA** | Malay | Chinese, English, tamil |
| **MALDIVES** | Divehi | |
| **MALI** | French | Bambara |
| **MALTA** | English, Maltese | |
| **MARSHALL ISLANDS** | English | Malay-Polynesian, Japanese |

**214**

| | | |
|---|---|---|
| **MARTINIQUE** | French | Creole |
| **MAURITANIA** | Arabic, French | |
| **MAURITIUS** | English | Creole, Bhohpuri, Hindi |
| **MAYOTTE ISLANDS** | French | Swahili |
| **MEXICO** | Spanish | |
| **MICRONESIA** | English | Malay-Polynesian |
| **MOLDOVA** | Moldavian | Russian, Ukrainian |
| **MONACO** | French | English, Italian, Monegasque |
| **MONGOLIA** | Khalkha Mongol | Kazakh, Russian, Chinese |
| **MONTSERRAT** | English | |
| **MOROCCO** | Arabic | Berber, FRench |
| **MOZAMBIQUE** | Portuguese | |
| **NAURU** | Nauruan | English |
| **NEPAL** | Nepali | Maithali, Bhojpuri |
| **NETH. ANTILLES** | Dutch | Papiamento, English |
| **NETHERLANDS** | Dutch | |
| **NEW CALEDONIA** | French | |
| **NEW ZEALAND** | English | Maori |
| **NICARAGUA** | Spanish | English |
| **NIGER** | French | Hausa, Ndjerma |
| **NIGERIA** | English | Hausa, Yoruba, Ibo |
| **NORWAY** | Norwegian | Lapp |
| **OMAN** | Arabic | English, Baluchi, Urdu |
| **PAKISTAN** | Urdu | English, Punjab, Pashto, Sindhi, Saraiki |
| **PANAMA** | Spanish | English |
| **PAPUA NEW GUINEA** | English | Motu, Pidgin |
| **PARAGUAY** | Spanish | Guarani |
| **PERU** | Spanish, Quechua | Aymara |
| **PHILIPPINES** | English, Philipino | Tagalog |
| **POLAND** | Polish | |
| **PORTUGAL** | Portuguese | |
| **QATAR** | Arabic | English |
| **REP. OF DJIBOUTI** | Arabic | French, Somali, Afar |
| **REP. OF CAPE VERDE** | Portuguese, Crioulo | |
| **REP. OF PALAU** | Paluan, English | |
| **REUNION ISLAND** | French | Creole |
| **ROMANIA** | Romanian | Hungarian, German |
| **RUSSIA** | Russian | Tatar, Ukrainian |
| **RWANDA** | French, Kinyarwanda | |
| **SAN MARINO** | Italian | |
| **SAU TOME & PRINCIPE** | Portuguese | Fang |
| **SAUDI ARABIA** | Arabic | |

| | | |
|---|---|---|
| SENEGAL | French | |
| SEYCHELLES | English, French | Creole |
| SIERRA LEONE | English | Krio |
| SINGAPORE | Chinese, English, | Malay, Tamil |
| SLOVAK REP. | Slovak, Czech | Hungarian |
| SLOVANIA | Slovene | |
| SOLOMON ISLANDS | English | |
| SOMALIA | Somali | Arabic, English, Italian |
| SOUTH AFRICA | Afrikaans, English | Zulu, Xhosa |
| SPAIN | Spanish (Castilian) | Catalan, Galician, Basque |
| SRI LANKA | Sinhala, Tamil | English |
| ST. KITTS & NEVIS | English | |
| ST. LUCIA | English | French |
| ST. PIERRE & MIQUELON | French | |
| ST. VINCENT | English | French |
| SUDAN | Sudan | English |
| SURINAME | Dutch | Sranan, Tongo, English, Hindustani, Javanese |
| SWAZILAND | English, Siswati | |
| SWEDEN | Swedish | |
| SWITZERLAND | German, French, Italian | Romansch |
| SYRIA | Arabic | Kurdish, Armenian, Aramaic, Circassian |
| TAJIKISTAN | Tajik | Uzbek, Russian |
| TANZANIA | English, Swahili | |
| THAILAND | Thai | |
| THE GAMBIA | English | Malinke, Wolof, Fula |
| TOGO | French | |
| TONGA | Tongan | English |
| TRINIDAD & TOBAGO | English | Hindi, French, Spanish |
| TUNISIA | Arabic | French |
| TURKEY | Turkish | Kurdish, Arabic |
| TURKMENISTAN | Turkmen | Russian, Uzbek, Kazakh |
| TURKS & CAICOS | English | |
| UGANDA | English | Luganda, Swahili |
| UKRAINE | Ukrainian | Russian |
| UNITED KINGDOM | English | Welsh, Gaelic |
| UNITED ARAB EMIRATES | Arabic | English, Fashi, Hindi, Urdu |
| URUGUAY | Spanish | |
| UZBEKISTAN | Uzbek | Russian, Kazakh, Tajik |
| VATICAN CITY | none | Italian, Latin |
| VENEZUELA | Spanish | |
| VIETNAM | Vietnamese | French, Chinese, Khmer |
| WESTERN SAMOA | Samoan, English | |

| | | |
|---|---|---|
| **YEMEN, ARAB REP.** | Arabic | |
| **YEMEN, P.D. REP.** | Arabic | |
| **YUGOSLAVIA** | Macedonian, Serbo-Croatian | Slovene, Albanian, Hungarian |
| **ZAIRE** | French | Kikongo, Lingala, Swahili, |
| **ZAMBIA** | English | Tonga, Lozi |
| **ZIMBABWE** | English | Chishona, Sindebele |

# APPENDIX V

## TRAVEL INSURANCE PROVIDERS

Some companies and organizations specialize in providing a variety of insurance coverage and travel related services to domestic as well as international travelers including coverage for medical expenses, accidental injury and sickness, medical assistance, baggage loss, trip cancellation or trip interruption. Check with your travel agent/agency, broker, or travel advisor for reputable insurers in your area. Members of travel clubs and automobile clubs may also check with their associations for availability of such policies.

Here are a few companies widely known in the country to provide travel-related insurance coverage. These companies also sell short-term policies.

**Carefree Travel Insurance**
120 Mineola Blvd.,
P.O.Box 310, Mineola NY 11501
(800) 323-3149 or (516) 294-0220

**Edmund A Cocco/Globalcare Travel Insurance**
220 Broadway, #201,
Lynnfield MA 01940
(800) 821-2488

**Mutual of Omaha**/Tele-Trip
Mutual of Omaha Plaza
Box 31685, 3201 Farnam St.
Omaha, Nebraska 68175
(800) 228-7669 or (800) 228-9792

**Travel Guard International**
1100 Centerpoint Drive,
Stevens Point Wisconsin 54481
(800) 782-5151 or (715) 345-0505

**Travel Insurance Programs Corporation**
243 Church St.
West Vienna, VA 22180
(703) 448-2472

**Travel Pak**
The Travelers Insurance Co.
One Tower Square, 15NB
Hartford, CT 06115
(800) 243-3174; (203) 277-0111

**Safeware** provides insurance coverage for computers. You should consider this since other travel policies do not often cover equipments such as computers. Safeware could be reached at 2929 North High Street, Columbus Ohio, 43202. (800) 848-3469; (614) 262-0559.

**ALLSTATE** provides insurance covering off-premises losses, including those due to theft. Check your local telephone directory for the nearest ALLSTATE insurance agent.

**218**

# *APPENDIX W*

## MEDICAL ASSISTANCE ORGANIZATIONS

**ACCESS AMERICA** offers travel insurance and 24-hour emergency travel, medical, and legal assistance for the traveler. One call to their hotline center, staffed by multilingual coordinators, connects travelers to a worldwide network of professionals able to offer specialized help in reaching the nearest physician or hospital. Services include medical consultation and monitoring of travelers by hotline center physicians, medical transportation and on-site hospital payments. Varying coverage levels available. For further information call: Toll Free: 800-284-8300 or write: P.O. 6600 West Broad St.,Box 11188, Richmond, VA 23230.

**ASSIST-CARD INTERNATIONAL**
444 Brickell Ave., Suite M130, Miami Florida 33131. (800) 221-4564 or (305) 381-9969

**CAREFREE TRAVEL INSURANCE**
Carefree provides health, emergency health evacuation, baggage and trip cancellation insurance. They are located at 120 Mineola Blvd., P.O. Box 310, Mineola, NY 11501. (800) 323-3149 or (516) 294-0220.

**EMERGENCY DATA BUREAU OF AMERICA INC.,** an international company, provides a complete Emergency Medical Identification System. The laminated membership card contains medical and personal history on four microfilm chips sufficient for Emergency Room use for informed treatment. Information includes treatment and surgical authorizations, and authorization to treat minor children if parents or guardian cannot be reached. EKG and other charts or records can be included on microfilm at no additional cost. EMERGENCY DATA BUREAU can be called without charge worldwide 24 hours if microfilm viewer is not readily available. Special decals are furnished to each member so that emergency personnel know the card is being carried. Membership cards can be easily updated. Individual memberships are $45 annually; spouse may be included for $22.50, children $11 each. Special group and corporate rates are available. For information write P.O. Box 4187 Mesa, AZ 85201 or call (602) 833-2583

**HEALTH CARE ABROAD**
243 Church Street West Vienna, VA 22180. (703) 591-9800.

**I.T.C. TRAVELLERS ASSISTANCE LTD** is an international assistance service with Coordination Centers in 174 countries. Trained, local multilingual personnel provide free medical aid 24 hours a day.

**219**

Worldwide membership includes: free telephone access to any eight ITC Emergency Control Centers, all required medical assistance (ambulatory, hospitalization, prescribed medication, transportation); repatriation, free return tickets for children left unattended because of the Member's hospitalization. Individual or family membership is available for any length of trip, up to 180 days. Membership to ITC MEDICAL DATA AND REFERRAL BANK is also available. This service records members medical history, making it readily available to emergency treating personnel and provides member access to worldwide network of English speaking doctors. For additional information call (403) 228-4685 or Fax (403) 228-6271, or write, P.O. Box G-759, Stn. G, Calgary, Alberta, Canada T3A 2G6.

**IAMAT (International Association for Medical Assistance to Travelers)** is a nonprofit tax-exempt Foundation financed by donations from its members. The purpose of the Foundation is to assist travelers in need of medical attention while traveling outside of their country of residence, and to advise them of the sanitary and health conditions in different parts of the world. IAMAT's North American locations are at 417 Center St., Lewiston, NY 14092 (tel: 716-754-4883, and at 40 Regal Rd., Guelph, ON, Canada N1K 1B5. Upon joining IAMAT, members receive a Directory which lists IAMAT centers in 450 cities in 120 countries, along with the names and addresses of individual English-speaking physicians associated with IAMAT and a schedule of agreed upon fees. Membership also includes a Traveler's Clinical Record, various charts and brochures with information pertaining to Climate, Clothing, Food, Water conditions, Immunizations and other Health related recommendations for travel to Foreign countries. Donations for World Climate Charts are requested.

**INTERMEDIC INC.,**
777 Third Avenue, New York, NY 10017. (212) 486-8900

**INTERNATIONAL HEALTH CARE SERVICE**
440 East 69th Street, New York, NY 10021. (212) 472-4284.

**INTERNATIONAL SOS ASSISTANCE, INC.**
1 Neshaminy Interplex, Suite 310, Trevosa, PA 19047. (800) 523-8930 or (215) 244-1500

**LIFE EXTENSION INSTITUTE'S Primary Care Center**, located at 437 Madison Ave., 14th Flr., New York, NY 10022, is open to the public for the administration of immunization required for travel abroad. For further information call (212) 415-4747.

**MEDEX/TravMed**--a worldwide travelers' assistance program that provides prompt access to medical and related assistance services 24 hours a day 7 days a week. By calling the nearest MEDEX Assistance Center, a multilingual specialist will immediately assist you in locating quality medical providers and services and assist you in overcoming language barriers by directing you to English speaking doctors/translators. MEDEX will coordinate and establish contact with your family, personal physician and employer and

**220**

monitor your progress during treatment and recovery and will make direct immediate payment of your medical bills. When necessary, arrangements can be made for emergency medical evacuation and repatriation. For TravMed information call Toll-free: U.S. 800-732-5309 or write: I.T.A.A. P.O. Box 10623, Baltimore, MD 21285.

## MEDIC ALERT FOUNDATION
P.O. Box 1009, Turlock, CA 95381. (800) 344-3226.

**MEDICAL ALERT FOUNDATION INTERNATIONAL** a nonprofit and charitable foundation that has since 1956 offered a lifetime emergency medical ID service--an alerting bracelet individually engraved with patient information and a 24 hour hotline phone number, so that physician and family can be contacted in emergency, plus an annually updated wallet card with medical and personal information. There is a one-time fee of $35.50 for all services; medically indigent patients are enrolled without charge at the request of physicians. Each year a new wallet card is issued and members' computer data can be updated with any change in medical or personal information whenever necessary for a small fee of $7.00. For additional information, write to Medic Alert Foundation International, 2323 Colorado Ave., Turlock, CA 95380. Tel. 800-344-3226.

**T R A V E L   A S S I S T A N C E INTERNATIONAL** by Europe Assistance Worldwide Services, Inc. provides comprehensive medical and personal emergency assistance 24 hours a day, 365 days a year through agent offices in 211 nations and territories. TAI emergency services include medical referral, On-The-Spot payment for medical expenses, unlimited transportation expenses for medical evacuations, medical monitoring and follow-up, shipment of medication worldwide, repatriation of a child under the age of 16 if left unattended due to your hospitalization, payment for a friend or family member to visit if hospitalized more than 10 days and payment of added travel expenses for a traveling companion. Individual and group coverage is available from one week to a year. For further information call toll free: Continental U.S. 800-821-2828 (in Washington D.C. area call (202) 331-1609 or FAX (202) 331-1588), or write to : 1133 15th Street, N.W., Suite 400, Washington D.C. 20005.

**TRAVEL CARE INTERNATIONAL, INC.** provides assistance or evacuation in the event of a medical emergency anywhere in the world, 24 hours a day, 7 days a week; communicates with the patient's physician; arranges for appropriate medical crew, fight escorts and necessary medical equipment; arranges medical ground clearance on all ends, ground transportation at every landing and coordinates all the logistics of the repatriation. Coordinators provide language translators. Bedside to bedside services offered. For information contact Travel Care International, Inc., Eagle River airport, P.O.Box 846, Eagle River, WI 54521. TEL: 715/479-8881, Continental U.S. & Canada 800-5 AIR-MED.

**TRAVELER'S AID INTERNATIONAL** provides medical and legal assistance, and a number of other services such as theft and illness. TAI can be reached at 918 16th St. NW Washington DC 20006. (202) 659-9468.

**TRAVEL GUARD INTERNATIONAL**
1100 Centerpoint Drive, Stevens Point, Wisconsin 54481, (800) 782-5151 or (715) 345-0505.

**WALLACH & CO., Health Care Abroad** provides medical assistance for insured travelers. Their policies cover hospitalization, prescriptions, doctor's office visits, medical evacuations to the U.S. For more information, Box 480 Middleburg, VA 22117; (800) 237-6615; (703) 687-3166

**WORLDCARE TRAVEL ASSISTANCE ASSOCIATION, INC.,** is staffed 24 hours a day by American physicians, nurses and paramedics as well as a team of multi-lingual assistance coordinators. WORLDCARE provides medical assistance, evacuation and hospitalization coverage, as well as immediate payment for medical costs incurred abroad. If a member is hospitalized for 10 days or more, round trip airfare is provided to a family member to visit the hospitalized member. Return transportation is provided for minors left unattended as a result of member's hospitalization. Memberships are available for any length of trip up to one year. Administrative headquarters located in San Francisco. For more information write to: 605 Market St., Ste 1300, San Francisco, CA 94105, or call: (415) 541-4991; or toll-free: 800-666-4993 or 800-253-1877. Worldcare can also be reached at 2000 Pennsylvania Ave., Suite 7600, Washington D.C. 20006 (800) 521-4822 or (202) 293-0335

**\*\*STUDENTS, TEACHERS, and YOUTHS may want to also contact the** COUNCIL ON INTERNATIONAL EDUCATION EXCHANGE (CIEE) at 205 East 42nd Street, New York, NY 10017. (212) 661-1414. CIEE offers very affordable short term policies called "Trip Safe" to holders of the International Student Identification Card (ISIC), International Teachers Identification Card (ITIC) or the International Youth Card (IYC). These cards are issued by CIEE and can be easily obtained from them.

# *APPENDIX* X

## MEDICAL EMERGENCY KIT

Listed below are some items you may wish to include in your medical emergency kit. These items are readily available (in various brands) in your local pharmacy. Consult your physician for advice on other useful items and health matters.

Aspirin, 5 gr., or Tylenol, 325 mg.
Aluminum Hydroxide with Magnesium Trisilicate Tablets
Milk of Magnesia Tablets
Chlorpheniramine Tablets
Antihistamine Nasal Spray
Antimicrobial Skin Ointment
Calamine Lotion
Liquid Surgical Soap
Tweezers
Antifungal Skin Ointment
Zinc Undecylenate Foot Powder
Vitamin Mineral Tablets
Oil of Clove and Benzocaine Mixture
Opthalmic Ointment
Throat Lozenges
Kaolin Pectin Mixture, Tablets or Liquid

Paregoric or Lomotil
Adhesive Bandages
3-inch Wide Elastic Bandage
2-foot-by-19-Yard Gauze Bandage
4-inch by 4-inch Gauze Pad
Adhesive Medical Tape
Medium-Size Safety Pins
Thermometer
Insect Repellent
Sleeping Pills
Small Pack of Cotton Wool
Tampons
Tissues
A Pair of Scissors

# *Appendix Y*

## CURRENCY EXCHANGE SERVICES

**Thomas Cook,** 1800 K Street, N.W. Washington D.C. 20006, Tel. (800) 368-5683

**Ruesch International,** 1350 I Street, N.W. Washington D.C. 20005, Tel. (800) 424-2923

**American Express Travel Services***, Salt Lake City Utah, 84184 Tel. (800) 221-7282

**Citibank***, Foreign Currency Dept., 55 Water Street, 47th Flr., New York, NY. 10043, Tel. (800) 285-3000, or (212) 308-7863

---

\*      These firms provide limited currency services.

\*\* See Appendix O for information on how to send money.

# *APPENDIX  Z*

## INTERNATIONAL EMERGENCY CODES

| Country | Emergency # | Ambulance # | Police # |
|---|---|---|---|
| Algeria | | | 17 |
| Andorra | | 182-0020 | 21222 |
| Andorra | 11/15 | | 20020 |
| Anguilla | 999 | | |
| Antigua | 999 | | 20045/20125 |
| Argentina | | | 101 |
| Austria | | 144 | 133 |
| Bahamas | | 3222221 | 3224444 |
| Barbados | | | 112/60800 |
| Belgium | 900/901 | 906 | 101 |
| Belize | | | 2222 |
| Bermuda | | | 22222 |
| Bolivia | 118 | | 110 |
| Brazil | 2321234 | | 2436716 |
| Columbia | | | 12 |
| Costa Rica | | 2158888 | 117 |
| Cyprus | 999 | | |
| Czech Republic | 155 | | |
| Denmark | 000 | | |
| Dominican Republic | | | 6823000 |
| Egypt | | | 912644 |
| Ethiopia | | | 91 |
| Fiji Islands | 000 | | |
| Finland | 000 | 002/003 | |
| France | 17 | 12/17 | |

| | | | |
|---|---|---|---|
| **French Guiana** | | | 18 |
| **Germany** | | 110 | |
| **Gibraltar** | 199 | | |
| **Great Britain** | 999 | | |
| **Greece** | 100 | | 171 |
| **Guyana** | 999 | | |
| **Haiti** | 0 | | |
| **Hong Kong** | 999 | | |
| **Hungary** | 04 | | |
| **Iceland** | | | |
| (Reykavik) | 11100 | 11166 | |
| (elsewhere dial 02 for the operator who will then place the call) | | | |
| **India** | | 102 | 100 |
| **Ireland** | 999 | | |
| **Israel** | | | 100 |
| **Italy** | | 113 | 112 |
| **Jamaica** | 110 | | 119 |
| **Japan** | | 119 | 100 |
| **Jordan** | 19 | | |
| **Kenya** | 999 | | |
| **Liechtenstein** | | 144 | 117 |
| **Luxembourg** | 012 | | |
| **Malaysia** | 0 | | |
| **Malta** | 99 | | |
| **Maltese Island** | | 196 | 191 |
| **Monaco** | | 933-01945 | 17 |
| **Morocco** | | | 19 |
| **Nepal** | 11999 | | |
| **Netherlands** | | | |
| Amsterdam | 559-9111 | 5555555 | 222222 |
| (elsewhere dial 008 for the operator who will then place the call) | | | |
| **New Zealand** | 111 | | |
| **Norway** | | 003 | 110011 |
| **Pakistan** | 222222 | | |
| **Papua New Guinea** | | | 255555 |
| **Paraguay** | | | 49116 |
| **Peru** | 05 | | |
| **Phillipines** | | | |
| | | | 599011 |
| **Poland** | 999 | | 997 |
| **Portugal** | 115 | | |
| **San Marino** | 113 | | |

| | | | |
|---|---|---|---|
| Singapore | 999 | | |
| Spain | 091 | | |
| Sri Lanka | | | 26941/21111 |
| St. Vincent | | | 71121 |
| St. Kitts & Nevis | 999 | | |
| St. Lucia | 95 | | 99 |
| Suriname | 99933 | | 711111/77777 |
| Sweden | 90000 | | |
| Switzerland | | 144 | 117 |
| Tanzania | 999 | | |
| Thailand | | | 2810372/2815051 |
| Tunisia | | | 243000 |
| U.S. Virgin Is. | | 922 | 915 |
| Uruguay | 401111 | | 890 |
| Venezuela | | | 169/160 |
| Yugoslavia | 94 | | 92 |

# APPENDIX 1A

## ORGANIZATIONS THAT PROVIDE SERVICES TO INTERNATIONAL TRAVELERS

**Academic Travel Abroad**, 3210 Grace St., N.W. 1st flr. Washington, D.C. 20007, Tel. (202) 333-3355

**Airline passenger of America**, 4212 King St., Alexandria, VA 22302, Tel. (703) 824-0505

**Airport Operators Council International, Inc.,** 1220 19th St. NW, Suite 200, Washington DC, 20036, Fax. (202) 331-1362.

**American Council for International Studies**, 19 Bay State, Road, Boston, MA. 02215, Tel. (617) 236-2051

**American Automobile Association (AAA)**, AAA Drive, Heathrow, Florida 32746 (404) 444-4000

**American Youth Hostels,** P.O. Box 37613 Washington DC 20013, Tel. (202) 783-4943.

**American Association of Retired Persons (AARP)**, 1909 K-Street, NW Washington DC 20049 Tel. (800) 441-7575 or (800) 927-0111.

**American Society of Travel Agents (ASTA)**, 1101 King St., Alexandria, VA

22314, Tel. (703) 739-2782

**Association of Group Travel Executives**, c/o Arnold H. Light A.H. Light Co., Inc. 424 Madison Ave., Suite 705, New York, NY. 10017 Tel. (212) 486-4300

**Association of Corporate Travel Executives**, P.O. Box 5394, Parsippany, N.J. 07054, Tel. (201) 537-4614

**Citizens Emergency Center,** Bureau of Consular Affairs, Rm 4811, N.S. U.S. Department of State, Washington DC 20520, Tel. (202) 647-5225.

**Council on International Education Exchange (CIEE)**, 205 E. 42nd St., New York, NY 10017 (212) 661-1414.

**Council on International Education Exchange (CIEE),** 205 E. 42nd St., New York, NY 10017 Tel. (212) 661-1414.

**Cruise Lines International Association**, 500 Fifth Ave, Suite

407, New York, NY. 10110, Tel. (212) 921-0066

Fly Without Fear (FWF), 310 Madison Ave., New York, NY 10017, Tel. (212) 697-7666

Freighter Travel Club of America (FTC), P.O. Box 12693, Salem OR, 97309, Tel. (503) 399-8567

Hideaways International, 15 Goldsmith St., P.O. Box 1270, Littleton, MA 01460, Tel. (508) 486-8955, (800) 843-4433

Institute of Certified Travel Agents (ICTA), P.O. Box, 8256, 148 Linden St., Wellesley, MA. 02181 Tel. (617) 237-0280

Interexchange, 356 W. 34th St., 2nd flr. New York, NY., 10001 Tel. (212) 947-9533

International Gay Travel Association, P.O. Box 18247, Denver, CO. 80218, Tel. (303) 467-7117

International Federations of Women's Travel Organizations, 4545 N. 36th St., Suite 126, Phoenix, AZ, 85018 Tel. (602) 956-7175

International Association for Medical Assistance to Travellers (IAMAT), 417 Center St. Lewiston, NY. 14092 Tel. (716) 754-4883

International Airline Passengers Association (IAPA), 4341 Lindburg Dr., Dallas, TX, 75244, Tel. (214) 404-9980

International Association of Tour Managers, 1646 Chapel St., New Haven, CT. 06511, Tel. (203) 777-5994

International Cruise Passengers Association (ICPA), Box 886 F.D. R. Station, New York, NY 10150, Tel. (212) 486-8482

International Visitors Information Service, 733 15th Street, NW Suite 300, Washington DC 20005, Tel. (202) 783-6540.

International Bicycle Tours, Champlin Square, Box 754 Essex, CT 06426 Tel. (203) 767-7005

National Association of Cruise Only Agents, (NACOA) P.O. Box 7209, Freeport, NY. 11520

National Campers and Hikers Association, 4804 Transit Rd., Building 2, Depend, NY 1404, Tel. (716) 668-6242.

North American Vegetarian Society, P.O. Box 72, Dolgeville, NY 1339, Tel. (518) 568-7970.

SCI International Voluntary Service, Innisfree Village, Rt.2, BOX 506 Crozet, VA 22932, Tel. (804) 823-1826.

Share-A-Ride International (SARI), 100 Park Ave. Rockville, Maryland, Tel. (301) 217-0871

Society of Incentive Travel Executives, 347 Fifth Ave., Suite 610, New York, NY. 10016, Tel. (212) 725-8253

Society for the Advancement of Travel for the Handicapped (SATH), 347 Fifth Ave., Suite 610, New York, NY 10016 Tel. (212) 447-7284. 858-5483

**Travel Information Service (TIS)**, Moss Rehabilitation Hospital , 12th St., and Tabor Rd, Philadelphia, PA. 19141, Tel. (215) 456-9600

**U.S. Department of Commerce, International Trade Information Center,** Tel (800) 872-8723.

**U.S. Department of Transportation, Office of General Counsel**, 400 7th St. SW, Rm. 10422, Washington DC 20590, Tel. (202) 366-9306 (voice), (202) 755-7687 (TDD)

**U.S. Public Health Services, Centers for Disease Control,** Atlanta Georgia, Tel. (404) 539-2574.

**Volunteers for Peace International Work Camps**, 43 Tiffany Rd., Belmont VTY 05730, Tel. (802) 259-2759.

**World Ocean and Cruise Liner Society**, P.O. Box 92, Stamford, CT. 06904, Tel. (203) 329-2787

**230**

# APPENDIX 1B

## INTERNATIONAL CRUISES AND CRUISE LINES

**Admiral Cruises, Inc.**
1220 Biscayne Blvd.
Miami, FL 33132
(800) 327-0271

**Adrift Adventures**
378 N. Main St.
P.O. Box 577
Moab, UT 84532
(801) 259-8594 or (801) 485-5971, for
reservations only (800) 874-4483

**Adventure Center**
1311 63rd St. Suite 200
Emeryville, CA 94608
(510) 654-1879

**Alpine Adventure Trails Tours**
783 Cliffside Drive
Akron, OH 44313-5609
(212) 867-3771

**Amazon Tours and Cruises**
P.O. Box 39583
Los Angeles, CA 90039
(800) 423-2791

**Ambassador Travel**
3080 S. College Ave.
Fort Collins, CO 80525
(800) 453-7314

**American Hawaii Cruise Line**
550 Kearny St.
San Francisco, CA 94108
(800) 765-7000

**American Canadian Caribbean Line**
461 Water St. Warren, RI 02885
(401) 247-0955 or (800) 556-7450

**Cruise International**
501 Front St,
Norfolk, VA. 23501
(800) 647-0009

**Coral Bay Cruises**
2631 E. Oakland Park, Blvd.
Fort Laudadale, FL 33306
(800) 433-7262

**Asian Pacific Adventures**
336 Westminster Ave.
Los Angeles, CA 90020
(213) 935-3156, (800) 825-1680

**Archaeological Tours, Inc**
30 E. 42nd St., Suite 1202
New York, NY 10017
(212) 986-3504

**Australian Pacific Tours**
512 South Verdugo Drive, Suit 200
Burbank, CA 91502

**231**

(800) 821-9513, (800) 227-5401
or (818) 985-5616 in CA

**Backroads International**
6901 Pritchard Place, Suite 101
New Orleans, LA 70125
(504) 861-8593, (800) 227-7889

**Belize Promotions**
720 Worthshire
Houston, TX 77008

**Big Five Tour Expeditions, Ltd.**
110 Walt Whitmen Rd.
South Huntington, N.Y 11746
(800) 541-2790, (800) 445-7002

**Carnival Cruise Lines**
3655 N.W. 87th Ave.
Miami, FL 33178-2428
(305) 599-2200 or (800) 327-2058

**Chandris Fantasy Cruises**
900 Third Ave.
New York, NY 10022
(212) 223-3003

**Clipper Cruise Line**
7711 Bon Homme Ave.
St. Louis, MO 63105-1956
(800) 325-0010

**Commodore and Crown Cruise Line**
800 Douglas Road, Suite 600
Coral Gables, FL. 33134
(800) 327-5617

**Costa Cruises, Inc.**
World Trade Center
80 S.W. 8th St.
Miami, FL 33130-3097; or

P.O. Box 019614
Miami, FL 33101-9614
(305) 358-7325 or (800) 462-6782
**Cruises, Inc.**
5000 Campus Blv. Drive,
Pioneer Business Park
East Syracus, NY 13057-9935
(315) 463-9695 or (800)854-0500

**The Cruise Line, Inc.**
4770 Biscayne Blvd, Penthouse 1-3
Miami, FL 33137
(800) 327-3021, (800) 777-0707 in
Florida

**Club Med**-New York Boutique
3 E. 54th St.,
New York NY 10022
(800) CLUB-MED, (212) 750-1687

**Costa Cruises**
World Trade Center,
80 SW 8th St.
Maimi, FL 33130
(800) 462-6782

**Cruise World**
(800) 874-3220

**Cunard Line**
555 Fifth Ave
New York, NY 10017; or
P.O. Box 2935, Grand Central Station
New York, NY 10163
(212) 880-7500 or (800) 528-6273
(800) 423-4264 in California

**Delta Queen Steamboat Co.**
P.O. Box 62787
New Orleans, LA 70162
(800) 543-1949

**Discount Cruise Hotline**
9495 Sunset Drive #B270
Miami, FL 33173
(800) 458-2840

**Dolphin Cruise Lines**
1007 North American Way
Miami, FL 33132
(800) 222-1003

**Epirotiki Cruise Lines**
551 Fifth Ave
New York, NY 10176
(212) 599-1750
(800) 221-2470

**Eurocharters, Inc.**
6765 South Tropical Trail
Merritt Island, FL 32952
(407) 632-5610 or (407) 453-4494

**Freighter World Cruises, Inc.**
1805 Lake Ave., Suite 335
Pasadena, CA 91101
(818) 449-3106

**German Rhine Line**
(914) 948-3600

**Glacier Raft Co.**
P.O. Box 264A
West Glacier, MT 59936
(406) 888-5454

**Great American River Cruises**
P.O. Box 276
Crystal Lake, IL 60014
(813) 262-6599 or
(800) 523-3716

**Hellenic Mediterranean Lines**
(415) 989-7434

**Holland America Lines**
300 Elliot Ave. W.
Seattle, WA 98119
(206) 281-3535 or (800) 426-0327

**International Cruise Center**
(800) 221-3245

**Interworld Tours**
(800) 845-6622
(800) 221-3882

**Norwegian Cruise Line**
95 Merrick Way
Coral Gables, FL 33134
(800) 327-7030

**Horizon Cruises Ltd**.
A Hemphill/Harris Co.
16000 Ventura Blvd., Suite 200
Encino, CA 91436

**KD German Rhine Lines**
(East) 170 Hamilton Ave.
White Plains, NY 10601-1788
(914) 948-3600; (West) 323 Geary St.
San Francisco, CA 94102-1860
(415) 392-8817

**Ocean Cruise Lines**
1510 S.E. 17th St.
Fort Lauderdale, FL 33316
(305) 764-3500 or (800) 556-8850

**Pacific Sea-Fari Tours**
2803 Emerson St.
San Diego, CA 92106
(619) 226-8224

**Premier Cruise Lines**
101 George King Blvd.
Cape Canaveral, FL 32920

**233**

(305) 783-5061 or (800) 327-7113

**Princess Cruises**
2029 Century Park East
Los Angeles, CA 90067
(213) 553-1770 or (800) 421-0522

**Regency Cruises**
260 Madison Ave.
New York, NY 10016
(212) 972-4499,
New York, (800) 547-5566 (elsewhere)

**Royal Cruise Line**
One Maritime Plaza, Suite 400.
San Francisco, CA 94111
(415) 788-0610, (415)  or 95 Merrick,
Coral Gables, FL 33134. (800)
227-4534
or (305) 447-9660

**Royal Caribbean Cruise Lines**
1050 Carribean Way
Miami, FL 33132
(305) 379-4731 or (800) 327-6700,
(800) 327 0270

# APPENDIX 1C

## References and Resources for Overseas Travelers

‒ ‒ ‒ ‒

<u>Note:</u>
1. Several of the publications (brochures) mentioned here are revised from time to time and so are their prices. Remember to request for the current editions.

2. Most of the publications listed here and marked with asterisks have been reprinted verbatim in the book *Americans Traveling Abroad: What You Should Know Before You Go* by Gladson I. Nwanna (Ph.D)
[ISBN: 0-9623820-7-8, paperback, 658 pages, $39.99]. This book is available at most public libraries in the U.S. and can be ordered through most bookstores or through Access Publishers at 1-800-345-0096.

3. Several references made elsewhere in this book, in which I have directed you to your local libraries or telephone books can also be found by checking the appendix section of the book *Americans Traveling Abroad*.

4. For additional information on country-specific do's and don'ts, you may invest in the regional titles in the book series entitled *Do's and Don'ts Around the World: A country Guide to Cultural and Social Taboos and Etiquette*, published by World Travel Institute. Alternatively consider contacting the **World Travel Institute,** at P.O. Box 32674 Baltimore, Maryland 21282. For $7 per report, per country, they will send you over 200 specific do's and don'ts for each country requested. Reports are also available (for purchase) on-line at **www.worldtravelinstitute.com.** Turn to the end of this book for additional ordering information.

<u>U.S. DEPARTMENT OF STATE</u>

*The following fourteen publications from the Department of State,(D.O.S.) Bureau of Consular Affairs (B.C.A) may be ordered for $1 each (unless, otherwise indicated) from the Superintendent of Documents, U.S. Government printing Office, Washington*

*D.C. 20402; Tel. (202) 512-1800: Also check out these State Department web locations: http://travel.state.gov/travel_pubs.html and http://travel.state.gov/travel_warnings.html*

**\*Your Trip Abroad** provides basic travel information - tips on passports, visas, immunizations, and more. It will help you prepare for your trip and make it as trouble - free as possible.

**\*A Safe Trip Abroad** gives travel security advice for any traveler, but particularly for those who plan trips to areas of high crime or terrorism.

**\*Tips for Americans Residing Abroad** is prepared for the more than 2 million Americans who live in foreign countries.

**\*Travel Tips for Older Americans** provides health, safety, and travel information for older Americans.

**\*Tips for Travelers to Sub-Saharan Africa.**

**\*Tips for Travelers to the Caribbean.**

**\*Tips for Travelers to Central and South America.**

**\*Tips for Travelers to Mexico**

**\*Tips for Travelers to the Middle East and North Africa.**

**\*Tips for Travelers to the People's Republic of China.**

**\*Tips for Travelers to South Asia.**

**\* Tips for Travelers to  Russia.**

Other Department of State Publications and Resources

**\*Americans Abroad** provides basic up to date information on passport, foreign laws, customs, personal safety and helpful travel tips. You may request for a free copy by writing to: Americans Abroad, Consumer Information Center, Pueblo, CO 81009. Multiple copies of 25 may be purchased from the Superintendent of Documents, U.S.

Government Printing Office.

*\*Foreign Entry Requirements* lists visa and other entry requirements of foreign countries and tells you how to apply for visas and tourists cards. Updated Yearly. Order this publication for 50 cents from the Consumer Information Center, Dept. 438T, Pueblo, CO 81009.

**Key Officers of Foreign Service Posts** gives addresses and telephone, telex, and FAX numbers for all U.S. embassies and consulates abroad. \*\*(NOTE: When writing to a U.S. embassies and consulates, address the envelope to the appropriate section, such as Consular Section, rather than to a specific individual.) This publication is updated 3 times a year and may be purchased from the Superintendent of Documents, U.S. Government Printing Office. Single copy purchase price is $3.75. One year subscription price is $5.

\*\***Diplomatic List** lists the addresses, and telephone and fax numbers of foreign embassies and consulates in the U.S. including the names of key offices. This publication is updated quarterly and may be purchased from the Superintendent of Documents. U.S. Government Printing Office. Price $4.75.

*\*Passports* provides information on where to apply, how to apply and the best time to apply for a U.S. Passport, including renewals; Everything you need to know about getting a passport- cost, requirements etc.

*\*Consular Information Sheets* is part of the U.S. State Department's travel advisory instruments. It covers such matters as location and telephone number of the nearest U.S. Embassy, health conditions, entry regulations, crime and security conditions that may affect travel, drug penalties and areas of instability. Consular Information Sheets are available for most countries. For a free copy of the Consular Information Sheet for the country you plan to visit write to the state Department, Bureau of Consular Affairs, Washington D.C. 20520.

**Traveling Abroad More Safely** - a 12-minute Department of State videotape, that provides practical advice to U.S. citizens traveling abroad. It is available from Video Transfer, Inc., 5710 Arundel Ave., Rockville, MD 20552, Tel: (301) 881-0270. Price: $12 for VHS or Beta 2, $27 for BetaCam.

*\*U.S. Consul Help Americans Abroad* explains some of the functions and services of U.S. Embassies and Consulates abroad.

**237**

**\*Crises Abroad-What the State Department Does** available free of charge from Department of State, CA/PA Rm. 5807 Washington D.C. 20520.

**International Parental Child Abduction** available free of charge. Write to Office of Citizens Consular Services, Bureau of Consular Affairs, Department of State, Rm.4817 Washington D.C. 20520.

**\*International Adoptions** discusses the issue of International Adoptions including valuable tips, guidelines and procedures. This circular (publication) is available free of charge from the Department of State, Overseas Citizens Services or call (202) 647-2688.

**\*Travel Warnings on Drugs Abroad** available free of charge from the Department of State, CA/PA Rm. 5807 Washington D.C. 20520.

**\*\*\*Travel advisories,** issued by the State Department, caution U.S. citizens about travel to specific countries or areas. If you are concerned about existing conditions in a given area, contact your travel agent or airline, the nearest passport agency or the Department of State's Citizens Emergency Center at (202) 647-5225.

**Foreign Consular Offices in the U.S.** lists all foreign diplomatic offices in the U.S. This booklet is available from the Superintendent of Documents, U.S. Government Printing Office, Washington D.C. 20402. Tel. (202) 512-1800. The cost is $6.50.

**\* Security Awareness Overseas: An Overview** provides guidelines and tips on a variety of topics relating to personal safety and security while overseas.(D.O.S. Overseas Security Advisory Council, Bureau of Diplomatic Security). This pamphlet may be ordered from the Superintendent of Documents. U.S. Government Printing Office.

U.S. DEPARTMENT OF TREASURY

**\*Know Before You Go, Customs Hints for Returning U.S. Residents** gives detailed information on U.S. Customs regulations, including duty rates. Single copies are available free from any local customs or by writing to the Department of the Treasury, U.S. Customs Service, P.O. Box 7407, Washington D.C. 20044. (U.S. Customs Publication)

**\*U.S. Customs: International Mail Imports** provides information on procedures and requirements pertaining to parcels mailed from abroad to the U.S. (U.S. Customs

238

Publication)

**\*U.S. Customs: Importing a Car** provides essential information for persons importing a vehicle into the U.S. It also includes U.S. Custom requirements and those of other government agencies whose regulations are enforced by the U.S. Customs. (U.S. Customs Publication)

**\*Pleasure Boats** provides essential information for persons importing pleasure boats into the U.S. It includes requirements and charges. This publication is available free of charge from the Public Information Office, U.S. Customs Service, P.O. Box 7407, Washington D.C. 20044. (U.S. Customs Publication)

**U.S. Customs: Highlights for Government Personnel** provides information for returning U.S. Government civilian employees and military personnel. Subjects discussed in this pamphlet include, duties, gifts, personal and household effects, automobiles, restricted and prohibited goods. Available from Public Information Office, U.S. Customs: Department of Treasury, P.O. Box 7407, Washington D.C. 20044. Tel. (202) 927-2095. (U.S. Customs Publication).

**\*Pets, Wildlife: U.S. Customs** (U.S. Customs Publication)

**\*G.S.P. and the Traveler** provides basic information regarding the Generalized System of Preference which allows some products from certain countries to be brought into the U.S. duty-free. The leaflet only treats those non-commercial importations intended for personal use only. (U.S. Customs Publication).

U.S. DEPARTMENT OF AGRICULTURE

**\*Travelers Tips on Bringing Food, Plant, And Animal Products Into the United States** lists the regulations on bringing these items into the United States from most parts of the world. Fresh fruits and vegetables, meat, potted plants, pet birds, and other items are prohibited or restricted. Obtain the publication free from the Animal and Plant Health Inspection Service, U.S. Department of Agriculture, 732 Federal Bldg., 6505 Belcrest Road, Hyattsville, Maryland 20782. Tel. (301) 734-7885.

**\*Shipping Foreign plants Home**. Provides tips and guidelines. Obtain the publication free from the Animal and Plant Health Inspection Service, U.S. Department of Agriculture, 732 Federal Bldg., 6505 Belcrest Road, Hyattsville, Maryland 20782. Tel.

**239**

(301) 734-7885.

**\*Travelers Tips on Prohibited Agriculture Products** Free copies may be obtained from the address above.

## U.S. DEPARTMENT OF HEALTH

**\*+Health Information for International Travel** is a comprehensive listing of immunization requirements of foreign governments. In addition, it gives the U.S. Public Health Service's recommendations on immunizations and other health precautions for the international traveler. Copies are available for $7.00 from the Superintendent of Documents, U.S. Government Printing Office.

## DEPARTMENT OF INTERIOR
**\*Buyer Beware!** tells about restrictions on importing wildlife and wildlife products. For a free copy, write to the Publications Unit, US Fish and Wildlife Service, Department of the interior, Washington D.C. 20240; (202) 343-5634.

## ENVIRONMENTAL PROTECTION AGENCY

**\*Buying a Car Overseas? Beware!** Free copies may be ordered from Publication Information Center PM-211B, 401 M Street S.W. Washington DC 20460 (202) 260-7751. (U.S. Environmental Protection Agency).

## DEPARTMENT OF TRANSPORTATION

**\*Fly Rights** explains your rights and responsibilities as an air traveler ( U.S. Department of Transportation).

Although essential requirements are provided in the leaflets listed above and, all regulations cannot be covered in detail. If you have any questions, or are in doubt , write or call the specific agency or organization mentioned. Their addresses including the type of subject matter they might provide some assistance are noted below.

**Agency/Source  and Type of Inquiry/Assistance**

**U.S. Public Health Services**
**Centers for Disease Control**

Division of Quarantine
Atlanta, Georgia 30333
Tel. (404) 539-2574

*[On bringing food, plant and animal products into the U.S.]*

**Animal and Plant Health Inspection**
**U.S. Department of Agriculture**
613 Federal Building
6505 Belcrest Road
Tel. (301) 734-7885,

*[On bringing food, plant, and animal products into the U.S.]*

**U.S. Fish and Wildlife Service**
**Department of the Interior**
Washington, D.C. 20240
Tel. (202) 343-9242,
(202) 343-5634

*[Fish and Wildlife]*

**Department of the Treasury**
**U.S. Customs Service**
P.O. Box 7407
Washington D.C. 20044
(202) 927-2095

*[Imports and Exports, duties (tariffs) restricted and prohibited products]*

**Food and Drug Administration**
**Import Operations Unit**
Room 12-8(HFC-131)
5600 Fishers Lane
Rockville, MD 20857

*[Import of food and drugs into the U.S]*

**241**

**Office of Community and Consumer Affairs**
**U.S. Department of Transportation**
400 7th Street, S.W., Rm. 10405
Washington, D.C. 20590
(202) 366-2220
*[To complain about an airline or cruise line or to check out the records of an airline or cruise line.]*

**Community and Consumer**
**Liaison Division**
APA - 400
Federal Aviation Administration
800 Independence Avenue, S.W.
Washington, D.C. 20591
(202) 267-3481

*[To complain about safety hazards.]*

**U.S. Environmental Protection Agency**
**Public Information Center**
PM-211B, 401 M Street
S.W. Washington, D.C. 20460
(202) 382-2504

*[Environmental issues dealing with imports of certain products or goods, including cars.]*

**TRAFFIC U.S.A.**
World Wildlife Fund - U.S.
1250 24th Street
N.W. Washington, D.C. 20520

*[On import of wildlife.]*

**U.S. Department of State**
CA/PA Rm. 5807 Washington, D.C. 20402
(202) 647 4000 or (202) 647 1488

*[Citizen safety, whereabouts, and welfare abroad, passports, visas, U.S. embassies and consulates abroad, foreign embassies and consulates in the U.S.*

**Superintendent Of Documents**
**U.S. Government Printing Office**
Washington, D.C. 20402
(202) 512-1800

*[U.S. government publications, including publications of various agencies and departments of the Federal Government.]*

**Office Of Foreign Assets Control**
**Department Of The Treasury**
Washington, D.C. 20220
(202) 566-2761

*[Import of merchandise from foreign countries.]*

**Quarantines, USDA-APHIS-PPQ**  6505 Belcrest Rd. (301) 436-7472

*[For permits and information on import of plants, meat products, livestock and poultry.]*

**Office Of Munitions Control**
**Department Of State**
Washington, D.C. 20520

*[Export/ import of weapons, ammunition and firearms.]*

**Bureau Of Alcohol, Tobacco and**
**Firearms**
**Department Of The Treasury**
Washington, D.C. 20226

*[Import of alcohol, tobacco and firearms.]*

**Office Of Vehicle Safety Compliance**
**(NEF 32)**

**243**

**Department Of Transportation**
Washington, D.C. 20590

*[Import of vehicles (standards).]*

**U.S. Information Agency**
Washington, D.C.
(202) 619-4700
*[Import/export of Cultural property.]*

**Consumer Information Center**
Pueblo, Colorado 81009
*[Publications of interest to the general public.]*

Series Title:*DO'S AND DON'TS AROUND THE WORLD: A COUNTRY GUIDE TO CULTURAL AND SOCIAL TABOOS AND ETIQUETTE*

Edition:    ISBN#:  Pages:   Price

**EUROPE**  1-890605-00-X;   332 pages;   $29.99

**SOUTH AMERICA**   1-890605-03-4;  245 pages;  $19.99

**AFRICA**    1-890605-04-2;  440 pages;   $34.99

**THE CARIBBEAN** 1-890605-02-6;  220 pages;   $19.99

**ASIA** 1-890605-01-8;  250 pages;    $24.99

**RUSSIA & THE INDEPENDENT STATES** 1-890605-06-9;   160 pages;  $12.99

**USA, CANADA & AUSTRALIA**  1-890605-08-5;  75 pages; $12.99

**OCEANIA & JAPAN**   1-890605-07-7;  185 pages;  $15.99

**THE MIDDLE EAST** 1-890605-05-0; 145 pages;  $12.99

*INDIVIDUAL COUNTRY REPORTS ARE AVAILABLE!!!*
at $7 per report per country.
Individual Country Reports can only be ordered directly from the
publisher or through the internet. Check out our web page at
(**www.worldtravelinstitute.com**)
for a list of available countries.

# ORDERING INFORMATION

# ORDER FORM

**Telephone Orders:**
Books may be ordered through Access Publishers at 1-800-345-0096 (Bookmasters at 1-800-507-2665, after 5pm). (BOOKS ONLY!!!).
Have Your Credit Card ready. Order any time, day or night, 7 days a week, 24 hours a day.

**World Travel Institute**
P.O. Box 32674-1A,
Baltimore, MD 21282-2674 U.S.A.
Fax: (410) 922-8115.

Make check or money order payable to **World Travel Institute (WTI)**. We also accept, international money orders; VISA & MASTERCARD.

Shipping/Postage Cost for books:
**U.S. Residents** add $4 U.S. dollars per book for postage.
**Canadian Residents** add $5 U.S. dollars per book for postage.
**Mexican Residents** add $7 U.S. dollars per book for postage.
**Other Countries**: add $15 U.S. dollars for airmail delivery; $7 for surface mail delivery.

Shipping/Postage Cost for Reports:
*[Save postage by ordering & downloading on-line version]*
U.S. Residents reports are mailed free-of-charge.
**Canadian Residents** add $2 U.S. dollars for postage.
**Mexican Residents** add $2 U.S. dollars for postage.
**Other Countries:** add $5 U.S. dollars for airmail delivery; $3 dollars for surface mail delivery.

Remember, individual country reports for COUNTRY DO'S & DON'TS are now available on-line for $7 (U.S. dollars) per country. Reports can be ordered through the publisher only!!! or through the internet at (**www.worldtravelinstitute.com**)

## ☐ Please enter my order for the following books:

- **Practical Tips For Americans Traveling Abroad..** $19.99 + $____postage
  [On-Line version available for purchase at www.worldtravelinstitute.com]
- **Americans Traveling Abroad..** $39.99 + $____postage Total $____
- **Do's and Don'ts**:

| | | |
|---|---|---|
| Europe | $29.99 + $____ | postage: Total $____ |
| South America | $19.99 + $____ | postage: Total $____ |
| Africa* | $34.99 + $____ | postage: Total $____ |
| The Caribbean | $19.99 + $____ | postage: Total $____ |
| Asia | $24.99 + $____ | postage: Total $____ |
| Russia/The Ind. States | $ 12.99 +$____ | postage: Total $____ |
| USA, Canada & Australia | $12.99 + $____ | postage: Total $____ |
| The Middle East* | $12.99 + $____ | postage: Total $____ |
| Oceania & Japan* | $15.99 + $____ | postage: Total $____ |

*( \* Please check availability/publication date)*
*(Please refer to the section containing postage/shipping information for applicable postage rates.)*

- **Do's and Don'ts - COUNTRY REPORTS:**
  for the following countries at $7.each     $____  + $____postage
                                                  Total $____

Please List Countries:_____
_____

**Sales Tax**: (Maryland Residents Only) Add 5%     $_____

**Enclosed is my Total Payment of $**_____by

☐ Check  ☐ Money Order  ☐ Credit Card  ☐ VISA  ☐ MASTERCARD
**Card Number:**_____**Card Holder's Name:**_____
**Expiration Date:**_____**Signature:**_____
                    ☐ This is a gift from:_____
**Ship to:**_____
**Address:**_____
**City:**_____**State:**_____**Zip:**_____**Country:**_____

# *NOTES*

# LIBRARY RECOMMENDATION FORM

*(This form should be hand-delivered to your local Head Librarian or Reference Librarian)*

Sir/Madam:

I regularly use the following book(s) published by **World Travel Institute**:

(1)_____

    ISBN #:_____ Price $_____

(2)_____

    ISBN #:_____ Price $_____

(3)_____

    ISBN #:_____ Price $_____

(4)_____

    ISBN #:_____ Price $_____

(5)_____

    ISBN #:_____ Price $_____

(6)_____

    ISBN #:_____ Price $_____

(7)_____

    ISBN #:_____ Price $_____

(8)_____

    ISBN #:_____ Price $_____

Your records indicate that the library does not carry these valuable and comprehensive travel reference books. Could you please place an order them for our library?

Name of Recommender:_____

Address:_____

_____

_____

Phone:_____

# INDEX

**251**

## OTHER WTI BOOKS BY THE SAME AUTHOR

*Americans Traveling Abroad: What You Should Know Before You Go* (2nd Ed.) Bestseller! paperback, 658 pages, ISBN: 0-9623820-7-8, $39.99 [Available at major bookstores throughout the United States. It may also be ordered from Access Publishers Network at 1-800-345-0096 (at 1-800-507-2665 after 5pm) or directly from the publisher-World Travel Institute].

*Do's and Don'ts Around the World: A Country Guide to Cultural and Social Taboos and Etiquette.* paperback, available in 9 different regional volumes: **Europe, Asia, Africa, South America, The Caribbeans, The Middle East, Russia and the Independent states, Oceania and Japan, USA-Canada-Australia.** These books contain hundreds of country-specific do's and don'ts and much more!.

[Available at major bookstores throughout the United States. It may also be ordered from Access Publishers Network at 1-800-345-0096 (at 1-800-507-2665 after 5pm) or directly from the publisher-World Travel Institute]. Also available on-line (at www.worldtravelinstitute.com) or directly from the publisher only are Individual Country Reports. Each report costs $7.

[See pages 245-247 for more details on the above mentioned titles]

254